EVERYONE IS ENTITLED TO MY OPINION

This is focused pretty locally, but I think/hope you will find it interesting. It was a fun project, but a real problem was deciding who the audience was — board, former residents, staff, social work types, etc — I may have told you that one of the great pleasures in spending so much time in Spokane was that it reminds me so much of Okla City in the days of our youth —

Thanks for being interested

The Hutton Settlement

The Hutton Settlement

A Home for One Man's Family

For Mildred, a true friend!

Doris H. Pieroth

Doris H. Pieroth

The Hutton Settlement
Spokane, Washington

The Hutton Settlement
422 W. Riverside, #931
Spokane, Washington 99201
509-838-2789
www.huttonsettlement.org

Library of Congress Cataloging-in-Publication Data
Pieroth, Doris Hinson.
 The Hutton Settlement: a home for one man's family / Doris H. Pieroth.
  p. cm.
Includes index.
 ISBN 0-615-12355-4 (alk. paper)
1. Hutton, Levi W., 1860-1928. 2. Hutton Settlement (Spokane, Wash.)—History. 3. Orphanages—Washington (State)—Spokane—History. 4. Children—Institutional care—Washington (State)—Spokane—History.
I. Title.
 HV-995.S662H886 2003
 362.73'2'0979737—dc21   2003007248

Front end-paper photograph:
Aerial view of the Hutton Settlement campus, ca. 1930. NMAC photo.

Back end-paper photograph:
Hutton youngsters working the Settlement's large garden plot, 1925. The campus remained a working farm until well after World War II. NMAC photo.

Frontispiece:
L. W. Hutton, ca. 1920. Hutton Settlement photo.

Graphic design by Diana L. Whaley

Table of Contents

Preface

Just north of Interstate 90 at Exit 287 near Spokane, Washington, stands one of that city's most venerable and least known institutions—the Hutton Settlement. Its magnificent buildings and its serene grounds call to mind an Ivy League college campus. Now listed on the National Register of Historic Places, this home for children was the creation of Levi W. Hutton, a generous and philanthropic Spokane capitalist.

Near the turn of the twentieth century, the Pacific Northwest lacked the enormous amounts of capital needed by its major extractive industries, especially mining. Thus, outside investors, mainly in the eastern United States, developed many of the region's mines, and much of the natural wealth extracted from them enriched the coffers of these absentee owners. The Hercules Mine in Idaho's Coeur d'Alene mining district stands as one notable exception to this pattern.[1]

The families of Harry, Eugene, and Jerome Day, majority owners of the Hercules, resided in northern Idaho, invested there, and wielded considerable influence in that state. Two of the mine's minority owners, Levi Hutton and August Paulsen, moved to Spokane in the first decade of the century, invested in real estate, and applied their mining wealth toward investments that enriched and benefited that growing city.

Spokane had been founded by settlers who saw economic potential in a site beside the dramatic falls in the Spokane River. In 1889 fire swept through the prospering town and all but destroyed its central core. The city immediately rebuilt. It rose from the ashes strong enough to survive the financial panic of 1893 and to flourish unrivaled on the route between the Twin Cities and Seattle. Railroading made it into a transportation and shipping hub; water power, timber, and agriculture secured its commercial dominance in the Inland Northwest. By 1909 Spokane boasted twenty-six millionaires.[2] The business district of the handsome and confident city was enhanced by buildings that these men, Hutton and Paulsen among them, erected. Hutton's commercial real estate ventures along with his mining wealth supported his personal philanthropy.

Orphaned early in life, this one-time farm boy harbored a desire to create a loving, caring, receptive home for similarly disadvantaged children. He satisfied that desire in 1919 when he opened the Hutton Settlement ten miles east of the city in the bucolic Spokane Valley. Much as his decision to invest his mine fortune locally had stood apart from a national tide, so, too, his decision to build a large home for children ran counter to child welfare thinking of the period, which deemphasized such institutions. A quiet, unassuming man, Hutton held firm to definite values and ideas born of his own experience. The home that he built to last 250 years continues into its ninth decade to reflect those ideas and values.

This book is the story of that home—its founder, the stewards of his dream who kept the faith through times of both difficulty and good fortune, and the children who grew to productive adulthood in its safe haven. It is also the story of sisterhood. The more than one hundred women who have served as trustees of the Hutton Settlement are bonded in friendship and loving association through long years of service in common cause. The Hutton Settlement is indeed a home. Those whose lives it has touched over the years truly constitute a family—one that reflects the strengths and frailties of all families. Looking back at the time of the Settlement's Diamond Jubilee, one member of that family said, "Home is a place where you are loved and cared for and given the opportunity to grow up to become someone," adding

> During my eleven years [at the Settlement], I lived with over two hundred children and, to this day, I still consider them my close friends. When we spend time together, we all look back and realize how fortunate we were the Hutton Settlement existed . . . [to] have a place to call HOME.[3]

As they guided the Settlement through decades of change and challenge, the women on the board of trustees remained true to the dream of its founder and benefactor. They and the three men who succeeded him in administering Settlement affairs diligently met his charge that they concern themselves with the lives of the children.

Note on sources

Official records of the Settlement constitute the major source for *The Hutton Settlement: A Home for One Man's Family.* I found the records to be uneven, to say the least. Minutes of all board meetings since 1920 survive, many minutes of committees and other records do not, and some that do are incomplete. All minutes and financial records are located in the Hutton Settlement office. Sources not otherwise located can be found in the Hutton Settlement papers in the Eastern Washington State Historical Society archives at Spokane's Northwest Museum of Arts and Culture. Secondary sources are in the end notes, cited in full at first references. In addition to the written record, sources include more than sixty interviews with Settlement board members, former residents, two administrators, other present and former staff members, and longtime observers of the Spokane scene.

Talking with these considerate, thoughtful people was both informative and a true pleasure; I am grateful to all of them for the time they were willing to spend with me. In researching and writing the book, I incurred many other debts of gratitude as well. Thanks go first of all to Laura Arksey. She not only introduced me to the Hutton Settlement story but also spent countless hours assisting me in the archives, gave invaluable advice and technical assistance, read the manuscript, and generously housed me during my numerous trips to Spokane. The Spokane Public Library's Nancy Compeau welcomed me to its Northwest Room and directed my use of the holdings there; she shared her knowledge of local history, and later agreeably responded to long-distance requests for help; for all of this I remain in her debt. Patsy Gottschalk made frequent searches in records, arranged many interviews, and provided good-natured and entertaining contact with the Settlement office. I thank the Settlement's board of trustees, many former residents, and all others who shared material from their own collections. A special thanks goes to the board's history committee, chaired by Jo Ann Nielsen; its members gave enormous support and encouragement to the project.

Obligations mounted west of the Cascades as well as inland. I thank my fellow historians Charles P. LeWarne and Margaret Hall, whose reading of the entire manuscript yielded helpful suggestions. Ruth Gale earned my great appreciation for her patience and the incomparable transcripts she made of the interview tapes. I am grateful for the superb editorial skills of Carol Zabilski; she always makes the task of rewriting seem like fun. I enjoyed greatly the interest and enthusiasm that friends and family showed in the project, and I benefited from their support.

Doris H. Pieroth
Seattle, Washington
February 2003

1

Prelude to Benevolence

T he roots of the Hutton Settlement run deep in the inland Pacific Northwest. The earth of Idaho's Coeur d'Alene mining district yielded the riches
that created the Settlement. Its guiding ethos, personified by the caring,
confident, conservative, optimistic, and work-driven people who have served it,
derives from values that have imbued the region since pioneer days. Levi Hutton's
investment of wealth from the Hercules Mine and his faith in the future of Spokane have sustained it for eight decades. Women who have composed the
Settlement's board of trustees trace family far back into the region's history, and
they have reaped the benefits of May Arkwright Hutton's labors in the cause of
women's rights in both Idaho and Washington.

Levi W. Hutton ranks among Spokane's pioneers, having first come there as a
young man in the summer of 1881, driving "a four horse team from Portland to
Spokane, which then had a population of a few hundred only. I pastured my team
on the flat about the corner of Post Street and Sprague Avenue, where the Davenport Hotel now stands."[1] The newly incorporated town at the falls in the Spokane
River was less than a decade old. Northern Pacific Railroad crews laying tracks
north and east from the Columbia River also reached Spokane that summer. Two
years later, approximately sixty miles west of Helena, Montana, they met NP crews
building westward from Chicago. On September 3, 1883, a memorable "last spike"
ceremony linked the tracks and gave the rest of the nation easier access to eastern
Washington and Idaho.[2]

Hutton's own route to Spokane had begun in Fairfield, Iowa, where he was
born October 22, 1860, the son of Levi Hutton and Mary Nancy Holsinger Hutton.
His father died when he was an infant. His mother's death six years later left him
and six siblings orphans to be dispersed among the households of aunts and uncles.
They were not allowed to grow up together, a fact that stamped the adult Levi's
philanthropy. In reflecting on his childhood, he wrote:

> Most of my early orphanhood, I spent in farm work, going to a country school some
> three or four months each winter and living in the home of my uncle, Stephen Hutton.
> I left Iowa in the spring of 1879, going to Salem, Oregon, where I spent a year,
> afterwards working among the Redwoods of California. Leaving California in the
> spring of 1881, I went to Portland and thence to Spokane.[3]

In a joyless childhood, he had carried a larger burden of work on his uncle's
farm than his cousins, and he felt the sting of ostracism from playmates who shunned

him as an orphan. The uncle's own children went to school, but farm duties prevented Levi from attending beyond third grade. He had run away to the Black Hills of South Dakota where prospectors had struck gold, but he soon realized that a mining town was no place for a twelve-year-old and returned to Iowa. After a time, he left the Midwest to join relatives in Salem and at eighteen struck out on his own.[4]

After a brief stay in Portland and Spokane, he spent eight or nine months as a steamboat fireman on Pend Oreille Lake, loading cordwood onto the steamer and tending the firebox. Returning to Spokane, he "took employment" with the Northern Pacific, first working in the roundhouse; then, tapping his steamboat experience, he moved into the locomotive cab as a railroad fireman. Completion of the transcontinental opened the next chapter for him. The railroad transferred him to its Missoula division and promoted him to engineer.[5]

Completion of the NP opened a new chapter in the region, too. Placer gold was discovered in the Coeur d'Alene mountains near Pritchard, Idaho. News of the find quickly spread. Although "many gold seekers rode the Northern Pacific to Idaho, pausing in Spokane to buy tools. . . . In the long run, there were too many men and too little gold." When it became apparent that the placer claims would produce no fortunes, action shifted from the north to the south fork of the Coeur d'Alene River, where "on Canyon Creek in May 1884 two [prospectors] staked a lead-silver claim. . . . In September 1885, downstream at Milo Gulch, Noah S. Kellogg . . . claimed lead-silver outcroppings and called this the Bunker Hill. Kellogg's find set off a new rush." Mining activity in northern Idaho would thereafter center around Milo Gulch and Canyon Creek.[6]

In 1886 the Northern Pacific again transferred Hutton, this time to its Wallace division in Idaho—to Wardner Junction and Milo Gulch. On his run from Cataldo Mission west of Wardner to Burke, near the source of Canyon Creek, the quiet, mild-mannered engineer soon became a favorite. He "rigged his engine whistle with a chime made by a Wallace plumber [and] his distinctive toot could be identified through the canyons."[7]

During his time in Missoula, Hutton had become a Freemason and a Shriner. When he moved to Idaho he became a founding member of the Blue Lodge in Wallace. On relocating to Spokane in 1907, he became active in the El Katif Shrine and remained a lifelong member.[8]

Al Hutton, as the young bachelor preferred to be known,[9] located the most outstanding food in town soon after his arrival in Wardner. By the autumn of 1887 he had become a regular diner in the boardinghouse owned and operated by May Arkwright. The best cook in the Coeur d'Alenes, outspoken May Arkwright relished life unabashedly, "did and said what she liked, . . . [was] the friend of plain people" and a champion of the underdog. Perhaps opposites do attract; or perhaps the wonderful meals and the cook's "lusty love of life" intrigued Hutton. Within a few weeks of their meeting, he proposed and she accepted. They were married on

November 25, 1887—Thanksgiving Day. Their first home was an inexpensive two-room flat above the railroad tracks in Wallace; the bride soon went to work as a cook in the Wallace Hotel.[10]

Mary Arkwright was born July 21, 1860, in Washingtonville, a coal-mining community near Youngstown in northeast Ohio. Along the way, Mary became known as May and, later, as Mame or Mamie to some in Idaho. As May Arkwright Hutton she left her mark on the Northwest—a leading activist in the struggle for women's rights and in Democratic party politics. Less well known are her compassionate and charitable endeavors and her openhanded philanthropy.[11]

May and Al Hutton had in common their far-from-idyllic childhoods. The illegitimate daughter of Isaac Arkwright, May had four half siblings. Her mother simply disappeared, and before May was ten years old, her father took her out of school and sent her to care for her blind grandfather. Despite the early separation, she maintained contact with her family; in 1908 she mentioned hosting "a houseful of relatives from Ohio." The record shows generous financial assistance to Arkwrights over the years.[12]

May became an excellent cook as she prepared her grandfather's meals. She also shepherded the old gentleman to meeting halls and the town square where, together, they would listen to speakers who interpreted current events and commented on political issues. Once after hearing William McKinley, then a young attorney with political ambitions, her grandfather invited him back to their house for cider and some of May's homemade doughnuts. The future president had talked about the late war and reconstruction as well as women's rights. At that point, she realized for the first time that women did not have equal rights.[13]

Two failed marriages in Ohio marked May Arkwright's young adult years, the first when she was eighteen years old. Four years later she married Gilbert Munn, and within a year that second marriage ended.[14]

In the early 1880s, labor relations and working conditions in the Ohio coal mines had become increasingly quarrelsome and difficult. Many miners began to leave the region, some to follow the lure of gold in the Coeur d'Alenes. A Northern Pacific Railroad pamphlet helped draw May from the Midwest. Claiming that the ores were so rich they yielded nuggets worth as much as $200 apiece, it declared that the Idaho mines were superior to those of the old world and "inexhaustible."[15]

Her grandfather Arkwright urged her to put no limits on her aspirations, to "hitch [her] wagon to a star," so in 1883, together with a collection of forty Ohio miners and their families, May Arkwright boarded a train for Spokane Falls en route to the Coeur d'Alenes. They hoped to strike it rich, or at least to better their lots in life.[16]

On the westbound train out of Chicago she met Jim Wardner, a self-styled town planner and entrepreneur who was promoting a town site on the south fork of the Coeur d'Alene River. May agreed to work in a café he would open in Wardner

Junction. It proved to be a makeshift lunch counter behind a saloon. She worked hard, saved her money, and by the time a narrow-gauge railroad was planned into the Bunker Hill and Sullivan Mine and on to Burke, she had the wherewithal to open her own boardinghouse. Her skill in a kitchen soon won her customers and friends in large numbers.[17]

Mining in the Coeur d'Alenes had become big business, and outside capital controlled most of it. Working conditions and labor relations resembled those in Ohio, and May came to embrace the cause of labor unions. People in the Coeur d'Alenes took sides, and lines hardened between supporters of the companies and those of the unions. In October 1887, just before she married Levi Hutton, the Bunker Hill & Sullivan cut wages, and the miners struck. On November 3, the men organized the district's first local—the Wardner Miners Union—which was followed by other unions and eventually the Western Federation of Miners.[18]

Al Hutton shared his wife's pro-union sentiments—up to a point. A quiet, friendly man "who always had a twinkle in his eye," he was a union man and labor man all his life, and he "paid his union dues right up to the very date of his death." But he remained circumspect on the subject, while May used the dining room in Wallace as a platform to proclaim the merits of organizing.[19]

Even as labor unrest grew, few people in the Coeur d'Alenes could resist speculating in mining. As a bachelor, Hutton had pursued some possibilities, and by the autumn of 1895 he and May had saved enough from her earnings at the dining room and his at the Northern Pacific to buy into a six-year-old operation called the Hercules Mine, begun by a young man named Harry Day. Another young hopeful, August Paulsen, also joined the Hercules partnership that October for $850— "paying $100 down and working in the claims at day wages to pay the rest." The Huttons purchased a 3/32 share in the mine for $880; Al, too, worked at the claim when not running his locomotive in the canyon. His manual labor and additional assessments eventually brought their percentage to a "five-thirty second interest or about one tenth interest in the mine."[20]

Lack of capital stood as only one impediment to development of the Hercules. The threat of violence hung over the divided labor scene in the Coeur d'Alenes when, in the spring of 1899, union miners struck the Bunker Hill over wages. The historian John Fahey recounts one memorable episode in the labor strife.

> The Mine Owners Association directed a covert warfare against union men, chiefly in Wardner, and the union retaliated. . . .
>
> On the night of April 28, 1899, masked men ordered the president of the Gem union to call a meeting. . . . [Unions] at Burke and Mullan voted their "moral support" of the Wardner union. . . [which] met all night. . . .
>
> The next day, 1,076 of 1,495 mine employees in the Coeur d'Alenes stayed away from work, . . . [and masked] union members commandeered Levi Hutton's train at Gem, backed it into the Helena & Frisco powderhouse to pick up dynamite, and ordered the engineer at gunpoint to carry them to Wardner.[21]

With a gun in his ribs, Hutton followed orders to stop his train at every town and blow his signature whistle; more masked men boarded at every stop. When they reached Kellogg just after noon, about 200 armed men got off and advanced toward the Bunker Hill. Near 2 o'clock the mill was blown up, rattling Wardner and Kellogg, where saloonkeepers had judiciously locked their doors. The union men whooped back to their train, directed Hutton to return, and at each station men jumped off and strolled home through the dusk.

In Boise, when he learned of the explosion five days later, Governor Frank Steunenberg declared martial law. Federal troops herded all men carrying union cards into a corrallike enclosure at Wardner known as the bullpen. Civil rights evaporated, and even when applications were made, "no men were released on writs of habeus corpus." Hutton, a reluctant participant at most, was held as a witness. He recounted the events of that day for authorities but could not, or would not, identify the masked miners, and knowing it would be suicidal to name names, he claimed not to recognize their voices.[22]

May Arkwright Hutton did not come close to the nineteenth-century ideal of American womanhood. A large woman, she was vocal and opinionated and no beauty. She had always held her own in the sometimes earthy give-and-take of life in the Coeur d'Alenes. Firm in her convictions and staunch in her support of labor, when her husband landed in the stockade, she lost no time trying to free him. A popular daily visitor to the prisoners in the bullpen, May harassed the authorities and harangued in their own salty language the troops sent to guard the miners. She finally appealed to Al's fellow Masons and, apparently through their intervention, won his release.[23]

An investigation followed the lifting of martial law, and a coroner's jury ruled Al Hutton to have been "a willing tool of the rioters." With this verdict, he lost his job with the Northern Pacific. He was now free to work full-time at the Hercules.[24]

In the years since the Huttons made their investment, a greater part of the backbreaking work at the mine had been done by Al Hutton, August Paulsen, and a stonemason named Claude Caro who hired on in 1898. Progress was slow and the work unimaginably hard, but the determined partners gave little thought to quitting. On June 2, 1901, Paulsen blasted through rock into "a cave of wire and lead carbonate" and "hauled a wheelbarrow of this ore outside, filled the suitcase he had brought his clothing in, and took it to show to his partners."[25] Paulsen's find validated the partners' hard work and confidence and took them to the next phase of underground toil.

May Hutton took great interest in the ongoing work at the Hercules and kept the miners well fed. The men gathered at the Hutton house for dinner and to display ore specimens and discuss their plans. Even as they delighted in both the amount of ore and its richness, the partners still had an enormous amount of work to do to realize the mine's potential. Work they all did, and "by the end of 1903, the Hercules . . . was yielding a net profit of $40,000 a month."[26]

Harry Day and his family owned controlling interest in the Hercules, and the minority stockholders willingly left managing its lead-silver business to him. The mine's dividends totaled more than $250,000 in 1903; two years later they rose to $626,300 and in 1906, the year before the Huttons moved from Wallace, $880,000. By 1925, before the mine was worked out and closed down, the Hercules had returned dividends totaling $19,067,816. The Huttons' investment and hard work had netted approximately $1,906,781.[27]

The silver strike enabled Al and May to move into a larger and better appointed house, but Wallace society, ruled by an elite of mine owners' wives, remained closed to them. Those ultraproper Victorian women could not accept May's assertiveness, her nonconformity and lack of formal education, her background as a boardinghouse proprietor, her size and flamboyant taste in clothes, and perhaps above all her pro-labor sympathies. In the wake of the Bunker Hill dynamiting and Al's incarceration, she had written a novel—*The Coeur d'Alenes: or, A Tale of the Modern Inquisition in Idaho* (1900). A scathing and satirical indictment, the book had thinly veiled characters that included Governor Steunenberg and the mine owners; it sold well, but once May joined the ranks of owners herself, she bought up all the remaining copies.[28]

Ostracism left her undaunted. May joined the Wallace Shakespeare Club; she read hungrily and widely—from classical literature to political tracts; she increased her vocabulary and, "with a considerable natural talent for vivid expression, became a convincing speaker." In their home the Huttons entertained many easterners of note including the suffragist Carrie Chapman Catt and the attorney Clarence Darrow. Both she and Al relished a good time, and they "whirled merrily through a plebeian society; they rarely missed a picnic, excursion, or union dance . . . and they liked costume balls . . . where May's fanciful clothing of her own stitching became legendary."[29]

Even after they moved to Spokane, they did not forget their friends from the mining district. May wrote to one:

> We celebrated our twenty-first anniversary on Tuesday. It doesn't seem possible that it has been twenty-one years since you played our wedding march but so it be. We had twelve guests to dinner . . . comparatively new friends whom we are learning to love and appreciate very much. After they were gone, Al and I talked it over and said how nice it would have been to have been back under the old roof-tree and had had around us twelve of the old crowd like one family to participate in our joys and sorrows in the days of the Coeur d'Alenes. Such is life and we are all too busy to indulge vain regrets but must make new friends among our new environment and work for the betterment of humanity. . . . [signed] Lovingly and sincerely.[30]

Working for the betterment of humanity in their new environment defined the rest of their lives.

The Huttons left the Coeur d'Alenes for Spokane in 1907. The city's leading business and professional men and its lumber and mining millionaires had built magnificent homes in Browne's Addition and on the developing South Hill, beautiful residential districts that distinguished Spokane for decades. The newcomers from Wallace, however, looked to downtown, where commercial real estate opportunities seemed unbounded.[31]

A year earlier, Al Hutton, seeing real estate as an appropriate pursuit, had started construction of the Hutton Building—a four-story edifice that went up on Washington Street. A lavishly furnished nine-room apartment on its top floor would be the Huttons' home until 1914. Hercules Mine business took him to Wallace two or three times a year, and the partners continued a regular correspondence. To counter any possible industrial espionage, Al sealed letters with wax imprinted with his monogrammed seal.[32]

While the Hercules and real estate occupied him, May Hutton was completely free to pursue the causes she cared passionately about. She met the same rebuffs from society leaders in Spokane as she had in Wallace, but she remained undeterred. Hutton understood his wife's enthusiasms and supported her in most of them. One Spokane friend said that, for May, "Al Hutton was the ideal husband. Rarely did he seek to restrain her [activities]. . . . At a time when women were fettered by custom and by convention, May Hutton was free to express her expansive . . . nature as she saw fit."[33] Reportedly, he admonished her only not to "make a holy show out of yourself" as she forged ahead.[34]

May had been involved to a small degree in the 1896 campaign that resulted in Idaho's adopting woman suffrage; an affirmed and committed Democrat, in 1904 she had run for the state senate from heavily Republican Shoshone County and lost by just eighty votes. Asked soon after whether men had taken kindly to her candidacy, she replied, "I can't say that they did, . . . but I got the vote of the women; that's one thing that I would like to have understood."[35]

Gaining the right to vote for women in Washington became her paramount goal. May had joined the National American Woman Suffrage Association in 1905 and through her suffrage activities had met Emma Smith DeVoe, a professional organizer sent from Illinois to lead suffrage campaigns in the Northwest. May joined the Washington Equal Suffrage Association and served as vice-president under the Seattle-based DeVoe. May recruited large numbers to the cause, and the Spokane Equal Suffrage Association became the largest in the state.[36]

But DeVoe's Seattle followers came to see Hutton as a threat to their prestige and power. Conflict between the eastern and western Washington groups took an ugly turn when DeVoe supporters dug for notoriety or scandal in May's past and tried to expel her from the state's suffrage organization. The state treasurer returned her 1909 dues payment, noting

> I believe you are ineligible to membership in the Washington Equal Suffrage Associa-
> tion because of your habitual use of profane and obscene language and of your
> record in Idaho as shown by pictures and other evidence placed in my hands by
> persons who are familiar with your former life and reputation.

Angry, but undaunted, the woman who had confronted martial law and survived
the rigors of the mining frontier promptly organized the Washington Political
Equality League. Operating from its office in the Hutton Building, she kept the
suffrage issue alive in eastern Washington.[37]

A wide gulf separated her from the other suffrage leaders. DeVoe, well educated, widely known, and successful, "must have felt politically and organization-
ally superior." May, former boardinghouse proprietor and staunch Democrat, sought
to take the suffrage battle into the area of party politics; DeVoe, a conservative
Republican, considered partisan politics unsuitable for the suffrage cause. And as
the historian Patricia Voeller Horner found, "Correspondence also suggests that
there was some antagonism toward May because of her newly acquired wealth."[38]

Soon after Washington's women finally won the right to vote in 1910, May
Hutton served on a Spokane County jury—one of the first women to do so. A
delegate to the Democratic party's 1912 state convention in Walla Walla, she cast
her vote for William Jennings Bryan and free and unlimited coinage of silver. The
convention did not award Bryan the state's delegates, but it did send May Hutton
on to Baltimore and made her the first woman delegate to a Democratic National
Convention.[39]

Her colorful reputation preceded her. Woodrow Wilson won the party's presidential nomination there, and May Arkwright Hutton won national celebrity. She
met with Mrs. William Jennings Bryan and "moved among the notable." She did
as she pleased: eastern reporters found her irresistible; they made much of her jury
service and happily recorded anecdotes about the blunt and plain-spoken woman
from Spokane. The most enduring tale centered on her laundry.

> She took a suite at one of the best hotels, did a small washing . . . and hung it out the
> window. The management protested. Then May protested. Had she not paid an outra-
> geous sum for the suite? She presumed that the window went along with the rooms.

She spoke on woman suffrage several times, accompanied by the sister-in-law of
the millionaire August Belmont.[40]

May Arkwright Hutton "dared to be herself at a time . . . [when] this was a
difficult thing to do. . . . [She] improved the lives of those around her and set a
worthy example." She and Al brought wealth and energy to Spokane and shared
both willingly to improve lives around them. She pushed for reform, spearheading
the creation of a juvenile court in Spokane and the drive to secure matrons to
supervise women prisoners in the city jail. The mayor appointed her to his newly
established city charities committee, and although the two did not always agree,

when her term expired he asked her to stay on, admitting that he knew of no one else with "her common horse sense and warm heart."[41]

Her husband joined her in philanthropic work in the private sector. She emphatically said, "I look after the charitable donations of the Hutton family," and as one who knew them said later of their charitable endeavors, often "May was the first to move into action." She had early discovered the Florence Crittenton Home for unwed mothers and established a long-term affiliation with its board, on which Al served for many years as treasurer. May related sympathetically to the young women at the home and frequently provided what amounted to a matrimonial bureau. She scoured surrounding farms and ranches for suitable husbands for them, and the Huttons' home became the site of many of their weddings. On at least one occasion the press recounted that "Mr. Levi W. Hutton gave the bride away."[42]

May also discovered an orphanage maintained by the Ladies' Benevolent Society in a building on Washington Street. In the spring of 1908, she reported: "All energies are directed this week toward raising $40,000 for the [new] Home of the Friendless in Spokane. . . .I am helping on that." The new building rose the following year and became known as the Spokane Children's Home. Levi Hutton related as sympathetically to the children in the orphanage as May had to the Florence Crittenton women, and when his wife became involved he, too, joined the work enthusiastically.[43]

The Huttons shared their wealth with Spokane, and they enjoyed it themselves. They traveled, they dressed well, they owned automobiles luxurious for the time, and they maintained a chauffeur for May, who did not drive. And they entertained. The Hutton dining room's well-fed guests ranged from politicians and bishops to family members and old friends from their Idaho days.

When May returned from the Democratic convention in Baltimore, she and Levi started construction on their dream home—a pillared white colonial at 17th Avenue and Crestline. It cost $68,000, an incredible sum for the time. The former Iowa farm boy bought sufficient land to build a small barn and keep a cow so that the one-time boardinghouse cook could have all the fresh cream she needed. Even with space for a vegetable garden and a greenhouse, they had more land than they could utilize. In typical fashion they "donated a portion east of the homesite for the Lincoln Park playgrounds. It was an enduring gift to the children of Spokane."[44]

Their house was completed in early 1914. Reveling in her new home, May held a housewarming for two thousand guests that July. But by then she had developed health problems. She had endured two bouts with the kidney affliction known as Bright's disease, and later that summer she suffered a third that confined her to bed. She had returned from the Baltimore convention a celebrity and such a potential force in national politics that William Jennings Bryan, by then Wilson's secretary of state, paid a visit to her sickbed during his peace-oriented tour of the West. She improved to some extent and even organized another action group,

Spokane Women for World Peace, but the illness left her a mere shadow of the woman who once weighed upward of 225 pounds. Even in decline, she managed one last social function—a lawn party for delegates to the State Federation of Women's Clubs convention in the summer of 1915.[45]

The following autumn, on the afternoon of October 5, "cheerful as usual," she received friends at home, but early the following morning she died peacefully in her sleep. Her funeral, held in the drawing room of the house next to Lincoln Park, drew a huge throng that overflowed onto the lawn. Mourners reflected a cross-section of Spokane, "society women and working girls, businessmen, rough miners and men from skid row and young girls with babies in their arms and tears in their eyes. They had all come to say goodbye to a friend." Floral tributes engulfed the house itself, including a spray of red roses from the Ladies' Benevolent Society. Newspapers in the city where society had once spurned her hailed her as "author, suffragist, philosopher, humanitarian and probably one of the best known women in the great northwest . . . [who] in Spokane was generally beloved for her charitable and public-spirited activities."[46]

Decades later, in Lincoln Park one Sunday afternoon in August 1973, the Spokane Chapter of the National Organization for Women (NOW) celebrated the anniversary of the Nineteenth Amendment to the Constitution. Acknowledging "a woman who was many years ahead of her time," the celebrants had issued a public invitation to a "picnic and program [to] be held under a tree planted about 50 years ago in honor of May Arkwright Hutton, Spokane's most colorful suffragette and wife of the founder of the Hutton Settlement, Levi Hutton." Another generation, a resurgent women's movement, had discovered her. Photographs show a gathering of strong, attractive, capable young women rallying that afternoon in the cause of women's rights.[47] May would have loved it and would have welcomed them to the shade of her tree with open arms.

After she died, Al Hutton stayed on in the large, comfortable home they had built. He continued their generous support of charitable organizations, especially the Ladies' Benevolent Society and its Spokane Children's Home. And he turned in earnest to planning his greatest philanthropy—the Hutton Settlement.

Although the Settlement certainly reflected May Hutton's interests and sympathies, it was Levi Hutton's creation; it became the consuming interest of the rest of his life. Many people assumed that he was simply carrying out her wishes, that the two of them planned it, or that he built it in memory of her. He later corrected such misimpressions in a letter to the Spokane *Spokesman-Review,* noting that they had never discussed establishing a children's home. However, of the woman who looked after the charitable donations of the Hutton family, he said, "I am sure were she here today she would heartily approve all I have done."[48]

2

The Founding Father
and Allies in Planning

W here there is a will there is a way. Levi Hutton had the will to improve the lives of orphans and others whose childhoods paralleled his own; he had found a way to do that by supporting the Spokane Children's Home. He continued to make generous contributions to the work of its sponsors, the Ladies' Benevolent Society, and by the spring of 1917 had begun to talk of building a new facility for them. But eighteen months after his wife's death, her heirs contested her will.

In December of 1913, May Arkwright Hutton had drawn a new will in which she bequeathed $1,000 each to her half sister and two surviving half brothers and the same amount to be divided between the children of a deceased half brother. A champion of labor to the end, she left $5,000 "toward the completion of a Labor Temple in the City of Spokane." The remainder of her estate went to her husband, "with full power to use, . . . for and during the term of his natural life" or until he should remarry. In the last eventuality, her portion would devolve to those named family members.[1]

Some of May's nieces and nephews had moved to the Northwest, but in March of 1917, a month before the estate was to close, the Ohio Arkwrights filed suit in Wallace, Idaho, to have Levi Hutton removed as executor of her estate and to prevent his receiving her half interest in the Hercules mining property. They contended that the estate had been fraudulently undervalued and that Idaho's community property laws differed from those of Washington, to their benefit. They sought "absolute title to all property, shares of stocks, bonds, notes and other personal property" from the estate. As one historian saw it, "Her generosity toward them while she was living so spoiled them that they felt entitled to a large portion of her estate."[2]

In the month after they brought the suit, Hutton had sought to reach a settlement with May's relatives. Although their claim had little legal merit, he estimated what they might receive on his death and offered these in-laws more than a fourth of the present value of their interest on condition that they "make proper conveyances of their entire interest in the estate to me." With a nephew in Portland as something of a go-between, the negotiations dragged on for months. Meanwhile, the Wallace probate judge rejected their petition.[3] Finally, in February of 1918, Hutton deposited $175,000 in Spokane's Old National Bank, for payment to the heirs May had named in her will, including the children of her now deceased half sister.[4]

Two months later, Hutton drafted a new will of his own. After bequeathing $10,000 each to his brothers, Asa and Stephen, and his sister, Laura Hutton Abraham, and lesser amounts to two cousins, he spelled out his intent to build a home for orphaned children on land acquired for that purpose. He directed that "the name of said home. . . shall be and permanently remain 'The Hutton Settlement.'" He made specific provisions, based on his real estate holdings, for constructing and maintaining the Settlement, pointedly adding, "no heir of mine . . . shall be entitled to the said real estate or any part thereof or to any of the income therefrom."[5] The Arkwright lawsuit had apparently made him wary of even blood relatives.

Throughout this year of turmoil, he had increased his support of the Spokane Children's Home. Early in his legal dispute with the Arkwright heirs, he received a note of thanks for a monthly donation: "How good it was of you, Mr. Hutton, to again remember the Spokane Children's Home with the magnificent present of $100 . . . [how] gratifying to the Ladies' Benevolent Society to have such a thoroughly good and loyal friend . . . as yourself." Hutton's dividends from the Hercules Mine totaled $486,718 in 1917 and $568,750 in 1918, two of the mine's best years; his generosity increased accordingly.[6]

Hutton met with the board of the Ladies' Benevolent Society on June 7, 1917, in the public meeting room of the Palace Department Store; he soon offered the board his own office for its meetings and the gift of his car for its use. The main topic of discussion that day was the mortgage on the Children's Home; he proposed paying the Home's operating expenses so that the board could use other donations to pay the mortgage. A week later the record shows that the women acknowledged "his wonderful kindness."[7]

Among the few extant written sources in Hutton's own hand is a small record book that he began keeping on August 27, 1917, when he entered the following: "I have this day purchased one hundred eleven acres of land ten miles north east of Spokane for a place to build an orphan's home. The following is what is needed to make a home up to date." He jotted down specific ideas in the book and over time noted milestones in its construction.[8]

Immediately after the land purchase, Hutton announced his intentions to the press, "I am giving the children's home to be erected on the site to the Ladies' Benevolent Society of Spokane without any strings. . . . I plan to spend about $100,000 on a modern brick building and will endow the home so that it will be assured an income of $700 to $1000 a month for maintenance." He bought the original tract from the Spokane Valley Land and Water Company for $29,329.20. Between November 21, 1917, and January 16, 1918, he also acquired adjoining parcels from Jacob Shrenk and F. H. Obermuller, bringing his total expenditure to $35,954.20 for land in the valley.[9]

He soon elaborated on his motives:

> I have a warm place in my heart for orphans because I know what it means to be an orphan. . . . I know by actual experience how lonely and absolutely unattached is [he]. . . . No orphan in the Inland Empire will be turned away from this home, no matter what his sect, creed or color may be. It will be a real home for boys and girls who have no home.[10]

And he explained further that

> I said nothing of these ideas, formed in my youth, until two years after Mrs. Hutton's death. . . . My ambition had always been to build such a home and in 1917 when I met with the Ladies' Benevolent Society, paid a $5,000 mortgage on the Spokane Children's Home of 10 years standing, and laid my plan before them, they approved it and the idea of my youth began to bear fruit.[11]

To say the women approved understates their reaction to his proposal. At the society's September meeting, President Fannie B. Lewis talked about the land Hutton had bought for the new home and repeated his promise that "an orchard would be planted soon and everything almost could be raised to support the Home." This rather meager account recorded in the meeting minutes translated into the following letter from the corresponding secretary:

> My dear Mr. Hutton—
>
> The last meeting of the board of the Children's home was a regular jubilee. Probably you are the only other person in town who is happier over the new prospects for the children than the ladies of the board—unless it is the children themselves. And some of them can't realize what it will mean to have all the milk and eggs and butter and other good things which are coming to them, for they have never had them in all their little lives. . . . we are all going to drive out to see the site of the new home. Mrs. Lewis is delighted with it.
>
> We want to tell you again how deep is our appreciation of all the splendid things you are doing and planning for the children.[12]

Even as he made his land purchase, Hutton hired an architect, Harold Whitehouse, who had moved to Spokane the same year as the Huttons had and worked for a short time with George H. Keith, whom Levi had hired to build the house on 17th Street; Whitehouse himself may actually have designed the residence. Seven years later, in 1914, Whitehouse formed a partnership with Ernest V. Price. The firm of Whitehouse and Price would go on to design many highly acclaimed buildings in the Northwest. The partners' numerous church designs include Spokane's magnificent Cathedral of St. John the Evangelist and Seattle's Church of the Epiphany. Their academic structures include buildings at the universities of Washington and Idaho and at Washington State University. They designed fraternity and sorority houses in Pullman and Moscow, Idaho, and for the Whitman College chapter of Sigma Chi. The campus of the Hutton Settlement stands as one of Harold Whitehouse's early triumphs. It received national exposure and recognition in 1920 when his three-part account of planning and construction appeared in the prestigious journal *Architectural Forum*.[13]

Whitehouse later recalled that the Hutton Settlement commission began with a trip to the East to investigate "the best orphanages in that part of the country." He visited "some thirty institutions and talked with heads of the same." On his return he met with Hutton and the Ladies' Benevolent Society board to share what he had learned.[14]

To understand and appreciate the unique place the Hutton Settlement holds in the annals of child care, some history is helpful. The role or status of childhood in the United States underwent dramatic change over the years. Colonists had brought with them the English traditions of both voluntary and involuntary apprenticeship. Parents of all but the upper classes "placed out" their children to learn a craft or trade. Adopting the philosophy behind Elizabethan poor laws to "suppress vagrancy and idleness and provide for the relief of poverty," local authorities "involuntarily 'bound out' orphans, bastards, abandoned children, and impoverished, neglected, or abused children" to work for and be educated by other families.[15]

The practice of involuntary placing out assumed new dimensions when the Reverend Charles Loring Brace founded New York's Children's Aid Society (CAS) in 1853. His main goal was to rescue impoverished children from the city's streets and "place them out West in good Christian families where they would be cared for, educated, and employed." In the spring of 1854, the CAS sent 138 children by rail from the city to farms in western Pennsylvania. By 1890, the phenomenon known as the orphan train had taken 84,000 children to the Midwest; by 1929, the number would total 150,000. Brace considered the children's chances of receiving ill treatment far fewer in the United States than in Europe and believed this country harbored "a widespread spirit of benevolence . . . [that] opens thousands of homes to the children of the unfortunate." But in fact these relocated youngsters were not always treated as sons and daughters in their new locales, and for some, their new situations were cruel and disastrous.[16]

The Reverend Brace continued his large-scale orphan resettlement while other child welfare reformers turned to orphanages. Following the founding of the New York Society for the Prevention of Cruelty to Children in 1874, a "multitude of anti-cruelty organizations sprang up" across the country. These joined other welfare agencies in placing abused and neglected children in large, congregate care orphanages. The nineteenth century has been called the age of the asylum; the number of orphanages tripled in the United States between 1865 and 1890.[17]

The carnage of the Civil War had left the nation with an enormous number of dependent and vagrant children; dealing with this problem produced unprecedented changes in child care policy. Northern state governments gave funds to private asylums "to house children of Union troops"; other states, both north and south, opened public institutions for children of the war dead. Postwar urbanization added to the numbers of dependent children and exacerbated the problem of caring for them. By 1890, the relatively new concept of children as a special category of citizens had gained acceptance, influencing child care immeasurably. In the following decade the state assumed a greater presence in the lives of the dependent and neglected. At the same time, the goal of "child saving" had also seized the attention and agendas of private sector social reformers, a goal that lasted well into the next century.[18]

The decade of the 1890s saw the incorporation of nearly 250 homes for children. Forty-nine umbrella groups also came into being, including the Children's Home Society of Washington in 1896. New institutions assumed different forms, and some reformers adopted the idea of preserving families instead of institutionalizing dependent children. One avenue for preserving the family lay in paying a "mothers' pension" to destitute mothers, enabling them to maintain their children at home. The nation's first mothers' pension legislation passed in 1911, forerunner of later depression-era Aid to Dependent Children acts. Large, impersonal orphanages fell from favor early in the twentieth century, and many closed their doors. New orphanages built on the cottage plan emerged, however, as an antidote to the stereotypical Dickensian institution—that large, dark, and dismal prisonlike structure that warehoused children in barren dormitories.[19]

At the landmark first White House Conference on the Care of Dependent Children in 1909, preservation of the family emerged as the top recommendation. With very few then defending the principle of congregate care in large asylums, delegates passed a declaration advocating that children be kept with their natural families whenever possible. When care by either the nuclear or extended family proved impossible, an extension of this philosophy would lead to placement in foster care. However, those who saw orphanages as unavoidable defended them. A small groundswell developed for the "formation of 'anti-institutional institutions' with family-style cottages." As one scholar put it, for some,

> and their numbers were not negligible, institutions remained the only solution. Even so, most child-savers argued, institutions should be made as much like families as possible, which meant dividing them into 'cottages' presided over by surrogate parents.

Ensuing debates centered on administrative matters such as size—"How many children could a cottage house and still be like a home?"[20]

When Harold Whitehouse traveled to the East Coast in 1917, it was to ask just such questions. His client's primary intent remained the creation of a *home* for orphaned, luckless, and ill-fated children. For guidance Hutton tapped into the currents of professional thought through his architect and the board of the Ladies' Benevolent Society. Those currents flowed from New York—from the New York

Orphans Asylum at Hastings-on-Hudson and from the Russell Sage Foundation, which was established, endowed, and named for her husband in 1907 by Mrs. Margaret Olivia Slocum Sage and which aimed at the improvement of social and living conditions throughout the country.

Whitehouse spent several days at the Sage Foundation where he received valuable information from W. H. Slingerland, special agent in its Department of Child-Helping, and from Hastings H. Hart, whose writings had influenced the trend away from large institutions. The architect also spent time with the head of the New York City Orphanage, Dr. Rudolph Reeder, who had converted that institution from regimented congregate care to the cottage plan and moved it out of the city in the process.[21]

Undoubtedly, Whitehouse visited the William L. Gilbert Home in Winstead, Connecticut. Gilbert, who derived a fortune from clock making and railroad investments, founded and endowed this home and school in the 1890s "for the improvement of mankind . . . [by] educating the young as will help them to become good citizens." A large, congregate care institution with a capacity for 225 residents, the Gilbert Home stood on a one hundred–acre site and operated its own school. Its admission policy rather than its format may have influenced Levi Hutton's thinking. The Connecticut asylum was a home "for normal children, mentally and physically, who for some cause are deprived of the advantages of family life. . . . Children are accepted as young as four years of age and many remain until they complete high school."[22]

On his return trip, Whitehouse changed trains in Chicago, and evidence points to his visiting two Chicago-area institutions. One of them recently completed on a 1,015-acre tract west of the city, was described as "the world's largest and greatest vocational school." Conceived in 1910, a time when fraternal organizations were ascendant, it was built by the Loyal Order of Moose. Thomas R. Marshall, vice-president of the United States and a member of the Order, had "dedicated the ground to the philanthropic uses of the Order under the name of 'Mooseheart.'" By the time of Whitehouse's visit, "permanent quarters for the housing of 500 boys and girls had been erected," and the architect saw a superb example of a large combined home and school in operation.[23] He later wrote that "allowing the orphan children to mingle with playmates at the public school seems the best system."[24]

His other stop in the Windy City was at the Chicago Nursery and Half Orphanage Asylum. This large three-story building housed children in dormitories, but Whitehouse found the building plans "well conceived," and "though not of the cottage type," they may have been one source of his own later thinking. He especially noted the infirmary "with isolation wards for both boys and girls."[25]

Convinced, however, of the advantages and soundness of the cottage system, Whitehouse returned to Spokane in November and brought his findings and recommendations to Hutton and the LBS board. The idea of a cottage-style orphanage strongly appealed to Hutton because his own childhood had not reflected the ideal envisioned by advocates of placement with extended family or in foster homes. But he wanted the final decision to rest with the women of the board. After careful contemplation and another thorough discussion, on November 24, 1917, they voted to "accept the cottage plan proposed by Mr. Hutton and [Mr.] Whitehouse for the new home. The President asked for a rising vote. The vote was unanimous." In anticipation of so important a decision, absent members "had telephoned their vote in favor of the cottage plan."[26]

As welfare concerns had grown more child-centered, women nationwide had played an increasingly important role. They spearheaded such reforms as mothers' pensions, child labor laws, and juvenile courts. In Spokane, women similarly had undertaken the improvement of life for the city's children in 1887 when they organized the Ladies' Benevolent Society intended "to provide a Home for the Friendless Children of Spokane Falls." The LBS had gone on to oversee operation of the Spokane Children's Home, the oldest charitable institution in the city. Now the Society's all-woman board, at Levi Hutton's request, was in on the ground floor of the Hutton Settlement. The founder wanted the women to "keep in touch with the building so they would understand all plans" for the new home; their advice and opinion counted. Reflecting what has been termed maternalist social policy, they also satisfied his goal of bringing a mother's point of view and disposition to his home for children.[27]

Board members stayed well abreast of current theory and practice; they read widely and actively sought information from experts to augment their own maternal inclinations. Once they subscribed to the cottage plan for the new home, they were determined to avoid any pitfalls in launching their new venture. In December of 1917, Mrs. Fannie Lewis, board president, turned for advice to Rudolph Reeder of the New York Orphan Asylum, who had set forth principles of child care in a 1909 book.

Dear Sir:

I have recently read with a great deal of interest your "How Two Hundred Children Live and Learn." . . . our society is to receive the gift of a complete set [of] community cottages and buildings for the care of 100 or more orphans. . . .

Our children range in age from the smallest infants up to 14 or 15 years, and naturally come from all classes and conditions of private homes. Have you found that one housemother can properly care for a family of 20 or more boys and girls of these ages? Have you ever had any difficulty from keeping boys and girls of these ages together in one cottage? That is any serious sex problems? Your answers and suggestions will be greatly appreciated by us.[28]

Reeder by that time had left for France with the Red Cross and was "already in the war zone helping to care for destitute orphans." Mrs. Lewis received no reply, but the influence of his book is apparent. One section of *How Two Hundred Children Live and Learn* contained compositions written by asylum children on "How I Spent Last Saturday."[29] Two decades later recollections of Hutton Settlement echoed those accounts of companionship and doing chores together.

In his hope to impart a feeling of family and keep siblings together in the new home, Hutton had thought to have boys and girls live in the same cottage. This idea no doubt motivated in part Mrs. Lewis's letter to Rudolph Reeder. Whitehouse shared her apprehension, and he, too, wrote for Reeder's opinion, explaining that his client contemplated

> an Orphanage on the Cottage Plan modelled as nearly after the plan of your institution as practicable; but he brings up the suggestion of building the cottages to accommodate ten boys and ten girls. . . .
>
> I advised against this quite strongly because of the fact that the children were not real brothers and sisters. . . . He thought that it would tend to make the family group still more homelike.

The New York Orphan Asylum's acting superintendent replied emphatically: "I know of nobody who has had experience in orphanage work who would dare to advocate the plan your client has in mind."[30] Thereafter, the Hutton Settlement planners agreed that separate cottages would exist for girls and for boys.

In the architectural vein of form following function, after working out administrative and operational plans for the new home with its benefactor and the LBS board, Harold Whitehouse undertook the design of four cottages and an administration building. He felt that, now that he had "thorough knowledge of the [operational] side of the work, . . . the architecture will. . . be fitting and proper, because utility and efficiency was the key note in all the planning."[31]

While continuing to run the Spokane Children's Home, the LBS board was closely involved in design decisions for the Settlement. Indeed, for the first three months after Whitehouse's return from the East Coast, the women met with him almost daily. The architect consulted them on numerous matters, among them "how large the Ladies would like the assembly room" at the new campus; anticipating annual Christmas programs, Friday night movies, dances, luncheons, and other gatherings, they decided it "should be large enough to accommodate three hundred or more."[32]

Levi Hutton may have been a bit utopian or naïve in hoping to house boys and girls together, but much of his thinking spoke positively to problems inherent in child care at the time—the breakup of family groups, rigidity and regimentation, isolation, loss of individuality, and the like. The home he had lacked as a child, the idea of home, was uppermost in his mind and informed every aspect of planning what might be described as an anti-orphanage.

He said he wanted "to get away from the uniform idea of most orphanages, where every child is molded after the same pattern . . . [and] the orphanage atmosphere is stamped on the very nature of every child." He knew that large and impersonal older institutions "typically required uniform dress, . . [and] children marched in columns into the dining room, where they sat at long tables." Hutton would have none of that. He opted for small dining tables, and an early entry in his record book stipulated that "cottage mothers must eat at the same table with the children." Toward greater individual freedom he specifically wrote, "Children must select the color of their clothing." His own childhood certainly determined his thinking, and it comes as no surprise that the man who had married May Arkwright would say, "Above all I want individualism."[33]

Raised on an Iowa farm, Hutton also saw great value in the healthful environment and activities of a working farm. In the spring of 1919, he recorded adding "more land to the Home, all told I have two hundred forty acres. About one hundred fifteen acres is pasture land." A month later the total was 280. He specified that the Settlement should include a "cow and horse barn [with] silo and hay capacity" as well as a chicken house. Anticipating favorable crop yields he also intended a "root house complete."[34] For decades, Hutton Settlement youngsters would work in these structures and care for the livestock they sheltered.

As for the rest of the Settlement buildings and grounds, Hutton seems to have overlooked nothing and to have spared no expense. He specified that the "lawn must be irrigated with the least possible work . . . [and the] water system must be complete in all details." From the sewerage system to the "garbage burner" and "sweeping machine," from the modern heating plant to electric lighting, he insisted on high quality and efficient function. A practical man appreciative of good food, he wanted state-of-the-art kitchens that would include a "bread mixing machine and up to date . . . electric oven." He also specified an "ice machine" and, with an eye toward laundry, a "washing machine and mangle."[35]

Determined that the Settlement be a true home where children "would learn to work as well as play," he anticipated that farm work and household chores would be part of resident life. Yet drudgery was to be avoided. He particularly noted that "all corners in floor and walk must be rounded up so they can be cleaned easy" and that "windows should be made to swing open so as to avoid weights and make them handy to clean"; such thoughts spoke to child-oriented labors. Addressing the play side of the equation, he said, "Each cottage must have a basement play house."[36] Window washing would remain among the least pleasurable of chores, but Settlement residents happily recalled that they had played and roller skated in the cottage basements.

He did not neglect the requirements of staff or their welfare, noting in one instance that "bath tubs should be raised so one can bathe children without stooping too much." Nor did he overlook health care provisions for the children. One wing would house a hospital, or infirmary, with a "sweat room and bath for the sick" and an "isolated ward." He stipulated that "each ward must have seven hundred fifty cubic [feet] of air for each person."[37]

Whether Hutton's ideas, including that "all buildings must have heavy slate roofs," originated with him or with his architect, they paralleled Harold Whitehouse's planning and designs and reflected the influence of the Russell Sage Foundation. Whitehouse continued to consult with the Foundation's Department of Child-Helping and W. H. Slingerland, who visited the campus during construction to advise.[38] In fact, hiring Whitehouse in the first place likely came as a result of the Sage Foundation's Hastings Hart, whose writings the LBS board likely had read. In one book Hart recommended that

> the architect should be selected early in the proceedings. If possible he should have had some practical experience in erecting institutions. If he lacks that experience, it will be economical to send him at the expense of the [planners] to study similar institutions. There are hundreds of institutions in the United States that have been made showy and pretentious, in order to produce a monumental effect, while the provision for children and employees is inadequate. The architect should know how to secure beauty by the lines and proportions of the building, rather than by expensive carving and other elaborate decorations.[39]

Although cost was not a primary concern of Hutton's, Hart's emphasis on child-centered utility and function resonated with Hutton and Whitehouse both. The architect intended to "let the final plan . . . spell efficiency from every angle . . . after all this is one of the fundamental principles of good designing." Hutton wanted the home "to last for two hundred and fifty years." To insure quality, he hired P. L. Peterson, one of Spokane's finest builders and "gave him carte blanche. . . . [He] built it just like the Rock of Gibraltar."[40]

Hutton followed every stage of planning and construction closely. He and Whitehouse, whose office was in the Hutton Building at the time, worked well together. The young architect considered his client "a wonderful man" to whom he was "very, very devoted."[41] His high regard clearly showed in planning for the bronze bas-relief that graces the entry of the administration building. Whitehouse, who had studied in Cornell's architecture program, engaged Christian M. S. Midjo, professor of art at that university, to create the likeness of Hutton based on photographs the architect supplied. Whitehouse and Peterson the builder bore the cost of the plaque. As the buildings neared completion, Midjo sent Whitehouse a photograph of the tablet soon to go to the foundry for bronzing. The delighted architect responded:

> I am over powered with joy with what you have started. It is perfectly delightful. There is almost no criticism to make of Mr. Hutton's likeness. . . his hair is just right. His eyes are perfect, in fact it is Mr. Hutton through and through.

He directed that the name on the inscription should read simply L. W. Hutton explaining, "He does not like his first name and does not wish it to appear [because] he is widely known . . . with the initials only."[42]

Most of the items Hutton had noted down in his record book found their way into the construction documents that the architect produced. For example, stairways and bathroom floors in the cottages would be made of expensive terrazzo, considered "far cheaper in the end," with the coved bases that Hutton wanted for ease of cleaning. Bathtubs would be raised to "make it much easier for the matron" in bathing younger children. Special kitchen sinks would allow dishwashing by several children at a time; the doors to the walk-in iceboxes would be kept low because loading the blocks of ice would be done by "boys who cannot lift as high as an adult." The infirmary occupying one wing of the administration building would have the isolation ward that Hutton wanted as well as a surgery and dental area for the use of visiting physicians and dentists. And all the roofs were to be heavy slate in "variegated grays, gray-greens and a few mottled purple and green."[43]

Whitehouse did everything possible to meet Hutton's desire that the Settlement "have a homelike atmosphere." Each cottage would accommodate up to twenty-five children. Built in the "late English style," the four cottages were virtually the same, but Whitehouse varied them "somewhat in general shape to create different exteriors." Each had a large living room, porch, locker room or "mud room," matron's quarters, kitchen, and dining room on the main floor. The second-floor bedrooms accommodated up to six younger children; older residents had single or double rooms, some on the third floor. Communal bathrooms served the children on residential floors; individual toilet facilities adjoined the mud rooms. In designing the bathrooms Whitehouse followed the advice of one authority: "for efficiency you should have an abundance of [plumbing] fixtures."[44]

With considerable foresight, patron and architect planned and spent for the long term. All five buildings boasted fireproof construction, with concrete foundations and walls "of hollow clay tile, faced with a tapestry brick." Roofs, framed with heavy timber, had "no exposed woodwork in the way of eaves or other structural members." To insure against rotting and erosion, slates at the eaves "start on the brick work which is corbeled out with special long-length brick." In a move virtually unheard of at the time, they placed campus electrical wiring underground.[45]

As he watched the buildings rise in the shadow of the foothills not far from the Spokane River, Levi Hutton took quiet pride in his creation. He even kept his litigious Arkwright in-laws informed of progress. Four months after at last settling with them financially, in the summer of 1918 he wrote to May's half brother Lyman, "I am getting along nicely with the Home. Have about sixty eight men working and will have it pretty well completed by the last of the year." However, it was not until June 28, 1919, that laying of the cornerstone would take place and, on September 21, construction conclude.[46]

To put the cost of his five buildings in perspective, consider that Hutton's carpenters received $6 per day; their counterparts in 2001 commanded $35 to $40 per hour. The campus was built when "the best brick cost $25 per thousand"; at century's end, best brick brought $830 per thousand.[47]

Fittingly, given Levi Hutton's long devotion to Freemasonry and the Shrine, the senior grand warden of the Free and Accepted Masons of Washington laid the cornerstone of the Settlement. A large crowd was on hand as he followed the ancient tradition of setting "a perfectly squared stone in the north east corner" of a building under construction, in this instance the administration building. His use of plumb, level, square, and trowel to set the stone "symbolically demonstrated moral concepts and standards of conduct of which all virtuous men approve."[48]

Many years later, Whitehouse's daughter suggested that on his East Coast tour the architect had observed what not to do as well as procedures to follow, and indeed he had returned determined to avoid "the many mistakes incorporated into the various institutions of the country." The close contact he established with the LBS board during the planning stage he maintained during construction, once bringing to a board meeting "samples of the woodwork for the Ladies to choose for the new Home."[49] For their part, the women took the lead in furnishing the cottages and developing plans for day-to-day living in them.

Who were the members of the Ladies' Benevolent Society board? They numbered among them wives and daughters of Spokane's founding fathers and early settlers and its leading business and professional men. Their own educational backgrounds exceeded the contemporary average for women, some having attended college. Their dedication to philanthropic causes mirrored that of their forebears, those "middle-class Protestant Americans [who] denounc[ed] rigid sectarianism in charitable affairs [while] inspired by an evangelical sense of mission." They personified Progressive Era child savers who empathized with the poor and the dependent and concentrated on such issues as "family violence, poverty, and the plight of children."[50]

Perhaps above all, the board women were practical. They directed every aspect of the Spokane Children's Home operations—from employing staff and negotiating annual contracts with the city for child maintenance to locating the best source for groceries and procuring the annual supply of firewood. Because that institution had minimal public financing, they had long experience in making a little go a long way. At a memorable meeting in 1917, they voted to "sell the horse and wagon immediately and . . . order . . . a car" to facilitate "gathering up things" such as donated clothing.[51] They devised inventive and effective plans for furnishing and operating the Hutton Settlement.

For example, they had long since agreed that, to ensure a homelike atmosphere, the dining rooms would "have small tables setting about five or six at each table." They determined to present this and other proposals to "the clubs in the city and let the good people understand just what is needed at the cottages and the administration building."[52] The board women also created cottage committees, still utilized eighty years later as part of a very "hands-on" management system. About six months before the Settlement opened, they decided to form "five committees, one for each house [and the administration building], and if those ladies get five captains and then get all the help they can, there would be no trouble in furnishing the new [cottages]. Several [people] have offered to furnish rooms." The Hutton Settlement's first cottage captains were Mrs. Kate Bean, Mrs. Ada Odell, Mrs. Miriam Ritchie, and Mrs. Mary Robison.[53]

The women did seek some consistency in furnishings. Toward that end Levi Hutton himself provided "beds and mattresses for all, which [they found] a very big help." The board also insisted that "those who furnish rooms must always consult the chairman of the furnishing committee in the cottage."[54]

They actively solicited help from possible donors, trying to "interest . . . the people of Spokane and vicinity in doing a bit for the home." One board member, Katherine Tate, approached Hutton's former compatriots in railroading. They responded: "What could be more appropriate than to submit [her] proposal to organizations of the railway brotherhoods and invite their attention to an opportunity for contributing to a worthy institution."[55] Railroad conductors agreed to furnish the matron's sitting room in Cottage Three.

Other completely furnished rooms in Cottage Three included the living room, which her Presbyterian friends provided in honor of Mrs. Margaret Dodd. Mrs. James L. Paine furnished the living room of Cottage One in honor of her father, the Reverend Henry T. Cowley. The matron's sitting room in Cottage Two was furnished in honor of Mrs. Harriet Ross Gandy, a Spokane pioneer and longtime board member of the LBS; one bedroom in that cottage was furnished by the wife of the former governor Marion E. Hay in honor of her mother.[56]

Raising money for the new campus buildings became a regular item for discussion at LBS board meetings. In August 1919, the idea arose that board members should hold a flower sale, "and all the street corners, Hotels, and stores should be filled with flowers." Immediately taking the form of a motion, it passed easily, and they authorized Mrs. Cole the secretary to get the necessary permit from the city council. At their September meeting they celebrated having netted $1,200 from the sale.[57]

Early that year the board women had endured a severe blow with the sudden death of their beloved colleague and highly respected president, Fannie Shaw Lewis. The Delaware native and her businessman husband, William A. Lewis, had come to Spokane in 1884. She had joined the Ladies' Benevolent Society shortly after its establishment and had helped operate the Spokane Children's Home, assuming the presidency by 1907. From Levi Hutton's first suggestion, she and the board had dedicated themselves to working in concert with Hutton and Whitehouse to create a new home for children. In her memory, her friends furnished the living room of Cottage Four at the Settlement.[58] Meantime, the LBS elected Mrs. James L. (Agnes Cowley) Paine president. At first reluctant to accept the nomination, "after thinking it over [she agreed that] for the sake of the little children she would do all she could for the work."[59] Under her leadership, the Society's work went on.

As construction of the Hutton Settlement neared completion, board members turned to the logistics of moving children from one home to another. Throughout planning and building, they had more or less assumed that the new cottages in the valley would replace their building in the city. However, other local welfare people thought, given the LBS's tradition of working with the city and county, "it would be a mistake to ever close [the] children's Home." The board had devised an application and admissions form for the Hutton Settlement but encountered an unforeseen obstacle when "some of the parents did not wish to sign and thought they preferred leaving their children in the Children's Home."[60] The Spokane Children's Home remained in existence for several decades more; some of the women continued to serve both on its board and that of the Hutton Settlement for many years.

L. W. Hutton, too, encountered the unforeseen as construction neared completion. Although 1918 had been one of the most profitable years for the Hercules Mine, the end of the war in Europe brought a decrease in the demand for lead and a decrease in his dividends. Dated April 1, 1920, the final statement for construction of the Settlement totaled $393,945.03. About $172,000 in expenses had accrued in the preceding fifteen months, and Hutton had needed to borrow $160,000. Banking laws at the time limited individual loans to $150,000. When he approached his friend D. W. Twohy at the Old National Bank for the larger amount, Twohy turned him down. Hutton served on the bank's board of directors; he finally convinced Twohy to lend him the money, arguing that with the Hutton and Fernwell buildings as collateral the bank would lose nothing. Had bank examiners "come around and checked up, [the two men] would have both got into trouble. . . . The president of the bank loaned [a director] $10,000 above the limit."[61]

The philanthropist's cash flow had benefited from his architect's tenancy in the Hutton Building. Whitehouse's fee was settled in December of 1921. Hutton's ledger explained an $886.77 item as "Balance due Whitehouse & Price used up as office rent in Hutton Bldg. 13 months @ 67.50 & $9.27 on Dec Rent." The ledger also shows that he made sizable payments in the fall of 1922 on "an additional loan from ON Bank of $15,000." By January 8, 1923, he had renegotiated his bank loans and "paid interest on note of $82,500. due on Jan. 7th and renewed note." Levi Hutton could not have relished carrying debt, but even when pressed himself, he dealt generously with others in financial straits. In September 1920 he closed the books on a prospector's account and even sent the man "$100 to keep him after his funds ran out." That same month he forgave $500 on another loan, because the "boys had bad crops, not able to pay."[62]

The burden of debt surely sat lighter when he recalled the accolades and warm letters of appreciation he had received for the Settlement. They came from everywhere. Frank Paine of Spokane's Union Trust Company told him the Settlement would be "a wonderful monument" and applauded "the thoughtfulness and generosity that prompted your splendid action." Senator Miles Poindexter weighed in from Washington, D.C., saying, "I . . . congratulate you on the splendid work you are doing in building a home for the orphans of Spokane"; he also sent an assortment of seeds for the Settlement farm and an offer to furnish federal agricultural bulletins. A woman in Seattle who had worked with May Hutton wrote:

> I congratulate you. Mrs. Hutton often spoke of the work that you did for the children and for the Florence Crittenton Home. [Your] gift proves that you are still deeply interested in the unfortunate and are not niggardly in dealing with them. Work of that sort blesses both ways as it helps the giver as much as the recipient.[63]

Children who would live at the Settlement and know their benefactor personally as "Daddy Hutton" appreciated and marveled at his generosity. Hutton carried the first of those children, four-year-old Jane Wiese, into Cottage One on a bitterly cold afternoon in late November 1919. She had fallen on the nearly frozen ground, and he swept her up into his arms and took her quickly inside. She recalled that day some forty years later and added, "He was the greatest, kindest and considerate person I've ever known."[64]

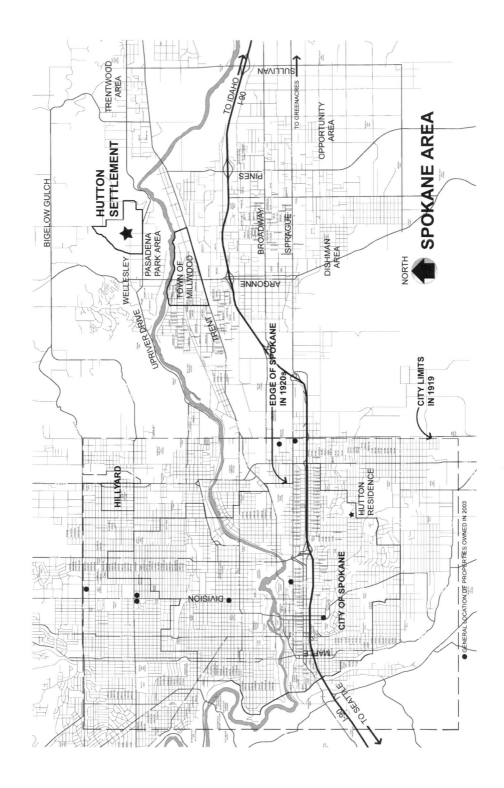

SPOKANE AREA

NORTH

HUTTON
SETTLEMENT

BIGELOW GULCH

TRENTWOOD
AREA

UPRIVER DRIVE

WELLESLEY

PASADENA
PARK AREA

TOWN OF
MILLWOOD

TRENT

TO IDAHO

I-90

SULLIVAN

TO GREENACRES

PINES

BROADWAY

SPRAGUE

ARGONNE

OPPORTUNITY
AREA

DISHMAN
AREA

HILLYARD

EDGE OF SPOKANE
IN 1920s

DIVISION

CITY LIMITS
IN 1919

HUTTON
RESIDENCE

CITY OF SPOKANE

MAPLE

I-90

TO SEATTLE

GENERAL LOCATION OF PROPERTIES OWNED IN 2003

● GENERAL LOCATION OF PROPERTIES OWNED IN 2003

3

Mission Accomplished:
Levi Hutton and the Board

Historically, the quality of care had varied enormously in America's private orphanages. Smaller places might be organized in homelike units but could be badly underfinanced; larger asylums could be better funded while failing to provide any sense of home or family.[1] Its founder's financial backing and unwavering intent that it be a *home* meant that the Hutton Settlement could offer uniformly good care under optimal conditions. Levi Hutton took great pride in his creation, saw to its incorporation, and as its chief executive officer—or supervisor—involved himself thoroughly in its operations.

On completion of the campus buildings in 1919, Levi Hutton contacted the Northern Pacific Railroad, hoping to acquire the bell from the locomotive he had operated in Idaho nearly three decades before. The company had long since sold Engine 109 but did locate it in a lumber camp in southwestern Washington. Obviously, the dynamite incident and his role in it had receded in company memory; in fact, in September 1921, NP officials from as far away as St. Paul came to present the bell to him for the Hutton Settlement.[2] Eighty years later, it was still in its place of honor just outside the administration building.

Nothing gave Hutton greater pleasure than hosting visitors to the campus. On one occasion soon after the Settlement opened, he escorted an important guest, a fellow Shriner, around the buildings and grounds. At that time the Shrine's Imperial Council sought to establish a charitable enterprise that would unite the entire membership in a worthwhile cause. Hutton's visitor was the imperial potentate W. Freeland Kendrick, who had come from Philadelphia to see for himself what Hutton had accomplished. Impressed by what he found, Kendrick told his host, "If one Noble can do what you have done alone, what can several hundred thousand Nobles do if we all put our shoulders together?" As a delegate from Spokane's El Katif, Hutton attended the Shrine's Imperial Council Session in the spring of 1920 where potential philanthropic projects were discussed. As an official version has it, "Out of that and other discussions The Shriners' Hospitals for Crippled Children became a reality" in 1922.[3]

Just as Hutton would play a role in the founding of the Shrine hospital in Spokane, so his fellow Shriners were early friends of his children's home. One of their first acts was the donation of $50 "to purchase cloth to sew . . . dresses, bloomers, and aprons for the children at the Settlement."[4]

Twenty-two children from the Spokane Children's Home, whose parents were willing to have them leave the city, numbered among those who moved to the valley campus in November 1919; by the end of the year the population totaled thirty-six. Official reporting began in January 1920, but before statistics and tallies supplanted informal head counts, the Settlement celebrated its first Christmas. Miss Jennie Dodd, chair of the Christmas committee, reported to the Ladies' Benevolent Society board that each child had received three or four presents. Foreshadowing Christmases to come, "each cottage had a Christmas tree with lots of candy, nuts, oranges and apples. A splendid Christmas dinner was served to all."[5]

After observing the holidays, board and benefactor set about formalizing the Settlement's organization. On January 31, 1920, Mrs. James L. Paine and L. W. Hutton, "desirous of forming a [Washington] corporation for a charitable society," appeared as witnesses to file articles of incorporation for The Hutton Settlement. That short four-article document, both practical and philosophical, contains the Settlement's essence.[6]

The corporation would "not be a joint stock company"; membership would come through majority vote of trustees. The trustees named therein constituted the initial membership, and no other membership body as such existed. Anyone living within a two hundred mile radius of Spokane would be eligible for selection, provided he or she was "a citizen of the United States of good moral character and reputation, and not an ecclesiastic, missionary, priest, rabbi or minister of any religious sect." This provision specifically established the basic and enduring nonsectarian nature of the Settlement. The corporation's purpose would be to acquire property and funds and

> to hold, administer, use and dispose of the same and the . . . income thereof for charitable purposes; and especially to take, acquire, hold and operate an orphanage and orphan asylum or settlement; and receive, care for or place out for adoption, and improve the condition of orphan, homeless, neglected or abused minor children.[7]

Reflecting Hutton's Midwest origins and Coeur d'Alene years, the articles state that those minor children would come both from Washington and from other states. The affairs of the corporation would be managed by twenty-seven trustees who constituted the board. The mayor of Spokane, the chairman of the Board of County Commissioners of Spokane County, and the presidents of three of Spokane's principal banks would serve as ex officio members of the board, and those five would have the same powers as any other trustees. Twenty-one women, essentially the board of the Ladies' Benevolent Society, and L. W. Hutton were specifically named as the other original trustees of the Settlement.[8]

Only one of the women designated did not then belong to the LBS board. The group addressed that matter at its next meeting when the members unanimously elected Mrs. Pearl Hutton Schrader to the board. A cousin of the benefactor, an accomplished musician and concert vocalist, Pearl Hutton Schrader became dedicated to the Settlement, and her continuing loyalty would see it through some difficult times that lay ahead.[9]

One week after incorporation, on February 13, 1920, Hutton conveyed the campus property—his entire valley holdings—to the Hutton Settlement corporation through a deed of trust. The deed stipulated that the land and buildings "shall be held and used solely and only as a home…for the care, education and preparation for the duties of life of orphaned and other poor children."[10] A practical man, Hutton placed limitations and restrictions on the conveyance that both reflected his pragmatism and expanded on the philosophy implicit in the articles of incorporation.

To insure the Settlement's nonsectarian character while not "exclud[ing] Christianity or Christian influence," the deed of trust specifically stated that as few trustees as possible "shall belong to any one creed, sect or denomination." Hutton hoped that at least "ten full orphans" should be residents at all times, none to be "adopted out or relinquished" before reaching the age of eighteen.[11]

The deed also set forth conditions for admitting residents to the Settlement. Children between the ages of five and fourteen years were eligible for admission, and age eighteen was the point at which a resident must leave. The lower limit was not cast in stone, however, and "should it be deemed advisable at any time that a child under five years of age be admitted," it would be on condition that the Settlement be given custody of that child. The flexible minimum age would allow for bringing an entire family of children into the Settlement, an important consideration for Levi Hutton, who had been separated from his siblings in childhood. No child would be admitted until examined by a physician and "pronounced normal mentally and physically." With an eye toward quality of life and a "desire that the children in the [Settlement] may be well and comfortably housed, maintained and educated," Hutton directed that their numbers "be kept as near one hundred . . . as practicable." Remembering the source of his wealth, he specified that "particular consideration . . . [be given] to applications . . . of orphaned children from [the] Coeur d'Alene Mining District of Idaho."[12] No doubt recalling mining accidents that left entire families fatherless, he envisioned keeping those children together by admitting them into the Settlement.

Looking to the future, Hutton specified that any violation of restrictions contained in the deed of trust should not annul the deed but be appealed to the courts. He was particularly concerned lest "sectarianism be allowed to secure any foothold." Also, having endured the challenge to his wife's will and having kept both his family and hers apprised of his plans for the Settlement, he also stipulated that no "heir or relative of mine may assert any claim to the property." One proviso for future action reflected the nation's climate in 1920—teaching and instilling loyalty to the government. Recoiling from the unrest that followed the Russian Revolution of 1917, Hutton added that any Settlement officer or employee guilty of an act of disloyalty or expressing "disloyal sentiments" or belonging to an organization that teaches any doctrine of disloyalty "shall be discharged and removed summarily."[13]

Hutton's notarized signature on the deed of trust was witnessed by his longtime secretary and property manager G. N. Crawford and by a young man recently added to the office staff following his discharge from the Navy—Charles A. Gonser. No name would loom larger in the history of the Hutton Settlement than that of Charlie Gonser.

When the board of trustees of the Hutton Settlement met for the first time on March 20, 1920, those present signed an oath that reflected the patriotic ardor of the time:

> I do solemnly swear that I will support the Constitution of the United States, the Constitution of the State of Washington, and faithfully and impartially perform my duties as a Trustee of The Hutton Settlement, so help me God."[14]

Agnes Cowley Paine, the LBS president, became Settlement board president "by unanimous standing vote." The other officers elected that day were Kate H. Bean, first vice-president, Maggie Dodd, second vice-president, Laura Northrop, recording secretary, Levi Hutton, treasurer, and Matilda Prescott, corresponding secretary. After discussing the office of supervisor, which approximated a chief executive officer, the women elected Mr. Hutton to that post also. In order to complete the formal organization of the new corporation, Mrs. Paine appointed a committee to draft its bylaws—Kate Bean, Louise Sargeant, and Laura Northrop.[15]

Although some changes would occur over the years, bylaws drafted by those three women endured from then on. They set morning hours of the first Tuesday of each month as their regular meeting time, and designated January as the annual meeting for election of officers and ex officio members of the board. A unique provision guaranteed stability and continuity and indelibly stamped the Hutton Settlement:

> The trustees, other than the ex-officio members[,] shall hold office until removed by death, resignation, or by a majority vote of the remaining trustees . . . [and] vacancies in the Board of Trustees may be filled at any meeting by a majority of votes of the trustees present.

Drawing on long experience with the Ladies' Benevolent Society, the drafters of the bylaws established a system of working committees. Many of the original committees survived all changes—those on finance, buildings and grounds, education, and admission and discharge. Cottage committees rounded out that list, each charged with keeping "a record of the furnishings and condition of the cottage, assist[ing] the matron with the care of the clothing and enter[ing] into the home life of the children."[16] Serving as a Hutton Settlement trustee required a colossal commitment—commitment that sustained the Settlement through years of change.

For an extended time, board rosters of the Hutton Settlement and the Ladies' Benevolent Society overlapped. Although meeting separately, the two boards operated somewhat in tandem as they ran two homes for children. Both boards continued to meet in Mr. Hutton's office during the 1920s. Dual memberships tapered off as Settlement board members severed their LBS connections. Some, however, stayed with both into the midthirties.[17]

Mrs. Paine still served as president of both boards in the spring of 1920 when six more children were transferred to the home in the valley, and she resolved to ask "if arrangements cannot be made to pay for those placed in the Hutton Settlement." The city of Spokane provided some financial support for the Spokane Children's Home, hence "any child in need [was] admitted." The privately funded Hutton Settlement was selective, but many children were transferred there from the home in the city. Although Hutton underwrote the Settlement's expenses, in some instances counties paid to have their children live there, and children with resources paid a small fee.[18] Hutton had been astute in naming the mayor and the chair of the county commission to the Settlement board.

Although the ex officio members lent some political leverage and no small amount of prestige to the board of trustees, the women members bore the ultimate responsibility for fulfilling Levi Hutton's dream. The founding board women, if only by extension, fit the category known as domestic feminists. Women of their mother's generation as well as their own "who were fearful of the radicalism of suffrage, . . . who scorned Carrie Nation's violence and Susan B. Anthony's arrest, who swore by motherhood and home, found in Domestic Feminism attractive possibilities for wider influence." In Spokane, those who had found the suffrage movement—and its principal exponent in the city, Mary Arkwright Hutton—too bold and audacious did not necessarily eschew the right to vote, however, and had increasingly moved beyond the home to engage in good works and laudable projects through church and club. Strong women with a clear sense of themselves, they stood in the progressive tradition, identifying with reform efforts to improve their city's increasingly urban and industrial society.[19]

Thus, "wives and daughters of the most visible and respected families" here, as in cities around the nation, established benevolent societies that were vehicles for the greater good and for their wider influence. Board women of the LBS and later the Hutton Settlement came to know, as had the generation before them, "the value of their own autonomy."[20] Lasting friendships and true sisterhood grew from continual association in common cause and remained an enduring hallmark of the Settlement board.

The appellation "Board Ladies" attached to the Settlement's board very early and persisted through the decades.[21] A quintessential Board Lady was Agnes Cowley Paine, who succeeded Fannie Lewis as president of the Ladies' Benevolent Society and became the Hutton Settlement's first president. In her service to the Settlement she epitomized both Progressive Era child savers and Protestant activists who bore some evangelical sense of mission. Born October 3, 1873, in Mount Idaho, Idaho, she grew up in an exceptional family. Her college-educated mother and her father, an ordained minister, created a home that radiated a deep sense of mission and a love of learning. It also reflected a regard for the rights and abilities of women that stamped Agnes and her three sisters and enabled their activities and contributions.

Henry Thomas Cowley, born in Seneca Falls, New York, October 9, 1837, was eleven when that city hosted the nation's first Women's Rights Convention. He worked at a number of occupations in New York and Ohio before deciding to pursue a college education. Lucy Abigail Peete was born July 22, 1838, the daughter of a Baptist minister in Castile, New York. In a time before certification requirements, she began teaching school at the age of sixteen. Later Cowley said of her, "She has a joyous spirit and a brilliant mind. . . . It was [her] love for education which took her to Oberlin [College] where unusual opportunities are given to women students."[22]

The first college to open its doors to women, Oberlin had early embraced the cause of abolition, and it remained a reform prototype. But as one scholar argues, Oberlin's "significance as a religious community" has been overlooked. Lori Ginsburg holds that Oberlin, founded in the 1830s when "Christian virtues were, increasingly, defined as inherently—and aggressively—female virtues," reflected the evangelical view of its founders and "demanded less that women perform on men's level than that men live up to the standards of women." Ginsburg found that many women went "to Oberlin for both an education and to fulfill a moral mission, . . . [and] many Oberlin women married men who shared their intense commitment to values fostered at Oberlin." Over time the reform impulse moved from evangelical fervor to pragmatic efforts in the political arena, and the social gospel came to the fore.[23] Much of the early Oberlin spirit lingered, however, and the college remained the seat of enlightenment, reform, and opportunity for both men and women.

Henry Cowley and Lucy Peete met when both were students at Oberlin during the Civil War. They married in violation of college rules that forced them to leave Oberlin in their senior year. Cowley finished his degree at Antioch College in 1867 and a year later entered Auburn seminary. On his graduation and ordination he learned of the Reverend H. H. Spalding's search for a young man to work with him in the West. He seized the opportunity to join forces with the pioneer Presbyterian missionary who, with the Whitmans, had been in the vanguard ministering to Northwest tribes. The Cowley family, which now included three children, arrived in Idaho in August of 1871. The Reverend Cowley spent the next two years teaching and ministering to the Nez Perce in the Presbyterian mission at Kamiah, ten miles east of Lewiston. Friction between Spalding and the government Indian agent coincided with disharmony in the Presbytery, causing the Cowleys to make a change. He taught public school in Mount Idaho briefly[24] and then acceded to the request of the Spokane Tribe that he establish a school and church for them at the falls in the river. His being the fourth non-native family in the fledgling community, the young minister established not one, but two schools—one for the tribe and one for the settlers, which began with six children in the Cowley log cabin, on present-day Sixth Avenue between Division and Browne streets. Cowley learned the Spokanes' language and established close relations with them; Mrs. Paine herself later recalled, "We never really knew what it meant to be afraid of the Indians. . . . [They] made themselves at home in our little house."[25]

Among his other firsts, the Reverend Cowley organized the first Protestant church in town, something of an amalgam of Congregational and Presbyterian. Nine charter members formed Westminster Congregational Church in May of 1879. Social life for its young members revolved around church activities that frequently centered in the Cowley home. James Lawrence Paine joined that group after arriving from Iowa in 1890; the twenty-five-year-old retailer eventually became chairman of the board of both the city's leading department store, the Crescent, and the Spokane Dry Goods Company. Agnes Cowley had followed her parents' paths to Oberlin where she studied piano and organ. After returning home to Spokane, as her daughter later recalled, "She played the organ in the Congregational Church. In those days, the bellows of the organ were pumped by hand and that pumper was" James Paine. The minister's daughter, now church organist, and the merchant who manned the organ pump were married in 1897.[26]

Joining the Ladies' Benevolent Society would seem almost preordained for the young matron, whose life from the earliest years had been infused with the ideal of service. She devoted countless hours to volunteer activities. Her daughter, Margaret, recalled that while she was Hutton Settlement board president, the Paines' "telephone would ring at meal time just because they knew she would be there…[she] worked hard . . . really pitched in" both in setting policy and working at the campus. In an era when few women drove, Margaret drove her mother to the Settlement on business.[27] As a college student Margaret tutored Settlement children and would herself join the Settlement board in 1935.

Agnes Cowley Paine, first president and prototypical board member, epitomized the spirit and qualities that sustained the Settlement over time. Strong, educated, and caring women followed her onto the Hutton Settlement board through the twentieth century. Their service mirrored hers in dedication to child welfare and the greater good of society as they guided the Settlement, assiduously following the dictates of the deed of trust.

Although Levi Hutton valued and deeply appreciated the contributions and work of those first women on the Settlement board, recognizing that without them "the success of the institution could not have been possible," he believed that a man should oversee day-to-day operations on the campus: "There must be a man Superintendent one that is big enough to handle an institution like this."[28] That stipulation proved difficult to meet.

Based on sparse Hutton Settlement personnel records, Waller Shobe appears to have served as the first resident superintendent. As chair of the board of the state Orphans' Home at Twin Bridges, Montana, Shobe had given advice to Harold Whitehouse in planning the campus. His wife had served as that home's matron. Hutton paid him $250 on December 1, 1919, and again on February 2, 1920. Mrs. Shobe also received payments ranging between $25 and $50 in that period. Yet it was Miss Nell Dondanville who filed the first superintendent's report—for January 1920. She had appeared on the payroll at $55 in December 1919; in March 1920 her salary increased to $100; she resigned as superintendent in October.[29] One hundred dollars per month remained the salary for the superintendent through Levi Hutton's tenure as the Settlement's supervisor.

The superintendent's monthly report proved essential to keeping the board women involved in life at the Settlement, and it occupied a prominent spot on their meeting agendas. Reports in the first years were little more than printed questionnaires with terse notations of admissions and discharges, health, and cash receipts. One line item asked for the number of full orphans at the Settlement; another, for the number from homes "wholly depending on charity." Yet another sought to know the number of children "whose guardian or parent is paying the fee." The number of full orphans increased in 1920 from three of the Settlement's thirty-seven children in January to fourteen of seventy-five in December. In July 1928, the number of true orphans among the seventy-three children reached sixty-five, but over time, as the Settlement grew and society changed, it proved impossible to comply with Levi Hutton's wish for at least ten full orphans in residence.[30]

In the wake of the catastrophic flu epidemic of 1918-19 that took the lives of 1,045 people in Spokane, the board placed high priority on the children's health. During the Settlement's first year, its well-equipped infirmary saw cases ranging from the common cold, measles, and mumps to whooping cough, smallpox, and acute appendicitis. Tonsillectomies and appendectomies appeared frequently in reports; the Settlement's first child death occurred August 7, 1920, when eight-year-old Bertha Bowles died "following an operation for appendicitis."[31] In the midtwenties, loss of a child through postoperative bleeding reportedly marked the end of in-house tonsillectomies; thereafter, children were taken into Spokane "kind of *en masse*" to a surgical facility in the Paulsen Building to have their tonsils removed.[32]

From its very beginning, the Hutton Settlement received excellent cooperation from the medical and dental communities. Physicians responded to calls, and dentists made regular visits to the campus to conduct routine dental exams and perform needed procedures. The board's corresponding secretary wrote countless letters of appreciation, as in June 1928 when she thanked dentists for six months of services: 15 extractions and 143 fillings.[33] The dentist's chair in the infirmary still loomed large in the memory of residents decades after they last sat in it.

Well-connected board members helped cement relations between the Settlement and the medical community, but on the campus itself the resident nurse personified health care. One whom the children called Nursie Martin came on the scene in mid-1922, bringing warm-hearted care to the sick and staff continuity to the infirmary wing of the administration building; elsewhere on the campus, however, continual turnover of personnel made for some uncertainty.

Mr. Hutton involved the board actively in personnel decisions during his years as supervisor; following Nell Dondanville's resignation as superintendent, he asked the women to meet with another candidate for the position. Edith Yeomans accepted the job, effective the first of December 1920, "and all the board ladies [were] glad." Superintendents carried a demanding and constant responsibility; the work was arduous, the salary less than commensurate. Miss Yeomans served until September 1921, when Eleanor Golden replaced her.[34]

Eleanor Golden served as superintendent from September 1921 through February 1924. Had Levi Hutton known of her penchant for uniformity, she might well have left sooner. At least one girl was told to straighten her naturally curly hair so as not to be "different from the rest of the girls." Lenore Spaid succeeded Eleanor Golden; Mrs. Spaid had been a cottage matron since June of 1922, and she remained superintendent until the end of December 1926.[35] Difficult though it may have been to find and retain superintendents, hiring and holding good matrons for the cottages was even more so.

Early conditions in Cottage Three, a boys cottage, are instructive. At the end of August, 1920, Mrs. Katherine Tate, cottage chairman, reported that everything was in order and that "the boys are very fond of Mrs. Price," the matron. A month later she deplored the state of the boys' clothes and attributed it "in part to the frequent changing of matrons during September." By the end of the year, after making four trips to the cottage in December, she reported a brighter picture: "They have a new house mother, Mrs. Chandler, and she seems to be the best one we have had yet." Her optimism lasted, and a followup report confirmed, "Everything [is] in splendid condition. Mrs. Chandler has wonderful control over the children." Ida Chandler did not disappoint; her stock rose over time, and although she took several months away from the Settlement in 1926 and 1927, she moved into the superintendent's office in January 1928.[36] Her promotion, however, left another vacancy in the ranks of the matrons, and filling such positions remained a constant concern for the board members.

Less than munificent salaries may account in part for constant staff turnover. When the Settlement first opened in 1919, its matrons received between $35 and $50 per month. The salary stabilized at $50 and remained so for another decade; superintendents got $100 during that period. All resident staff received free room and board.[37]

Mrs. Tate's four trips to the campus in December 1920 illustrate the time-consuming personal involvement that remained a hallmark of service on the Settlement board. Committee assignments meant numerous meetings in addition to the monthly gathering of the whole board. Education, finance, and buildings and grounds committees required significant amounts of time, as did the committee on admission and discharge, which evaluated each child's coming and going from the Settlement. Cottage committees spent considerable time in annual inventories of equipment and linen supplies; they oversaw refurnishing and refurbishing; and they kept track of their cottage's children in countless ways. In the Settlement's first decade, board members took children into town on shopping trips and into their homes for short emergency stays. In 1928 Mrs. Merryweather took in a Settlement young person who was attending business college; the board gave her "a rising vote of thanks." Women of the board also gave financial support to the Settlement, donating money to specific needs or to the emergency fund.[38] With the exception of caring for children in their homes, the Hutton Settlement board members continued these patterns of service at century's end.

Levi Hutton and the Board Ladies worked in harmony for a decade with mutual respect and admiration that approached affection. He sought their opinions and clearly trusted their judgment on virtually every aspect of Settlement operations save one. As treasurer, he retained the financial sphere as his own preserve, even though the board had a six-member finance committee that, under the articles of incorporation, had "general supervision of the financial affairs of the corporation." Only once, at its February 1921 meeting, likely while Mr. Hutton was away on his customary vacation in Hawaii, did the board receive a Settlement financial report, which Crawford, the property manager, presented. There were no further general financial accountings during Hutton's lifetime. He paid all bills himself; records show Settlement affairs intermingled with his own personal transactions, and no separate annual statements are extant.[39]

That first and only financial report attests to Levi Hutton's financial support of the Settlement. Income for 1920 came from residents' boarding fees, which amounted to $5,556.52, and from sales of farm produce, $214.57. Expenditures included $14,897.91 for campus maintenance, $5,925.97 for farm operations, and others. The "net cost to L. W. Hutton" was $24,334.21. The founder of the Settlement "continued to pay [the bills] until the day of his death in 1928. . . . It cost him the last year about thirty-seven thousand dollars."[40]

Openhanded though he was, as supervisor of the Settlement he could drive a hard bargain when a county had responsibility for any of his children. A 1925 letter to Yakima County commissioners indicates a resolute, no-nonsense businessman:

> I have . . . [two] girls from your County who were County charges. It doesn't make any difference to me what Department of your County they came from. They are from Yakima County. I have children from different Counties in the State and I have children from Idaho where the County buys their clothing.

Now, these children have got to be clothed and cared for and I will expect Yakima County to clothe [them]. If you can't clothe these children you certainly can care for them. Can you make arrangements to receive these children. I can send them to you any date you suggest.[41]

Board minutes show no mention of a Settlement treasurer other than Hutton until January 1927, when a motion carried that "Mrs. Osgood the Treasurer be authorized to devise a plan for the financing of the different funds." Nonetheless, it is abundantly clear that Hutton never relinquished financial control. His last motion as a board member, fittingly, spoke to fiscal matters: "That absolutely no one outside of the Captains and their committees be permitted to purchase or charge supplies or goods of any kind to the Treasurer's account for the Settlement."[42]

His control of the purse strings notwithstanding, as Hutton and the Board Ladies shared untold hours conducting Settlement business, over time and within the bounds of the era's social restraint, an easy familiarity developed. He sometimes hosted luncheon meetings in his home bordering Lincoln Park, and he enjoyed an occasional joke with them. Charles Gonser recalled that Mr. Hutton delighted in a shell game that he had learned during his railroading days: "It seems he always had a sack with three shells and a pea in it," and no one "was ever able to guess which shell the pea was under." At board meetings Miss Jennie Dodd was Hutton's favorite victim, and he especially enjoyed confounding her.[43]

Jennie Dodd continued to serve until World War II, but by the midtwenties death and resignations had begun to alter the board composition. Her mother, Maggie L. Dodd, second vice-president of the Settlement board and the first treasurer of the LBS, died in 1922. Another original board member and Spokane pioneer, Harriet Ross Gandy, died in the spring of 1925. The Board Ladies lost their president that same year with the death of Kate Bean; she had served the LBS for twenty-five years before the Settlement opened.[44] Her daughter Dorothy Bean Humbird joined the Settlement board in 1932, and another daughter, a journalist, Margaret Bean followed in their footsteps later on.

Selection of new members appeared frequently on board meeting agendas, but minutes provide few clues about who actually went on to serve. At one noteworthy meeting in the summer of 1927, the women unanimously elected the first man other than Hutton himself and the ex officio members. It was David Glasgow, Levi Hutton's personal attorney; he would play a crucial role in Settlement affairs in the 1930s, but his name never appeared on a board roster; however, on December 6, 1927, "in the usual way *Mrs.* D. A. Glasgow was elected a member."[45]

From the beginning the board had sought and welcomed involvement and support from the greater Spokane community. By the end of 1922 the women had secured some fifty individual and group contributions, ranging from the gift of a single bed to furnishings for an entire room. Donations came from a wide spectrum of the community, both in the city and the valley—from the Council of Jewish Women to the First and Second Churches of Christ-Scientist, from Spokane's Lincoln Park Community to the valley's Pasadena Park and Orchard Avenue Ladies groups, from the philanthropy of Mrs. August Paulsen to "funds given by Labor Unions."[46] The medical and dental communities donated services. Throughout the years, other community organizations contributed both money and time to the Settlement.

Masonic groups and Rotary International and its women's auxiliary underwrote many projects. Women's church and service groups volunteered sewing and other skills; they made the children new clothes and mended the old. One resident from the 1920s recalled that, at the beginning of the school year, a group of ladies would come with fabric and samples and let the children choose their new clothes. Cottage sewing machines were busy for weeks. One of those sewing groups from the early years was the Ladies of Browne's Addition, likely a subgroup of the LBS.[47]

In the Settlement's first spring, while the lines were still a bit blurred between its board and the Ladies' Benevolent Society's, at a meeting of the latter there was talk of keeping the public interested in the Settlement. Both bodies were mindful of the importance of the public's support, and indeed the Hutton Settlement hosted its first open house that summer. In her president's report for that year, Mrs. Paine said that strangers visiting the campus "always seem impressed with the home life of the children." She also "spoke of the harmony with which the Board always worked together, and of the kindness and generosity of their many friends, . . . particularly of Mrs. Runyon who left a bequest of $2,000.00 to the home.[48]

Mr. Hutton reflected back on the first year of the Settlement and declared it "the shortest year of his life." The midtwenties were busy and full: he entertained members of the Washington State Conference of Social Work when that group convened in Spokane in 1923[49]; he took particular satisfaction when representatives of orphanages that Whitehouse had consulted in planning the Settlement visited the campus.[50] In the fall of 1924, he invited friends of the Hutton Settlement to the first annual banquet marking the anniversary of its founding. The Marie Antoinette room of the Davenport Hotel was his favorite venue for these celebrations; the 1925 banquet and dance took the form of a Halloween party, and 150 seated guests included the Settlement board, Rotarians, Masons, many members of the medical and dental communities, and all their spouses. The following year, the guest list numbered 190; attendees enjoyed a vocal solo by Pearl Hutton Schrader and the remarks of their host. As a public speaker Hutton was at his best with a fork in his hand, and he addressed every banquet at length, thanking everyone and reporting on the Settlement farm's production as well.[51]

By 1928, the man whose physical labor had helped the Hercules Mine to prosper now served on boards of directors, his friends included leaders in the business and financial communities, he had membership in the elite Spokane Club. That spring he received an unexpected letter from Stephen B. L. Penrose, the president of Whitman College. Having toured the Settlement and marveled that "a man of wealth should devote himself as well as his money" to such a work, Penrose asked permission to recommend Hutton for an honorary Master of Arts degree. He explained:

> The particular art of which I think you are a master is the art of humanity for you have shown to a hard-hearted world a noble example of generous warm hearted service . . . and this virtue, humanity, is one of those which mankind must learn to honor properly and to cherish.[52]

On June 18, Levi Hutton, the man who had gone no farther than third grade received the degree in Walla Walla at Whitman's forty-sixth commencement celebration.[53]

By the following autumn, Hutton's chronic diabetes had gained the upper hand, and he made fewer trips to the Settlement campus. As his health had deteriorated he had come to depend ever more heavily on Gonser, now his manager, for handling his business affairs. Near the end of October, he asked his chauffeur to drive him to Sacred Heart Hospital. He died there on November 3, with Gonser and two Board Ladies, Pearl Hutton Schrader and Miriam Ritchie, at his side.[54]

Although invitations to the annual banquet had already gone out, Gonser and the Board Ladies decided to cancel the celebration. The chief celebrant was gone. His physicians believed that "he would not have lived his 68 years had it not been for the joy he gained from the Hutton home."[55]

His longtime friend, the banker D. W. Twohy, visibly shaken when told of his death, offered both tribute and summation:

> I have known Mr. Hutton for 25 years. In my opinion he was the outstanding figure of this community. He has done more for humanity . . . than any other Spokane man. He was a wonderful character, modest, unassuming, of the strictest integrity and always looking for an opportunity to do good for others.[56]

Over the years, his outstanding philanthropy and steadfast, dependable relationships in business and the community had made the young man who had driven his four-horse team into town in 1881 into Spokane's first citizen.

4

Life at the Settlement: Levi Hutton and His Children

*L*evi Hutton had clearly relished his role in planning and building the Settlement campus. In the decade after he carried the first child through the door of Cottage One, he thrived on the intangible rewards of day-to-day life on the campus and the vicarious nurturing of the children he regarded as his. Other facilities, including the Spokane Children's Home, provided child care in the region, and their operating approaches spanned a wide philosophical spectrum. But the Hutton Settlement continued to function under the guidelines that Mr. Hutton had set down, and as he had desired, the children did consider it their home.

During the eight years that Hutton directed the Settlement himself, most of what he had envisioned became reality. The Settlement more than fulfilled his dream of enabling siblings to remain together. The percentage of full orphans increased, reaching 89 percent by the summer of 1928.[1] Long residence lent continuity to the concept of a Settlement family. Admissions records do not exist for the early years, but later recollections of Settlement children of the 1920s show that, as he had desired, children from the Coeur d'Alene mining district accounted for a part of those percentages.

In 1924, the Coeur d'Alene connection brought children of a Kellogg, Idaho, miner to the Hutton Settlement. Their mother had died earlier, and when their father was killed, the mine superintendent recommended the Settlement. One of the four siblings lived there for ten years and declared the Settlement "the best thing that could have happened" to them. That same year, the four Trounce children were also orphaned, and as Jack recalled later, "My father had been a miner and Mr. Hutton had also been a miner, [so] Mr. Hutton opened the home to us, … the nearest thing to home a child could have."[2]

Forever known as Baby Jane, the child carried into Cottage One by Mr. Hutton in 1919, Jane Wiese had a sister and two brothers; they numbered among the fully orphaned sibling groups that came together to the Settlement in its first years. An aunt had "contacted Mr. Hutton when she learned the Hutton Settlement was ready for occupancy and we four children were accepted."[3] Hutton also had a personal role in the admission of six siblings whose widowed mother, before her death in 1921, wished that they all stay together. Esther Roos recalled, "She met Mr. Hutton before she passed away and felt hopeful that we would be together and well provided for."[4] The Roos children lived at the Settlement through their high school years.

The three Scott sisters arrived in the fall of 1922 from near Colville in northern Washington. Their mother, also widowed, "wanted to find a good place" for her girls. After she got them admitted to the Settlement, she lived on a while longer in Spokane and visited her daughters on the campus. One, Clara Scott, remembered, "They'd bring her a cup of tea and some cookies—the kids were really nice to her. So we had her for a little while while we were there." The Scott girls lived at the Settlement until each graduated from high school. Clara, the oldest, was ten when they moved in; "My two sisters and I were put in Cottage One. And we had a room right above the dining room, so we three were always kept together, so that was nice. Made it more family-like. So we were pretty happy."[5]

Susie Dubuque and her three brothers moved from Seattle to the Hutton Settlement in 1924. They had been separated and living in two different orphanages. She later recalled,

> My older sister and an aunt, struggling to keep the four of us together, heard about the settlement through a former matron at the Seattle home where I was living, who came [to the Hutton Settlement] to act as housemother. . . . The Settlement became my home for 10 years, until I graduated from high school.[6]

Levi Hutton's determination to see siblings raised together made a difference for the Wieses, the Rooses, the Scotts, the Dubuques, and many others.

Of course, not all the children who came to the Settlement in its first years had brothers or sisters. Five-year-old Mike Mateef found a home there in 1919. Mike was born in Spokane; his mother died when he was six months old. Until his father died two years later, he was cared for by the grandmother of the woman he would one day marry. Following his father's death, he went to live with his aunt who "had trouble raising her own family on the farm." Somehow she found out about the Settlement[7]; Mike Mateef lived there for twelve years.

Mabel Maley, born in Cul-de-Sac, Idaho, in the summer of 1910, came to the Hutton Settlement in 1922. Her mother and stepfather had moved to Spokane, and after her mother died, he sought a good place for her to live. Mabel recalled:

> He had heard about this orphanage, and he was trying to find a home for me. I didn't have a place to go, and he couldn't take care of me, so he said, "How would you like to go out and live where there's girls and boys?" . . . I said, "Well, I have no place to go, I guess I'd be fine."

The eleven-year-old, who was "kind of depressed, and everything, and didn't know anybody," plucked up her courage and joined in cottage life. Before long, she "really and truly enjoyed it."[8]

In his early thoughts on building an orphans home, Levi Hutton had assumed that it would include a school. But Harold Whitehouse, after visiting combination home and school facilities in the East, recommended that the children attend public school. This arrangement accorded with Hutton's desire for individualism and the opportunity for his children to "mix with other youngsters" as other children would.[9]

From its very beginning, the Settlement children attended schools in the West Valley School District. In 1920, in addition to a regular property tax of $858, Mr. Hutton's ledger shows a payment of $3,000 to School District 143.[10]

A sudden influx of "Hutton kids," as they soon came to be known, strained the district's elementary schools. After they completed the primary grades at Pasadena School, Settlement children attended Millwood Grammar School. At first, Millwood could not accommodate them all; as Mike Mateef recalled, "There were so many of us kids going to grade school, that they'd divide us up." Everyone walked the two miles or so to Millwood, whence buses distributed them to Parkwater, Orchard Avenue, and Dishman schools. The reverse pattern brought them back to Millwood in the afternoon, and all walked home from there.[11]

No one really minded the long walk; it was "kind of nice, when the weather was good." But as Clara Scott said, "In wintertime, oh, that was cold work." In really bad and snowy weather the children were driven to school, riding on benches rigged onto the Settlement's flatbed truck. Similar arrangements held for them through their years at West Valley High School.[12]

On the whole, Hutton kids had good experiences in school. Most liked their teachers, who treated them no differently from any of their classmates. Mabel Maley said that "we were not considered like, 'Hey, you're an orphan, we don't want anything to do with you.' Nothing. We just went right in with the rest of them. . . . I had no problems at all." Clara Scott echoed her, "We really liked our teachers. . . . [Other kids] were nice to get along with . . . we were all just kind of equal."[13] In high school, they took part in athletics and other after-school activities.

The Board Ladies rated education as pivotal and vital. Assigning it high priority, they took a strong, immediate, and ongoing interest. The board's education committee became something of a liaison with the school district. Within a year of its opening, the Settlement established a library in the administration building based on initial gifts of 800 volumes and an assortment of child- and youth-oriented magazine subscriptions. At that point, too, the education committee was visiting the schools once a week and could report with pride that "we have 7 honor children from the Hutton Settlement." By the spring of 1928, committee members had begun to explore "the question of college finances"; they contacted the dean of women at Washington State College in Pullman for information about work-study possibilities for Settlement graduates from high school.[14]

Both Levi and May Hutton had held a practical view of education. He considered learning and working on the farm an important experience for the Settlement boys. She shared his view, writing in 1912 that "we believe Practical Vocational

Training of the youth of the country is vastly more important than book culture
. . . [its lack is] 'The greatest problem before the people today.'" Moreover, she
believed that girls should have vocational training too. She had contacted John D.
Rockefeller two years earlier, urging him to support "an institution for the training
of housekeepers" that she wanted to establish in or near Spokane. She told him
such training "would come nearer solving problems that affect women principally,
and humanity in general, than any and all other means hitherto employed."[15]

Academic success did not go unrewarded however. To encourage children to
do well in school, Mr. Hutton gave cash prizes "to the Millwood School for those
children receiving the 'Highest Degree of excellence.'" He surely felt great pride in
1923 when three Settlement children received prizes—$2 each for second place to
a sixth-grade girl and a fourth-grade boy and $1 for third prize to a boy in second
grade.[16]

The visit of S. B. L. Penrose, president of Whitman College, in the spring of
1924 may have expanded Hutton's views on educational opportunity. Penrose wrote
praising the buildings and the remarkable planning that had produced the campus. Apropos of education, he said:

> I was even more impressed with the spirit of the children themselves, and the admi-
> rable arrangements which you have made for their up-bringing. . . .
>
> Only one suggestion occurs to me. Most of your boys and girls will probably go into
> trades or other occupations for which a high-school education will serve as a prepa-
> ration. . . . I do not believe that every body ought to go to college, but it would be
> unfortunate if boys and girls who ought to go, were prevented from doing so. A
> college education . . . will fit [a boy] for greater influence in the world and make him
> a leader among men.
>
> My suggestion is, that you should establish a Hutton scholarship for such occasional
> boys or girls at Whitman College. . . I would like very much if we might receive, now
> and then, from the Hutton Home, a bright boy or girl, who we could help prepare for
> larger usefulness.[17]

No record shows that Hutton acted on this suggestion. The seed of possibility
had been planted, however, and over time he invested thought and effort in plans
"for a fund to be used for educating the boys and girls at the Hutton Settlement
after leaving the home." Although he did not establish such a fund, his attorney,
David Glasgow, maintained that "had he lived I am sure this ambition of his would
have been realized."[18]

As in any home with school-age children, the school-year calendar and school
schedules shaped the pattern of daily living at the Hutton Settlement. There, as on
any family farm, the children rose early to complete their chores before school.
Many assignments cut across gender lines. In their cottages the boys worked in the
kitchen and did their own housekeeping, and outdoors they had farm jobs; milking

was a relentless, twice-a-day responsibility for the older boys. Girls, less involved with farm work, had kitchen and housekeeping duties in their cottages along with the job of caring for younger children, and some waited table in the administration building's staff dining room.

During the school year everyone was out of bed by 5:30. Susie Dubuque remembered that "we all had our chores. The boys helped with milking cows and gathering eggs and girls worked inside." The farm supplied the Settlement: after the morning milking, the older boys "delivered the milk to the cottages. . . . in big pails"; the girls strained it into smaller pails that went into the refrigerator.[19] Egg gathering worked along the same general lines.

Even the younger boys did their share. Mike Mateef recalled the morning routine for the twenty boys in his cottage:

I used to help the Matron—she'd prepare breakfast, you know, and I would kind of help there. And then [two of us would do] the dishes . . . one on each side [of the sink] washed, and one on each side dried, and boy we used to get into those dishes, and twenty of them—have them done in no time . . . and then we'd make lunches.

Memories of preparing sack lunches to take to school remained vivid for boys and girls alike. With sandwich ingredients and paper bags arranged assembly-line fashion on the spacious countertops, they put together sandwiches enough to satisfy the hungriest. Peanut butter was a staple. Mateef said, "The older boys, some of them would take three sandwiches, and some two. Gosh, we had twenty sacks, you know, and everybody'd grab them."[20]

Girls also did dishes and kitchen duty. During her years at West Valley High School, Mabel Maley was a kitchen helper in her cottage. She remembered it as

hard, because I had to get up early to get the breakfast going with my house mothers. . . . most of [whom] were really nice. . . . [One would] tell me what she wanted me to do, and I'd go ahead and do it all, and I had another girl with me, too. And then we had to go and set up the dining room [for dinner] . . . we had to start at 7:30, because by 8:00, or a little after 8:00, a great big bell [from the] engine from one of Mr. Hutton's trains, would ring, and that meant we were to walk to our school.

She also waited table in the administration building dining room where Settlement employees ate, and remembered going over there early in the morning to serve breakfast.[21]

Another morning duty in the Settlement's early years called for older girls to care for the youngest in their cottages. Cottage One usually housed twenty girls, but as Mabel Maley said, "Sometimes we had twenty-two; if we had little ones the older people took care of the little guys." She usually had a little girl assigned to her to look after, to see "that she would dress properly, and had all the buttons on her clothes, and [they] weren't torn, and . . . then after I got her all ready, well then I'd go get myself ready for school."[22]

The routine after school mirrored that of the morning. Older boys reported to the barn for the afternoon milking; girls and younger boys returned to kitchen duty. With the dinner tables set earlier, the main tasks for both boys and girls centered on helping with meal preparation. Clara Scott remembered that "the larger girls would help in the kitchen—help the Matron with the cooking, and those large kettles and things"; smaller children also had assignments, such as sweeping sidewalks. Mike Mateef went to his cottage kitchen to work on "a big canister of potatoes. I'd have to peel all those potatoes. Boy, I used to peel them fast so I could go out and play." During dinner in the Settlement cottages, as in most homes, the children served and afterward cleared and washed the dishes.[23]

Assignment of chores fell to the matrons. The Board Ladies left it to them "to tell children what work they are to do, or do over," and the children were to "have work changed once a month."[24]

Each person kept his or her own room clean, and on Saturday everyone turned to broader housekeeping responsibilities in the cottage. Children vacuumed the rugs, polished the floors in the hallway, cleaned kitchens and bathrooms, and washed windows. The cottages competed to see which could do the best job; a portrait of Mr. Hutton was the prize to hang in the winning cottage for the following week. The boys in Cottage Four delighted in consistently besting both girls cottages. Looking back decades later, Mabel Maley thought "the worst thing I ever did was wash the windows, and scrub the floor in the kitchen. And I hated that with a passion."[25] Mr. Hutton's insistence on bathroom floors that would be easy to mop made that job a favorite, but almost without exception his children loathed window washing.

Of large congregate care children's homes, one scholar has written: "Orphanages brought together a mass of children from troubled families . . . and concentrated them in one place, where they had ample opportunity to make one another miserable. Orphanage asylums had ways for dealing with this difficulty, but they were costly."[26] Levi Hutton had an excellent, cost-effective means of averting such difficulties at his new home out in the valley—the farm. The Board Ladies, too, saw the value of keeping youngsters busy. Soon after the Settlement opened, they tried to persuade parents to transfer their older boys from the Spokane Children's Home in the city. Mrs. Paine explained that "it would be so much better for the boys to be where there was work to take their spare time."[27] The vaunted work ethic of the Settlement, which in retrospect evoked both praise and commendation from Hutton kids of the early decades, was part and parcel of campus life.

Levi Hutton had always considered the farm basic to his plans for the Settlement. So central was it to his thinking, he hired a head farmer, Carl Olson, as soon as he purchased the land for the Settlement in 1917. In an article written during campus construction, the *Spokesman-Review* emphasized that Hutton expected "to do extensive farming on the acreage around the site of the new children's home he is building." True to form, Hutton involved himself in farm details. He personally purchased the farm's first tractor, proudly explaining that it was "equipped with some of the latest features. . . . The engine is the four-cylinder type, valve-in-head . . . [and] runs with either distillate or kerosene."[28]

The entire acreage in the valley stayed under cultivation in the 1920s. In addition to producing wheat, oats, barley, other grains, and a variety of garden vegetables and orchard fruit, Olson and the Settlement boys raised cattle, hogs, and chickens. The list of produce for 1926 included 1,555 tons of hay, 75 of silage, and 40 of baled straw. Foodstuffs destined for campus kitchens that year included, among other things, 1,200 boxes of apples, 1,400 sacks of potatoes, 1,000 pounds of both beans and onions, 600 pounds of dried sweet corn, 300 pounds of honey, 3 tons of dried prunes, and 5 tons of tomatoes, 3 of cabbage, and 2 of both squash and pumpkins. Such impressive annual yields made the Settlement nearly self-sufficient. Hutton's personal role in running the farm continued, and as late as 1927 he still outlined the summer work program for the boys.[29]

In the fall of that year, Gordon Windle arrived at the Settlement as a high school freshman; he recalled that "we raised nearly all of our own food." He said, having grown up on a dairy farm, "I wound up in a job milking the cows. . . . I had the cows to take care of twice a day—Christmas, New Years, Thanksgiving, you milk those things twice a day."

> We also did the farming, and raised our own wheat and . . . had a thrasher come in to thrash it. . . . we raised the hay that we needed for the cattle, . . . we raised the wheat for the pigs and the chickens. And then we planted big gardens . . . [and] had a lot of orchards where we raised all the fruits that you raise in this part of the country: apples, and cherries, and pears. . . . And in the [gardens] we raised all the summer vegetables we used, plus the keeping vegetables—squash. Girls . . . worked too . . . they did weeding, and planting.[30]

As Mike Mateef grew older, he took care of the chickens and received high school credit for it. "We had about 200 chickens, and that was my job, to take care of them. . . . out of 200 chickens I got almost 200 eggs [a day]—now that's something. And of course, we'd cull them out, you know [and] those that wouldn't lay" became Sunday dinner. The other livestock included "about twenty-some cows, four work horses, and one pony, and they had a big place for hogs." He remembered having "all the milk you could drink."[31]

The girls did their agricultural bit primarily during the summer. "Mostly," said Mabel Maley, "we picked the vegetables as they got ready." Susie Dubuque recalled, "The week we had to pick gooseberries was always the worst, but girls who did that were rewarded with an extra swim in the pool and that we liked."[32]

The Settlement pool approached midtwenties state-of-the-art construction, although it was filled with water from the irrigation ditch that ran behind the cottages. Diving board and tower provided the boys with ample opportunity to show off. Swimming sessions were supervised; however, in the twenties there was no instruction and "you learned on your own." Pool hours were regulated; boys and girls swam at separate times. Swimming pool privileges went a long way toward allaying potential discontent on any number of fronts.[33]

The summer routine at the Settlement differed from the school year routine. After completing the milking and other early morning chores, the boys worked on the farm from 9:00 until 11:30 when they had a thirty-minute prelunch dip in the pool; work resumed from 1:00 until 3:00, and then it was back to the pool for a longer swim.[34] Some children spent a vacation week or two away from the campus with relatives, and many relished going to Boy Scout or Camp Fire camp. The Settlement had its own Boy Scout troop . Any boys who wanted to could be scouts; Hutton and the board saw to it that they were properly uniformed and encouraged to earn Eagle Scout status. In 1927 the board voted to establish Camp Fire on the campus, and on a Sunday in February Dorothy Bean Humbird and a friend created "much enthusiasm" when they drove out from town to organize the group. The girls came to relish making their own gowns with beading on them and in summer looked forward to going to Camp Swayalockan on Lake Coeur d'Alene.[35]

Hutton kids in the twenties found any number of avenues for fun throughout the year. The open area between cottages and administration building became the place for touch football, stick hockey, softball, and such old favorites as run-sheep-run and red rover. The slopes behind the cottages made sledding and skiing top winter favorites. Before television and computers, indoor hours were devoted to toys, pleasure reading, and card and board games.

Cottage basements proved ideal for roller skating, but the girls in Cottage One puts theirs to a different use. Clara Scott said that each girl

> mark[ed] a place off in the large basement which was your space, [to] sit there, sew, do your own thing, you know. You had to have a private place, and it was a large basement, like a playroom. Nobody disturbed . . . my favorite dolls—things like that, and the things you used to sew with. You have to have a little space of your own.[36]

In the basement of Cottage Four Mike Mateef made a pair of skis. He recalled picking up oak slats left over from the cottage flooring and soaking them "in the sink downstairs where we used to wash our own socks. Yeah, real hot water, see, and they start bending, and you put them in the [rungs of the] step ladder, and keep bending them a little."[37] From his molding them around and through the ladder rungs, the skis had enough camber and bend at the tip to give him reasonably safe runs down the slope behind the cottage.

Winter fun endured in the memories of most. Mateef recalled some details:

> We'd go way up, and follow that ridge right down. And I remember when they had snow all of us forty kids [from the boys' cottages] . . . we'd [line up] side by side and pack that snow down. And then when it would freeze, boy, you'd have an ice lot. You could put ice skates on—those old flat ones—and whoosh! Oh, that was great.

He also relished memories of making a ski jump from an old door, a project that was a spectacular failure.[38] And there was the time-honored fun of sneaking out on clear winter nights. He said, "I thought that skiing was great. I used to sneak out at night just when the moon was shining."[39] Climbing out the cottages' windows and down their brick walls posed a challenge, but the real trick lay in getting back in unnoticed. Every generation rose to the challenge, but few if any made it completely undetected.

Seeing that his children had fun ranked high among Levi Hutton's priorities. The board's initial standing committees included the entertainment committee. Among the most popular and eagerly anticipated entertainments were the Friday night movies shown twice a month in the auditorium in the administration building. H. B. Hickman, a movie operator with a theater chain in Spokane, brought the films, and someone played piano to accompany the silent pictures on the large screen. The Hutton kids eagerly watched for Hickman to come up the road and then lined up by cottages to march around into the auditorium. Those movies inspired everything from Mike Mateef's ski-jump experiment to Tarzanlike swinging in trees.[40]

The Settlement welcomed neighbors to the Friday movies, "and under no circumstances were any admission fee or collections received from the visitors." The goodwill gesture was suspended, however, during the winter months for health reasons. Since many of the neighbor children "walked as far as two miles through muddy roads and unfavorable weather in order to attend the vaudeville and moving picture attractions," Hutton and the Board Ladies determined not to risk "chances of carrying contagious diseases" between the Settlement and private homes.[41]

One unforgettable entertainment of the 1920s was an impromptu visit by Babe Ruth; in the off-season the famed New York Yankee traveled on the Pantages vaudeville circuit, which one winter brought him to Spokane. As Charles Gonser related it, Ruth himself grew up in an orphanage, and when he "heard about the Hutton Settlement [he] wanted to go out there. He went out and had breakfast with the boys. . . . Then he and Mr. Hutton and the boys played baseball [for] quite a while." Far from regarding it as a mere photo opportunity, the baseball legend stayed a considerable time and met the girls, too, and shook hands. Playing with Babe Ruth, getting "right close to him," was the thrill of a lifetime for the budding second baseman–shortstop Mike Mateef. More than seven decades later he still remembered the day and marveled at Ruth's power with a bat.[42]

In addition to events at the campus, the Hutton kids enjoyed going into town for assorted amusements. In the Settlement's first summer, Levi Hutton took 60 children to the circus, each child wearing a red ribbon. Various businesses and service organizations later underwrote trips to whatever circus played Spokane. The circus outings became something of standard treat. Another popular recurring excursion was a visit to Natatorium Park, Spokane's outstanding amusement park that boasted a magnificent merry-go-round with hand-carved horses. Once described as the "young folks mecca," it attracted Settlement children until it closed in the mid-1960s.[43]

Some entertainment was provided on the campus by the children themselves for guests and supporters of the Settlement. Christmas and Easter pageants were a staple. First produced under the direction of Pearl Hutton Schrader, a professional musician and perennial chair of the entertainment committee, they remained the single most memorable event for the participants decades after their last performances on the auditorium stage. Hutton children debuted as singers at the Settlement's initial open house on July 24, 1920, with a song dedicated to Mr. Hutton. They sang "Children's Voices," composed by Mrs. Schrader with words by Stoddard King; King, a *Spokesman-Review* editorial staffer, was known nationally as the lyricist of "There's a Long, Long Trail," a popular song from World War I.[44]

The pageants and the traditions begun at the Settlement's first Christmas endured as annual highlights. Each child always received a number of gifts and candy; each cottage always had a Christmas tree; gifts were opened on Christmas Eve; and all who remained on campus enjoyed a celebratory Christmas dinner next day. A large tree in the auditorium welcomed guests from town to the annual programs.

The 1920 celebration was a sort of benchmark. Mrs. Schrader had yet to establish the pageants; the program in the auditorium that year included carol singing and poetry reading followed by silent films provided by the manager of a Spokane movie theater. In a truly extraordinary event in the fledgling air age, "At two o'clock Santa Claus arrived in an aeroplane right out of the clouds. He was quite real for he came in and distributed gifts to the children." He came courtesy of Symon-Russell Aviation Company. Although fifty or so children went to spend the rest of the holidays with families or friends that year, the thirty who stayed on campus enjoyed various activities and a special dinner party.[45]

Christmas observances came naturally for the Hutton Settlement's Board Ladies. Most of them, typical Progressive Era child savers dedicated to service and responsibility, held strong religious convictions and had early arranged for the children to attend Sunday School. Although the Settlement maintained the nonsectarian character set forth in the Deed of Trust, as late as 1933, "four regular Sunday school services were held in [the] auditorium, [with] all children attending."[46] High school-aged Hutton kids often taught the classes, and Sunday services were a major part of the week's routine.[47]

Because of the holiday productions, Pearl Hutton Schrader was the Board Lady best known to every child during the twenties and thirties. As the monthly cottage committee reports indicate, however, other board members spent considerable time in the cottages throughout the year, fulfilling their mandate in the bylaws to help with clothing and generally "enter into the home life of the children." Cottage committee members had close contact with "their" children and considerable impact on their upbringing. They saw to it that those who wanted to take music or dancing lessons had the opportunity. They encouraged the children to invite friends to the campus. And they underscored the efforts of entertainment and education committee members, who encouraged participation in school music, sports, plays, debate, and the like.

Above all, perhaps, the Settlement board seems to have embodied the credo of the lyricist Julia Ward Howe: "To keep up the tone of society is part of every woman's duty." These women brought to the campus children a sense of style and gracious living. One former resident recalled the late Mrs. Walter Merryweather, captain of the Cottage One committee during the ten years she lived there: "I credit her with all the manners and training we received. . . . These are things you really don't appreciate until you look back. She was a stickler on manners. Mrs. Jones, the housemother, also was strict where manners and behavior were concerned."[48] Clara Scott remembered how nice mealtimes were: "wonderful food," seating, "just like home,"[49] at small tables "set with good dishes, linen tablecloths and napkins. We all learned how to set a proper table. We were taught manners—always said our 'please's and thank-you's.' The blessing was given before each meal."[50]

Some Settlement children had board members as individual sponsors, Susie Dubuque among them.

> I was one of those fortunate ones. Mrs. F. J. Walker . . . took me to her home on weekends and special occasions and after she moved to the Davenport Hotel, I spent weekends there with her which was a real treat. . . . She always told me Hutton Settlement was like a finishing school and she was right. We had linen table cloths on the tables at night and sterling silver flatware. We also had our own initialed napkin rings in silver.[51]

Clara Scott recalled Board Ladies who were "especially interested in me, and they'd take me in to the Crescent at the Tea Room for lunches so I'd learn nice things."[52]

The boys, too, remembered the napkin rings, linen tablecloths, and four-person tables. Mike Mateef also recalled that Hutton kids, like those in any family, had rules, chief among them being "what you took, you ate."[53] There was no wasting of the plentiful food at the Hutton Settlement.

Among the more than 100 Hutton kids of the Settlement's first decade a sense of family prevailed, and they enjoyed regular reunions. The life they recalled seems to have been remarkably full: "If we wanted to bring a friend for dinner we could," said Susie Dubuque; "There were movies on weekends and dances and other entertainment. . . . I went into Spokane every week for a dancing lesson."[54] Clara Scott's younger sister O'Ce remembered that anyone who showed talent or had a special interest was given lessons or further schooling. "We felt we were one big family and the feeling still exists. I wouldn't trade those years for anything."[55]

As many former residents admitted, they were not always so sanguine during the years they lived on the campus. Some children left the Settlement discontented with life there, and some were sent away for various reasons. For the most part, however, the first generation of Hutton kids had the sort of home experience that Levi Hutton had envisioned.

The Settlement came into being at a time when most institutional and private homes in the country routinely employed corporal punishment to deal with rules infractions and antisocial behavior. Hutton kids from every decade reported "paddlings"—either their own or those of friends. The Scott sisters lived in Cottage One; Clara recalled that "the matron's room was right next to our room, and if we were naughty, we got paddled. . . . I didn't get it, but my two younger sisters did." Other minor infractions might lead to a trip to the administration building and a session with the superintendent, and in some instances boys would simply be sent away from the Settlement. Actual lawbreaking resulted in one boy's being sent west of the Cascades to the state correctional center at Chehalis.[56]

Addressing the matter of discipline, at the May 1927 Settlement board meeting, Hutton moved that

> No officer or employee of the Hutton Settlement except the cottage mothers will be allowed or permitted to reprimand or punish a child without the superintendent, cottage mother, and the one reporting the offense being present.
>
> The time for reprimanding and punishing a child must not exceed a total of more than fifteen minutes.[57]

Seconded by Mrs. Agnes Paine, the resolution carried easily.

Two years later, the Board Ladies revisited the rules. They emphasized that "punishment of children must be taken up with Superintendent," and explicitly stated that "there must be no corporal punishment except in the presence of Superintendent and Captain."[58] Since board members served as captains of the cottage committees, board involvement in campus operations at that time was intimate indeed.

Mrs. Margaret Martin may have made a greater difference to the Settlement children, day-to-day, than any other adult. Nursie Martin staffed the infirmary for more than a decade, starting in June 1922, at a monthly salary of $85, soon reduced to $75, where it remained.[59] The children thought her wonderful, especially those who spent time in the infirmary.

"She was so good to all of us," declared Clara Scott. Mike Mateef never forgot being nursed through a long bout of pneumonia. Mabel Maley, who once spent a week in the infirmary, remembered:

> Oh, she was a doll. Nothing bothered her, and she had so many people come in there . . . she just kept busy all the time. She was a very, very lovely person. I think of all the staff, I loved her most because she just was so loving to everybody, . . . if you were hurting she'd put her arm around you, . . . and just say, "We'll have that all taken care of in a little bit." And she would.[60]

But no one loomed larger in the lives of Settlement children in the 1920s than Levi Hutton himself. They eagerly anticipated the frequent visits of Daddy Hutton. Clara Scott said, "We all loved him—he meant a lot to us. He'd come out . . . and bring his dog. . . . and we loved his dog, too." Susie Dubuque remembered him as "a very fatherly man who loved to show people through the Settlement. . . . He used to ask the children to do things for his guests and we all ran to greet him when he came to visit."[61] He was a man "you could go up and talk to and he'd answer everything," said Mabel Maley; "I can remember that car come driving out there, and everybody [shouting] 'There's Mr. Hutton! There's Mr. Hutton!'"[62]

Settlement children were intrigued by everything about Hutton, from his dog, a German Shepherd named Peter Von Hindenburg, to his automobiles. Mike Mateef described him as a sturdy man who stood "oh, five-ten or so"; he remembered that "we'd kind of watch for him. He had a car—a REO . . . a Flying Cloud"; and the habitual Hutton cigar appealed to the young Mateef, who said, "I used to follow him all around all the time. He smoked that one cigar, and it sure smelled good."[63] Renowned as one of the slowest drivers in Spokane, Hutton "never drove over twenty-five miles an hour and that was his peak." Until he bought the REO sedan in 1927, he always owned an open car, despite Spokane's freezing winters, "because he thought a lot of people would think he was stuck up" if he drove a closed one.[64]

Whatever the season, closed car or open, Hutton frequently drove the ten miles between his home in Spokane and the campus in the valley. A Settlement date book for 1927 confirms Charles Gonser's assertion that "he was out there all the time. When they threshed in the fall, he was there and helped them thresh. He helped them plant and everything. He enjoyed it." Daddy Hutton made several trips a week. His missions ranged from bringing supplies and planning the farm's summer work schedules to escorting new children from town to their assigned cottages; and sometimes he just visited—"Mr. Hutton came out [in the] morning and talked to the cottage 2 girls."[65]

Levi Hutton delighted in the Settlement kids, calling them "my children." Indeed, he claimed the eighty-some children as dependents on his income tax return, and the Internal Revenue Service allowed the deduction. He returned the love and affection of the children many times over and took pride in their accomplishments. His feeling for them crossed generation lines; when he learned that one of the early residents "had married and had a baby, [he] jovially and proudly termed the infant 'my first grandchild.'"[66]

Death was a fact of life for Hutton kids in the early years. Most had lost one or both parents, and a few children at the Settlement died during the 1920s. When Mrs. Alice McVay, Board Lady and cottage captain, died in August of 1927, "her going cast a gloom on all," but no team of grief counselors rushed to console the boys in Cottage Three, six of whom attended her funeral.[67] However mindful of mortality they may have been, no one and no thing could have mitigated their loss of Daddy Hutton in November 1928.

Nine years had passed since Levi Hutton had carried Jane Wiese into Cottage One. She later wrote, "His death was the greatest disaster in my life. I can remember that Saturday morning when we were told he was dead. It was almost unbearable." Mike Mateef always felt that things changed when Mr. Hutton died, and Mabel Maley, older than the other two, recalled, "I was down at College, down at Cheney, and I said, 'I'm going to go to that funeral,' and I did. I don't remember how I got up here. . . . but I went."[68]

Ever practical and modest, Levi Hutton had directed in his will that "simple services [be] conducted at my home, [followed by a] Masonic burial service." Although the regard for him throughout the region virtually demanded a large public funeral, arrangements did follow the general outline of his wishes. The service was held in Spokane's 1,800-seat Masonic Temple on November 6, 1928. The Reverend E. Leslie Rolls read the Episcopal rites, after which Knights Templar conducted the long Masonic service. Floral tributes crowded the stage, and white chrysanthemums adorned the casket along with Mr. Hutton's own plumed hat and sword of the Knight Templar.[69]

Long before the services began, the large hall had overflowed; after all seats quickly filled, many stood and more were turned away. All the Settlement children sat in the main floor's center section. The press reported next day:

> How well had been [Hutton's] care of his large family was evidenced yesterday. All were better dressed than the average youngster and every boy looked as if he had just had a hair cut. . . . as the service proceeded many of the girls broke down, unable to stand their sorrow longer, for to many of them Mr. Hutton was the only father they had ever known.

Harold Whitehouse served as a pallbearer. A long procession of automobiles accompanied the hearse to Fairmount Cemetery—to the burial site Levi and May Hutton had selected high above the river.[70]

The funeral service made an indelible impression on the Settlement children, and gave them some sense of how admired Daddy Hutton had been and how wide his philanthropy. For some of the children it marked the first time they had seen a black person; members of Spokane's leading African-American church had come to pay respects to their honorary member—the man who had contributed to their building fund at a crucial point in the congregation's history. The floral tributes had represented a cross-section of the community and various stages of his life. They came from, among others, business colleagues, tenants, and bankers, the Central Labor Council and Electrical Workers Union Local 73, and old Idaho connections, too, including the Harry Day family and Shoshone Lodge 25 in Wallace. Even his Ohio Arkwright in-laws sent flowers.[71]

Things could never be the same with Levi Hutton no longer on the scene. It remained for the Board Ladies and Charles Gonser to assume complete responsibility, and they soon faced enormous challenges that threatened the future of the Hutton Settlement.

Levi Hutton and May Arkwright met in Idaho's Coeur d'Alene country when she ran a boardinghouse and he operated a train for the Northern Pacific Railroad. Here they pose near the engine. NMAC photo.

The Hercules Mine, ca. 1905. The mine north of Burke, Idaho, was the financial foundation for Levi Hutton's dream of building a home for orphaned children. NMAC photo.

Newfound wealth from the Hercules Mine did not alter priorities for the down-to-earth Huttons, who still did the yardwork in their home in Wallace, Idaho, ca. 1905. NMAC photo.

The Hutton Building in 1920. Completed soon after the Huttons moved to Spokane, it held both monetary and symbolic value for the Settlement trustees, who reluctantly sold it in 1979. NMAC photo.

The Fernwell Building in downtown Spokane, 1905. When he bought it in 1914, Mr. Hutton said it showed his faith and confidence in the city's future. NMAC photo.

May Arkwright Hutton, ca. 1914. An ardent and audacious leader in struggles for woman suffrage and social reform, she matched her husband's compassion and generosity toward the less fortunate. NMAC photo.

The Huttons' Spokane home, built in 1914 just beyond the city limits at 17th Avenue and Crestline. They gave most of the land east of the house itself to the city for the Lincoln Park Playground. NMAC photo.

The architect Harold C. Whitehouse, ca. 1932. The young Whitehouse had worked closely with Mr. Hutton in creating plans for the Settlement. Photo courtesy of the Whitehouse family.

·L·W·HUTTON·

BENEFACTOR·OF·CHILDREN·WHOSE·GENEROSITY
HAS·PROVIDED·THE·HUTTON·SETTLEMENT —
THIS·TABLET·IS·AFFECTIONATELY·DEDICATED
BY·HIS·FRIENDS·IN·APPRECIATION·OF·THE
INESTIMABLE·VALUE·OF·HIS·GIFT·IN·MOULDING
THE·FUTURE·CITIZENSHIP·OF·THE·COMMUNITY

The bronze bas-relief that graces the entry of the administration building portrays Levi Hutton to perfection. Hutton Settlement photo.

Levi Hutton at the wheel of his state-of-the-art tractor in 1918. He took a special interest in planning and equipping the Settlement farm. Photo courtesy of the Spokane Spokesman-Review.

Pearl Hutton Schrader composed music for "Children's Voices," with which the children serenaded Mr. Hutton at the Settlement's first open house on July 24, 1920. Hutton Settlement papers, NMAC.

The fondest memories of former residents are of Christmas at the Settlement. In 1921 "Daddy" Hutton and all his children gathered in front of their tree in the auditorium. NMAC photo.

The Settlement has always enjoyed community support and contributions. Barbers union members gave children free haircuts for decades, as on this visit to the campus in 1921. NMAC photo.

The children always looked forward to Mr. Hutton's visits to the campus with his dog, Peter. Here a group presents him with a piece of cake while Peter lounges in the foreground. Hutton Settlement photo.

Cottage Three, ca. 1921. In winter the hills behind the cottages have always afforded the children hours of sledding and skiing fun. NMAC photo.

Children and Mr. Hutton on the steps of the auditorium, ca. 1921. Harold Whitehouse's plans for the administration building included a clock tower that became the Settlement's trademark. NMAC photo.

5
Keepers of the Flame

The Board Ladies had worked with the Hutton Settlement's founder during its first decade, assiduously following the provisions set forth in the Deed of Trust. In his absence, they would carry forward his plans, ideals, and expectations, and Charles Gonser, too, would assume a burden of exceptional stewardship. Growth of the social work profession would affect the Settlement as board and administrator sought both to embrace modern methods and to maintain independence. The decades of depression and war would prove difficult, bringing changes and challenges that included legal and financial threats to the Settlement's very existence.

The day after they had paid tribute to Levi Hutton at the impressive and poignant funeral services in the Masonic Temple, the pragmatic Board Ladies ushered in a new phase in the conduct of the Settlement's business. Meeting "in the usual place with eighteen members present," they officially noted that "Mr. L. W. Hutton, Great Benefactor of needy children was called to his eternal home," and the minutes show that Mrs. Merryweather moved that "Mr. Gonser be elected a member of the Hutton Settlement Board to fill the vacancy caused by Mr. Hutton's absence. The motion was seconded by Miss Dodd and carried in the usual way." After Hutton's attorney D. R. Glasgow read the will, Mrs. Paine made a motion, seconded by Mrs. Prescott and carried, that the will be filed for probate that very afternoon. To expedite matters, President Miriam Ritchie appointed the executive committee to act if required by the executor. Although facing an institutional crisis at that juncture, the women remained focused on their basic concern and held "an informal discussion about the Thanksgiving dinner for the children of the Settlement."[1]

That Mr. Hutton had named thirty-one-year-old Charles Gonser as his executor came to light only with the reading of the will. Just a year earlier he had designated the Old National Bank and Union Trust Company as executor and trustee of a trust "for the benefit of the Hutton Settlement" that would take in his entire estate.[2] When the news of his appointment became public, Gonser received a flurry of congratulatory letters. A local investment broker, Joel Ferris, noted that Hutton had "believed in individuals, their honesty, ability and capacity, and this is reflected in his making you executor." The head of the city's finance department termed the appointment "a striking tribute to your honesty, [that] shows great faith in your judgment, and is highly complimentary to your sense of responsibility." The president of the National Association of Building Owners and Managers, wrote from Chicago: "I am sure you feel deeply the compliment that he has paid you, and I am also sure that your administration of his affairs will be even more than he could have hoped for." Hutton's hopes were considerable: one of his final requests of his young manager had been that he "see that the work [at the Settlement] was carried on."[3]

As the reality of change settled in, the Board Ladies, too, expressed appreciation to Gonser for his "splendid cooperation, patient helpfulness and eagerness to assist during these trying days in an endeavor to carry out the wishes of Mr. Hutton." Acknowledging his "familiarity with the workings" of the Settlement, they saw that they would "feel keenly the need of your advice and counsel on many occasions." He responded, saying:

> The real work . . . of the Hutton Settlement activities has been done by the Hutton Settlement Board. It is true that Mr. Hutton furnished the money and also injected his splendid personality into it but he nor no one else could do it alone. . . .
>
> I intend to be just one of the Board. . . . I will call on the Hutton Settlement Board for counsel and advice. This is one large family and we must all work together.

With the stage set for a working relationship based on mutual appreciation and trust, and in accord with Hutton's wishes, at its next meeting the board officially elected Gonser "manager of all properties owned by the Hutton Settlement Estate."[4]

The procedural and organizational actions taken by the Settlement board in the wake of Hutton's death had been in fact specified in the will. The rush to probate, for example, was intended to prevent any interruption in staff payroll. Hutton left no detail unresolved. He even bequeathed $100 to each woman who had served on the board, in "appreciation for . . . untiring service . . . without which the success of the institution could not have been possible."[5]

With the exception of a $10,000 bequest to his brother Stephen, Hutton left the remainder of his considerable estate to the Hutton Settlement. He directed that all mining stock and property, stocks, bonds, mortgages and other securities "be sold or converted into cash within six months" and that his house on 17th Avenue be sold and its contents taken to the Settlement to be "used to the best advantage." In one final instruction he directed "that the Hutton Settlement, . . . shall not encumber the property coming into its hands or incur indebtedness aggregating more than five thousand dollars ($5,000.00) at any one time."[6]

The burdens of working under that directive during the Great Depression and dealing with litigation challenging Hutton's will fell to the youthful Charlie Gonser, whose family had moved to Washington in 1898, just after statehood, from Falls City, Nebraska, where Charlie was born June 25, 1897. They "settled on a farm near the Whitman Monument near the state line" and farmed there for a number of years before moving into Walla Walla.[7]

Charlie went through school in Walla Walla and in 1916 arrived in Spokane to enroll in a two-year course at the Spokane Expert School of Business, which he completed in record time. He passed the civil service examination and had job offers, but he was intrigued by a job opening at the Hutton Building. He applied, got the position, but almost immediately enlisted in the navy. Still in uniform, he returned to Spokane on February 18, 1919, where as promised, his job was waiting. But Charlie had not seen his mother for some time and wanted to go to Walla Walla for a few days. Hutton reacted in typical fashion, telling him, "You go down and visit your mother for two weeks. Your pay started this morning."[8]

Gonser resumed his clerk's job in the Hutton Building office just before completion of the Settlement campus. As he grew in favor with Mr. Hutton, he progressed from clerk to assistant manager and assistant secretary.[9] His connection with the Settlement itself grew over time, and in November 1928, he found himself responsible for the entire real estate and philanthropic empire built by Levi Hutton.

Along with a prodigious work ethic, Gonser brought to his new task the admirable traits that Hutton had perceived in his young clerk a dozen years earlier—loyalty, reliability, total honesty. Ed McWilliams, his longtime friend and business associate, saw Gonser as largely a self-made man, adding, "I'm certain that Mr. Hutton pointed him in the right direction. He learned . . . what things to do, and what positions to take, [which] seemed a basic formula that he lived all his life, [but] he did his own blossoming." Charlie Gonser "walked faster than anybody else, and he always had an unlighted cigar in his mouth," said McWilliams; and his common sense led him to "listen to every side of [a debate] before he made up his mind, and when he did, well that was it. . . . He didn't mind a vote of eleven to one against him. . . . and he was seldom on the short end of a vote."[10]

Gonser's standing in the business community grew out of his working with the bankers on the Settlement's Financial Advisory Committee. The Board Ladies' respect for him increased over time. The Settlement children had favorable recollections. Clara Scott remembered, "When I graduated from high school he and his wife bought me a baccalaureate outfit—a suit. They were really kind people." Anita Abramson, who moved to the Settlement in 1935, remembered the Gonsers as "really neat, sweet, people." Bob Grater, another 1930s Hutton resident, admired him as "really a good business man to hold [the Settlement] together here."[11]

Holding the Settlement together during the Great Depression certainly proved no mean feat. But before focusing his efforts solely on that Herculean task, Charlie Gonser had to steer the Settlement and its board through a lengthy court challenge to its financial underpinnings. In the midst of all this, adversity suddenly and unexpectedly struck him personally—his wife died in 1932, leaving him to care for their two young sons alone until he re-married in 1937.

With Levi Hutton's estate valued at $1.25 million, claims against the will were not long in coming. The only surprise lay in the direction from which they came and the direction the arguments took.

On May 6, 1929, relatives of both May and Levi Hutton filed a petition in Spokane County Superior Court contesting probate of the estate. The Arkwrights involved were sons and daughters of May's three deceased half brothers—Lyman, Delaney, and William Arkwright; her late half sister's offspring were not a party to the litigation and in fact aided Gonser somewhat in his efforts to fight the challenges. In addition to the sons and daughters of Hutton's two deceased brothers, Asa and Jacob, his brother, Stephen, whom he had named in the will, was a plaintiff.[12]

The Arkwrights contended that May had clearly meant for her estate to revert to her heirs on Levi's death, that he "had only a life interest in his wife's estate and had no authority to will it at [his] death" and thus deprive them of their share of her wealth.[13] The Huttons, incredibly, charged that for several years before he drew his final will in August of 1927, Levi's mind had been unsound and he had thus been incompetent to dispose of his property. They further alleged that Gonser, "conspiring with other persons" had exercised undue influence, hence "the will does not represent the will or desire of Mr. Hutton."[14] Presumably the "other persons" were the members of the Hutton Settlement board.[15]

The crux of the argument from both sets of plaintiffs centered on the intent of May and Levi Hutton in drawing their wills in 1913. Testimony in support of their arguments, including that of a spiritualist named Cora Kincannon Smith, who had been a frequent dinner guest of the Huttons, might have merited headlines in the *National Enquirer* half a century later.

Witnesses, not all of whom supported the plaintiffs' claims, dredged up sixteen-year-old memories to address whether in 1913 the Huttons had "made an oral agreement that the estates of each should be utilized to the benefit of heirs of each." It was also contended that they meant the 1913 wills to be final, leaving the estate of each in trust for the life of the survivor, with their respective relatives to share the residue. Levi's relatives insisted they were "entitled to his half of the estate and that Mr. Hutton had no right to leave it in trust to the Hutton Settlement."[16]

But in fact Levi Hutton had made it crystal clear to his family that he had taken care of them financially and that they would receive nothing from his estate. In 1922, when he sent his brother Asa $250, he told him then:

> I have recently made a will and have thoroughly considered everything, and especially those who I consider might be in need when I am gone. You having ample for anything . . . I have not mentioned you in my will, therefore I thought it advisable to have you know this at the present time, but should you call on me at any time I may be in a position to assist you.[17]

A month later he wrote to a nephew noted for boasting of what he would inherit, "I want you to understand for all time to come there will not be one cent left to you or yours."[18] And the Settlement Deed of Trust, signed February 13, 1920, left no doubt about Levi's intentions: "It is not my wish that . . . any heir or relative of mine may assert any claim to the property . . . or any part thereof."[19]

As for the spiritualist Kincannon Smith, Gonser learned from a Hutton relative that "Mrs. Hutton was scarcely gone before Cora was laying her plans to get her fingers on the Hutton money, by hook or crook. When she found she could get no place with L. W. she began to use other methods." Ingratiating herself with them, she connived with his nephews and other cousins.[20]

Arguments supporting the alleged oral agreement of 1913 and Levi's alleged incompetence failed to persuade Judge Charles Leavy. On October 30, 1929, he dismissed the case and absolved Charles Gonser of "any charge of wrong doing."[21]

The Arkwright plaintiffs returned in the spring of 1931 to federal district court in Spokane, this time to challenge the legitimacy of the financial settlement Levi had made with their fathers in 1918; it appears that they had already approached Gonser and the board. The Board Ladies, impatient, if not indignant, had voted to "refuse to settle or compromise in any way with the Hutton relatives in regard to their legal action against the Hutton Estate."[22]

The Arkwrights' 1931 suit charged that the 1918 agreement between Levi and May's half brothers, in which they relinquished any and all claims to her estate, had been obtained by fraud. Their claims reopened the challenge to May's will and required verification of the value of the 1915 Hercules Mine holdings that had formed the basis of Mr. Hutton's dealings with the Arkwrights.[23] On June 8, Judge Stanley Webster "held there had been no fraud and denied the heirs any part of the Hutton estate." The Arkwrights appealed. Final resolution of the conflict came a year later when the Ninth Circuit Court of Appeals in San Francisco ruled in the Settlement's favor.[24]

Charles Gonser devoted more than three years to litigation. Not until 1935 could he report to the board that he had been released as executor of Mr. Hutton's estate. He would now be free to focus full time on managing the Settlement's real estate holdings and administering the business side of its campus operations.

The downtown commercial property owned by Mr. Hutton at the time of his death consisted of a small building at Second and Washington, the Hutton and Fernwell buildings, and the City Ramp Garage. Although the garage was a recent, somewhat speculative acquisition, the other properties were old investments. The Fernwell Building, for example, which he bought for $275,000 in 1914, showed Hutton's "faith in Spokane" and "confidence in its future."[25] The Cobweb Bar, a longtime popular rendezvous in Spokane, had occupied one corner of the ground floor; it came close to preventing the purchase. May Hutton adamantly opposed liquor, and the Huttons refused "to derive revenue from the liquor traffic in any way, or permit the sale of liquor on any property" they owned. There was some consternation in the city when they did not renew the tavern's lease, forcing it to close in April 1915. They had, meanwhile, instructed their property manager "not to deposit the saloon rent to their account, but to devote it to charitable purposes." The Huttons' liquor aversions had earlier affected a tenant in the newly completed Hutton Building. The chamber of commerce had occupied the entire second floor and announced plans to open a bar to help meet its expenses. The Huttons did not renew the chamber's lease, either.[26] Both properties brought the Huttons and later the Settlement handsome returns. The City Ramp Garage was a different case.

A venture by Levi Hutton, the Paulsen Estate, and the Old National Bank intended to counter a large development planned at the far west end of downtown, the garage was built to anchor the city's business center at the east end, in the vicinity of the Hutton and Paulsen buildings. It was the first structure in Spokane designed specifically for parking automobiles. As he had Harold Whitehouse in planning the Settlement campus, Mr. Hutton dispatched Gonser "up and down the Pacific Coast looking at garages to get ideas." The Whitehouse and Price-designed art deco building opened three weeks after Hutton's death. It had reduced the estate's cash to little more than $14,000, and it proved a financial albatross throughout the 1930s and 1940s.[27]

The law suits had cost the Settlement at least $40,000 in attorney fees and court costs; income from the Fernwell and Hutton buildings had plunged—the Fernwell from annual net revenues of $23,799 in 1927 to only $7,241 by 1935 and the Hutton from $24,295 to $1,723. Keeping the Settlement solvent during the depression required ingenuity, great effort, and constant vigilance, sending Gonser and the board in search of other revenue sources.[28]

In the 1920s the Settlement had received a few small bequests. The board earmarked interest from these investments for specific uses, such as that of the $2,000 Sherwood fund, which went to improving the tennis courts in 1929. The cool-headed and unflappable Board Ladies had considered the treasurer's first report after the stock market crash simply as "most interesting," but six months later, reality compelled them to redirect that interest income for emergency and educational use. In the summer of 1935, the Settlement received a $50,000 bequest from the estate of Grace Z. Smith; the board designated it as the Grace Z. Smith Income Fund. It contributed substantially toward Settlement operations during the depression; even so, and during a lamentable investment climate, careful stewardship left it valued at $34,593 a decade later.[29]

Similarly, the Settlement benefited in the midthirties from the estate of Mary J. Thomas, sharing jointly with the Salvation Army ownership of buildings on North Lincoln and on Sprague Avenue. Eventual sales of the two properties bolstered the Settlement's finances during a time of true emergency. The Smith and Thomas assets may have been the inspiration for Gonser to express publicly his hope that people with philanthropic ideals would provide for the Hutton Settlement in their wills.[30]

During the depression, the Hutton Settlement received funds from the Spokane Community Chest. But such help was somewhat problematic in that Settlement affairs became public. As the role of public welfare expanded in the 1930s, the board walked a fine line trying to avoid entanglement with state Department of Welfare social workers.

The Hutton Settlement Board Ladies had carried over from the Ladies' Benevolent Society characteristics of the typical nineteenth-century board member, "no remote figure who met from time to time with other directors to ponder broad questions of policy." They participated actively in the day-to-day conduct of Settlement affairs and continued that dedication and involvement through the twenties and into the thirties as social work jelled into a profession that worked "to impress upon board members the fact that wealth, social standing, and good intentions were not substitutes for training and skill." Nationally, "evangelical zeal and the mystique of personal service had been replaced by a bureaucratic machinery geared to efficiency, [and] philanthropy remained an opportunity to promote business and social contacts and fulfill expected social obligations without the burdens of intimate participation."[31] But the Hutton Settlement board continued to reflect that zeal for personal service; even as new people replaced the charter members, the women hewed diligently to the charge spelled out in the Settlement's Deed of Trust.

Social work can trace its professional roots to the reform movement that emerged in reaction to the orphan train phenomenon. The goal of keeping families together that had led to the cottage system adopted by the Hutton Settlement "became the *raison d'être* of professional social workers" and the linchpin of public welfare. Early reform leaders, such as the Russell Sage Foundation's Mary Richmond, had "viewed themselves as exponents of a holy cause."[32]

In the 1890s some charity workers began to feel it necessary for people to "take charge of this work who are specially trained, who have a calling for the work, and who mean to devote themselves to it." Training specifically for social work began in 1898; with efficiency as a watchword, the pace picked up during the first two decades of the new century, and in 1921, the Child Welfare League of America opened its New York headquarters. Embracing sixty-five member organizations, it soon became "the most important private national agency for child welfare." The American Association of Social Workers also was established that year, and by 1930 its membership was 5,000 strong. By the time of the Great Depression, through schools, associations, and agencies and "by the test of efficiency, not zeal," social work had justified its professional existence.[33] Reform legislation of the New Deal welded it to public welfare.

But along the way, "a chronic tension between public and private welfare" developed. "This legacy of suspicion," as one scholar terms it, was nowhere more evident than in the relationship between the Hutton Settlement and social workers in Washington's new Department of Welfare, which, during the depression, began to pressure the Settlement to add case workers to its staff. As the profession had gained influence and leverage, even the Sage Foundation's Mary Richmond criticized a "certain opinionated and self-righteous attitude in some of the trained social workers."[34] Although not on record, the independent-minded Board Ladies probably echoed her sentiments.

Even though Charles Gonser did not suffer social workers gladly, the Hutton Settlement tried to find some ground for accommodation with the state Welfare Department. During the thirties board members began to attend professional conferences and seminars. Stalwart Agnes Paine represented the Settlement in February 1936 at the Eastern Washington Public Welfare Conference. The next month two women from the state Welfare Department visited the campus. Mrs. Paine explained Hutton's vision to them; other Board Ladies outlined the Settlement's policies and practices. Jessica Mooney, a department supervisor, visited fairly often and usually "seemed favorably impressed"; however, "a set of rules for child welfare care" that she sent in 1940 was simply "placed on file for future reference." Staying on Levi Hutton's course while navigating public welfare currents required vigilance and skill. In April of 1943, the board voted to "take a $5 membership in the Washington State Conference of Social Workers."[35] That step had not come easily, but having turned to Community Chest funding, the Settlement could not avoid the world of the social work professional.

Forerunner of the United Way, the Community Chest had arisen nationally during the twenties because it "could amass more money with less annoyance to givers" than numerous separate appeals by individual charities; it soon "established an elaborate, systematic canvassing machinery designed to reach every potential contributor." Recipient agencies, however, found strings attached to its funds. As one historian has said, "Through its budgeting procedure, . . . [the Community Chest] exerted an influence over constituent agencies more potent than moral suasion." It also "became a public relations arm of professional social work." Positioning professionals between donors and agencies, the Community Chest may have "eliminat[ed] any sense of personal identification between giver and ultimate recipient."[36]

Levi Hutton had been an early and generous contributor to the organization; his name appeared on the first committee of the Community Welfare Federation of Spokane, as it was called in its first campaign in 1921. Board Ladies' husbands regularly served on its executive committee and headed annual fund drives. Their sense of duty led the women to join in annual Community Chest drives. Mrs. Paine was a leader of the 1925 fund drive; rosters of workers in both the South Hill and Browne's Addition included many Settlement board names.[37]

Member organizations of the Community Chest that first year of 1921 included the Spokane Children's Home, which requested, under "gifts needed," $6,500, "including $2,500 for children at Hutton Settlement." From that rather stealthy beginning, the Settlement's reliance on the Community Chest grew. After Hutton's death, the board continued his tradition of contributing to the annual drives. Throughout the 1930s, the Settlement requested funds from the Community Chest even as it continued to make donations and board members continued to work in Community Chest fund drives. Its standard annual allocation was $4,500, but in 1936 the figure was $5,000.[38]

As the depression deepened, both the Hutton and Fernwell buildings had to be mortgaged. The cost of operating the Settlement in Hutton's last year at the helm had been approximately $37,000. Cutting expenses to the bone lowered the outlay to $17,000 in 1932. After securing a mortgage on the two buildings, in December 1934 Gonser told the board that debts amounting to $56,000 had been paid and there was $2,200 in the bank.[39]

The situation became more grim. In 1936 expenses were more than $18,000, and income was less than $4,000. The following year Gonser borrowed $5,653.04 from the Washington Trust Company to pay the first half taxes on the downtown buildings. Washington Trust, whose president, Fred Stanton, long served on the Settlement's Financial Advisory Committee, remained the only bank willing to lend to the Settlement during the depression. Stanton's son later said

> That was my father's doing. But I think that was based upon Charlie Gonser's management. . . . Dad knew that Charlie was not . . . [going to] get into a situation that would hurt the Settlement, and he backed him a number of times. They didn't like debt any more than anybody else, but in order to protect their investment several times they had to take on some debt.

In September 1937, Washington Trust agreed to reduce the interest on the Hutton and Fernwell buildings' mortgage and "waive the right to call the loan in five years."[40]

In the autumn of 1941, as the state geared up for war and Spokane's economy improved, real estate revenues began to rise. The Settlement received some bequests and even a special dividend from a reorganization of the Hercules Mining Company. Gonser buoyed the October meeting of the Financial Advisory Committee with the good news that the debts were paid with money to spare. A jubilee, on the order of that greeting Hutton's 1917 announcement that he would create the Settlement, might well have followed the Board Ladies' receiving the canceled mortgage.[41] Their next goal was to free the Settlement from Community Chest oversight.

In her study of private maternity homes, the historian Regina Kunzel found that the Community Chest "urged and eventually required allied organizations either to cooperate with local casework agencies or to hire their own caseworkers." The Hutton Settlement, like those maternity homes, found that "only when the depression cut private funding . . . threatening many with financial collapse, were maternity home workers forced to acquiesce to the demands of Community Chests."[42] Among those demands were that recipients of funding submit their books for auditing and their programs for approval; Charles Gonser and the Board Ladies remained loathe to surrender any degree of independence.

An early indication of board uneasiness with outside intrusion came in the summer of 1936. In June the Settlement received a letter from the Community Chest "suggesting that a case-worker be assigned to investigate applications for admission to the Settlement and to conduct the follow-up work when the child leaves." Having performed both of these functions themselves, first with Mr. Hutton and then with Charlie Gonser, the Board Ladies endorsed Mrs. Paine's motion to "postpone consideration of the matter until a later day." Two years later another letter from the Community Chest recommended "restricting the term of office of trustees to not more than two consecutive terms of three years each." Once again the women resisted the interference, though voting that their president, Pearl Hutton Schrader, "write a letter . . . stating our Board is carefully considering the matter and will advise them of our decision when the matter is acted upon."[43] No copy of her letter survives, but board members have continued to serve "until removed by death, resignation, or by a majority vote of the remaining trustees" as provided in the original bylaws.

Such encroachment together with on-going audits very likely fueled the desire to withdraw the Settlement from the Community Chest. Open discussion of withdrawing began in the spring of 1942, and a year later, finances made it possible. With characteristic diplomacy, at a special meeting on June 15, 1943, the board members voted that "due to our present financial status, we [feel] that with economical management we can retire from the Chest . . . thus releasing funds to supply some of the very heavy demands that will be made upon the Chest for 1944." In their letter to the Community Chest, Board Ladies expressed gratitude for its help in the past. After receiving one final payment in December of 1943, the Settlement became a nonparticipating agency, though, at the request of the Community Chest, two members of the board attended annual meetings.[44]

Even as legal affairs and financial problems had beset the Settlement, Gonser and the Board Ladies sought to keep an even keel on the campus itself. They remained determined to keep Settlement traditions insofar as possible.

The annual banquet to honor friends and benefactors of the Settlement stood high on the list of traditions. Having sorrowfully canceled the 1928 affair, they reinstated it the following year, again at the Davenport Hotel. Now called the Founders Day Annual Banquet, it proved to be "a most gratifying occasion." The following year Ben Kizer, a civic leader who had known both May and Levi Hutton, gave the evening's major address. In 1931, financial considerations forced the Board Ladies to move the event to the Settlement auditorium, where they returned in 1932. Eric Johnston, husband of a board member, Ina Hughes Johnston, spoke that evening to an assemblage that for the first time included former residents of the Settlement.[45]

The 1933 banquet was the largest and most celebratory since Mr. Hutton's death. One hundred eighty-six friends and patrons gathered in the festively decorated auditorium for a "supper [that] consisted mainly of Settlement farm products, deliciously prepared by Mrs. Jackson, the cateress, and efficiently served by the girls of the Settlement." There were impromptu speeches, a special music program, the crop report, and the main address outlining "the aspirations and high purpose of Mr. Hutton's life."[46] That evening marked the last of the annual banquets.

Meanwhile, three months after Mr. Hutton died, dependable Mrs. Ida Chandler had resigned as superintendent of the Settlement. She had served since January 1928. A search found in nearby Lewiston Mrs. Dell Tunstall, whom Gonser considered "a woman and executive well qualified" for a position that was hard to fill. She had managed the student cafeteria at Kansas State College in Manhattan, and at Lewiston Normal School she managed two dormitories and the dining facilities on campus. At the Settlement Mrs. Tunstall handled constant matron turnover and dealt with a child population that numbered near ninety on average. After a year on the job the board voted that she should "have 24 hours off duty each week," but she left just a few months later.[47] Her replacement was the first man to serve as Settlement superintendent.

Mr. and Mrs. O. S. Burkholder came to the Hutton Settlement in October 1930 as a team—he as superintendent, she as his assistant. They received a monthly salary of $300, plus the standard room and board. The Board Ladies made a point of encouraging them to "consider their suite of rooms in the Administration Building as entirely private, having the status of a home." Mrs. Burkholder had worked with the YMCA, but his background is not clear. His reports to the board and the programs he ran at the campus indicate plainly that he came with experience in youth and group work. In what appears to have been a first for a superintendent, he attended the December 1930 board meeting to explain those programs. He began the practice of holding monthly meetings of the staff and welcomed board attendance at them. Burkholder maintained a presence in the larger community; he spoke frequently to service clubs and maintained close connections with the West Valley School District.[48]

He resigned abruptly in December 1934, when an opportunity opened for him in "Public Lecture Work and Radio Broadcasting in Vocational and Youth Guidance Activities." He and his wife left "with the kindest feeling toward every child, the Staff and members of the Board." But Burkholder shortly took a job in Oakland, California, at the Finch Children's Home, from where he kept in touch with the Settlement board.[49] Although Charles Gonser and the Board Ladies were favorably impressed with him, Burkholder received mixed reviews from Settlement residents who lived there during his tenure.

The Board Ladies apparently grew comfortable with Burkholder's take-charge leadership style, which his successor did not possess. Mr. and Mrs. Waldo Smith and their two daughters moved onto campus in January 1935. The Board Ladies hired the couple as superintendent and assistant superintendent at half the salary of the Burkholders, promising an increase "as soon as we are financially able." More than four years later, the pay jumped to $175. In the meantime, the superintendent got a day off each week and permission to smoke in his own quarters. The board also allowed "that the Smith children shall be governed by their parents and not by the rules of the Settlement." In the summer of 1936, the board met to discuss the Smiths' performance and whether to retain them. Some members

> felt their institutional training had not fitted them for this particular work; others believed [they] had not been given sufficient authority. . . . It was the general feeling that Mr. Smith is giving too much time personally to the farm work . . . and not enough to the children, the Cottages or the supervision of housemothers. . . . that the school work should be followed more closely . . . [and] that our girls should be properly chaperoned.

Reservations were laid to rest, and the Smiths stayed on until May 1941, when they were guests at a luncheon of appreciation at the Davenport Hotel. Settlement children of the Smith years remembered them favorably for the most part; the Smith daughters had become their friends and schoolmates.[50]

With the departure of the Smiths, the entrance to the superintendent's office became a revolving door. Between May 1941 and August 1944, five different people served as superintendent. The Settlement could not compete with wartime salaries in Spokane. Soon after Pearl Harbor the 2,400-acre Spokane Army Air Depot (now Fairchild Air Force Base) rose west of the city; downtown streets teemed with men in uniform—airmen from the new air depot and trainees from the navy's Camp Farragut in Idaho. At a time when local high school graduates found a $200-a-month typist job with the Army Air Corps more appealing than a $79 entry-level job in a bank, the Hutton Settlement was hard pressed to attract and retain employees of the caliber the board desired.[51] Difficult as it was, the problem of finding and retaining a superintendent paled beside that of finding good housemothers for the four cottages.

In March 1942, the board contacted O. S. Burkholder in California, both for his advice and to ask him to return as superintendent. He agreed to return for three years at a monthly salary of $400 and some unspecified expenses. The women realized that they could not afford his salary demands but "unanimously agreed that under no circumstances would anyone but a trained worker be employed." At a rare joint meeting of the board and the Settlement's Financial Advisory Committee in April, Fred Stanton and Joel Ferris opined that "a competent Superintendent and wife could be employed at $300 a month." Gonser had consulted Jessica Mooney of the state Welfare Department, who agreed.[52] Burkholder did not return; there was a quick succession of three superintendents before the board hired Clair W. Blair in August 1942.

Into the early thirties, the number of children living at the Settlement hovered between seventy and seventy-five, the majority full orphans; and in 1932 they included twenty-two sibling groups. By June 1936 the average had dropped to fifty-five, and many were considered boarders, having parents or guardians who visited regularly. The Settlement's financial bind had caused the board to contemplate closing and consolidating cottages as early as 1933, and as the population fell, it considered that prospect again. Early in 1939 the Board Ladies did close Cottage Two, but contributions from the Community Chest and other organizations helped them reopen it in 1940. The Spokane Woman's Club, for example, completely furnished a four-bed room in memory of May Arkwright Hutton, who had been a charter member.[53]

Monthly applications for admission to the Settlement numbered near ten in the early forties, and the population reached sixty-three in the spring of 1943. That August, Superintendent Blair told the board, "We are forced to continue with more changes, even though our children suffer the greater injury that attends the coming and going of Matrons." In October alone, three cottages lost matrons, two without warning. Louis Maynard, one of the older boys, kept his cottage going during a search for replacements. The situation disheartened the Blairs "because it means that our children are not receiving the attention and care . . . that they have received in former years." Mrs. Blair took on matron's duties in one cottage, but the situation was untenable. She and her husband came to ask themselves, "Is it possible that we are without the ability to inspire and direct others through our example and encouragement, to do a difficult job in a satisfactory manner?"[54]

By then the Settlement's financial picture was much improved, yet the near impossibility of staffing the campus forced the board to consider alternatives. Closing the Settlement remained unthinkable; the women chose instead to condense operations to a bare minimum and move everyone into the administration building. They asked parents or guardians to begin moving children from the campus, and the campus population dropped from forty-eight in November to twelve in December. Blair's report for that month was concise and to the point: "All Cottages were closed the evening of December 31st. The first meal was served that evening in the Administration Dining Room to all children. . . . [They had] assisted with moving . . . and the cleaning."[55]

The Blairs themselves left the Settlement in March 1944, after seeing the twelve children, all full orphans, settled into the administration building—six girls on the second floor and six boys on the third. Mrs. Harriet Ashton moved into the building, too, as girls matron; on the Blairs' departure she was named temporary superintendent. Three months later, when she left, the Board Ladies turned to one of their own—the estimable Miriam Ritchie—as her replacement.[56] Under Mrs. Ritchie's watchful eye, the "small family," of Settlement children and employees rode out the rest of the war.

The Settlement's empty cottages presented a tempting possibility out in the valley for Spokane School District 81 and the Spokane County Juvenile Court. Early in June 1944, the school district's guidance officer, a Mr. Ferguson, met with the board, citing the rise in juvenile delinquency and an increase in the number of Spokane County boys below the age of fifteen sent to the state training school. He offered a community committee proposal for a jointly administered "protective school" for such preadolescents, girls as well as boys, that would incorporate the Settlement children; three Settlement board members would join school district and county representatives in running the new institution. After considering all this, the board expressed its feeling that the venture could not succeed. Anxious to be a good neighbor, however, the Settlement board offered to lease one cottage to the Spokane school district for a trial of the program so long as it remained independent of the Settlement. The board also noted that "when competent help is available it is the intention of the [Settlement] to operate again at full capacity." The community committee's spokesman, Judge Webster, who had worked with many of the Board Ladies since the Settlement opened, declined the offer in view of the "difference in programs" and the protective school's need for a permanent home.[57] Thus the Settlement board, having only recently severed its connection with the Community Chest, remained true to the Deed of Trust and maintained the separation of private and public philanthropy.

Despite staff shortages that necessitated the reduction of the campus population, the war years put the Settlement in a healthy state financially. New government agencies leased much of the Hutton Building in 1943, and Gonser's report of the Settlement's net worth in January 1944 must have been a glimmer of light at the end of a rather gloomy tunnel—"assets owned by the corporation showed a total in excess of $1,556,282.52 in valuation with no outstanding obligations."[58] He and the Board Ladies had taken the Settlement through some very challenging and thorny times.

6

Life on the Campus and Beyond: The Great Depression and World War II

Bereft of the personal warmth and devotion of Daddy Hutton, life at the Settlement would assume a different air for those children who had loved him and eagerly looked forward to his visits. But the memory of Levi Hutton permeated life on the campus, and his pioneering exploits and incredible generosity grew into legend. Visits to his grave site became annual pilgrimages for Settlement children. On the first Father's Day after his death, all attended a service there, and Mrs. John Bruce Dodd, "placed a wreath on the grave in silent tribute" to the man who had become Spokane's leading father. On Memorial Day 1932, Governor Roland Hartley headed a list of dignitaries gathered to honor Spokane pioneers and to mark their graves with bronze plaques. The first so honored was Hutton. Fourteen-year-old Jack Trounce, then a resident of Cottage Four, positioned the plaque, after which an honor guard from nearby Fort George Wright fired in salute.[1]

Always looking forward, Hutton had provided for the future, and the stewardship of the Board Ladies and Charles Gonser preserved the essence of the home that he had envisioned. Traditions begun in the Settlement's first years continued through the difficult decades to come. As longtime residents moved on and newcomers moved in, board and administrator did their best to maintain the Hutton Settlement as a secure refuge from the harsh realities of economic depression and war.

Providing for siblings to be raised together continued as a Settlement priority; in 1932, twenty-two groups of brothers and sisters composed two-thirds of the campus population. New arrivals continued to come from northern Idaho as well as eastern Washington. Relations with the West Valley School District remained amiable, due in no small part to the board's education committee long chaired by Cazenovia Cowley Weaver. By the end of 1933, a total of 316 children had lived at the Settlement since it opened, and a summary of statistics that year reported that "the children all seem to be happy with perhaps a very few exceptions."[2] For residents, the Settlement's second decade paralleled its first. Daily chores, the school routine, farm and garden work, Sunday School, Christmas pageants, cottage living arrangements, summers and the swimming pool—all continued to define life on the campus through the thirties and into the forties.

Among others, Jane Wiese, Mike Mateef, and the Scott sisters had grown into teenagers at the Settlement; by 1930 they attended West Valley High School where they took part in student government and participated in sports and other after-school programs. Clara Scott served as president of the High School Girls Federation in 1931, and Jane Wiese was elected vice-president of the student body in 1933. Another Hutton kid, Gordon Windle, who graduated from West Valley in 1931, remembered it as a "typical farm-area school" that offered a good general program in the still rural valley. He played football, managed the track team, and "entered into the social life, and the political life, and the athletic life" of West Valley "just like any other student." Most Settlement alumni of the late twenties and thirties echoed his assessment; one woman allowed that the advantages that she appreciated in retrospect "may not have overweighed the stigma placed on us as Settlement Kids at that period of my life."[3]

The Board Ladies never wavered in their commitment to the education of the Settlement children. The education committee chair, Mrs. Weaver, who lived in Pasadena Park in the West Valley School District, kept a close eye on the progress of the grade schoolers and personally steered many into the high school program and on to graduation. She regularly met with eighth graders "to consider the choice of their high school subjects" and make a check "on High School students . . . to [see] who needs to make up certain credits in order to graduate."[4] Although West Valley offered a good range of academic and vocational classes, it lacked a strong art program. Clara Scott recalled that her youngest sister, Ethyl, "was kind of an artist, and really good." Because of her talent, the board arranged for her to go into Spokane and attend Lewis and Clark High School, "which had a better [art] course."[5]

Cooperation between the Settlement and the school district continued. In the autumn of 1930 West Valley students held a party in the Settlement's administration building and the school provided the chaperones, who included the principal. The first generation of Hutton kids continued to meld with the rest of the student body and built lasting friendships.[6]

The issue of dating did not arise officially, either at school or on the Settlement campus. But Don Fleetwood and Leo Billings, first-generation boys, recalled an "imaginary line—one that kept the boys out of the girls' cottages." Fleetwood added that "we knew we better not get caught crossing [it]. . . . We would get 15 swats if we were caught. I got swatted many times."[7]

On the other hand, Hilda Lawson recalled from the early thirties that "we had parties together and were allowed to invite our school friends [and] we were allowed to go on dates with boys." Clara Scott said she and her future husband "started going together" as freshmen. She recalled that even though his family lived near the school and the Settlement was nearly two miles distant,

> he'd walk home from school with me, and carry my books. He'd walk clear across, and then clear [back home]—but he had a bicycle. . . . He'd let one of the other Hutton Settlement children ride his bike, so he could walk with me home and carry my books. I had to carry my own violin.

Most Settlement high schoolers walked to and from school, but the Settlement provided transportation for those who wanted to stay for sports and other activities.[8]

Although Mr. Hutton had not established funding for his children's post-high school education, the Board Ladies encouraged their charges to seek vocational training or a college education, as the founder had intended. In 1928 the board had contacted Washington State College in Pullman in an effort to help fund the Settlement's first generation of college-bound youngsters. Funding became more difficult as the depression deepened. The board arranged loans from its education fund and closely monitored repayment.[9] Some sponsors made contributions to further schooling, and individual board members underwrote some expenses. Minutes of most board meetings in the early 1930s show discussions of loans for former Hutton youngsters to complete courses at schools of nursing, beauty schools, business colleges, normal schools, and four-year colleges.

In autumn 1931, five Hutton youngsters were attending Washington State College. The Board Ladies had authorized that gifts of "$50 from Mrs. Bender and $20 from Mrs. Blackwell be used for [one student's] college entrance expenses," and they followed keenly the recipient's progress and that of all the others. They did not hesitate to provide small loans and gifts throughout the academic year. They convened a special meeting to authorize a loan for Georgina Petheram's senior year in Pullman and proudly reported her graduation in June 1933. They must have taken considerable pride when Georgina was employed three months later by Wenatchee's premier hotel, the Cascadian, with promise of greater things as a hotel dietitian in what became the Westin Hotel chain. Thirty years later, another generation of Board Ladies saved the 1963 summer edition of *Pow Wow*, a Washington State University alumni publication, which spotlighted Georgina Petheram Tucker, then assistant director of the food and beverage division of the hotel chain, overseeing operations from Anchorage to Guatemala, Denver to Tokyo.[10] Clearly, Georgina Petheram had succeeded when opportunity for corporate advancement eluded many qualified and accomplished women.

Nursing and public school teaching stood as virtually the only professional opportunities for young women when the first generation of youngsters left the Settlement. The normal school in nearby Cheney drew more than a few of them. Peggy Trounce went to Idaho and earned a teaching certificate at Lewiston Normal School in the spring of 1932; the Settlement education committee reported that for the coming year she had "a splendid position as teacher and does the janitor work and gets $10.00 extra for it."[11] Because newly-minted elementary teachers who started in rural, one-room schools typically handled janitorial duties, Peggy Trounce's extra pay made hers an exceptional case.

Wanda Swindler, who had come to the Settlement in 1919, earned her credential at the Cheney Normal School. She began teaching in a rural school at Bickleton, between Grandview and Goldendale, in autumn 1933, and at semester's end wrote the Board Ladies "a nice and newsy letter." She also wrote in the spring of 1937 to say that she was coming to Spokane for a teachers' institute and "hoped to secure a position in the city schools." When the education committee reported in May that she had been hired, the board unanimously instructed the corresponding secretary to "write Wanda expressing the pleasure of the board" at her success.[12]

Wanda Swindler's story exemplifies the genuine interest the board took in the Settlement children and in their later lives. Swindler in middle age wrote that the Settlement "inspired [her] to study for a higher education" and added that "had it not been for the Hutton Settlement I very much doubt that I would have had the fulfilled life which I have enjoyed."[13]

More than a few young women from the Settlement became registered nurses, graduating chiefly from programs at Spokane's St. Luke's and Deaconess hospitals. The Board Ladies played a large role in securing tuition funds and providing uniforms. When Clara Scott made the decision to enter training at St. Luke's in the spring of 1932, the board discussed the "matter of Clara Scott's uniforms" with the volunteers of the Browne's Addition Chapter, "the plan being to furnish the material if the chapter would make the uniforms."[14] That sewing group had kept the Scott sisters well dressed for years.

The Settlement's longtime and beloved Nursie Martin left her position in the campus infirmary in July 1932. In replacing her, the Board Ladies turned to one of their own. Esther Roos, who had come to the Settlement with her five siblings in 1921, graduated from the Deaconess nursing program in February 1931 and began caring for the Hutton kids the following year. After three years she resigned seeking "wider opportunity to engage in her profession," a move that took her to the East Coast.[15]

The concern for the future of one young woman in the midthirties illustrates the personal involvement of the board in the lives of the Settlement children. The women did not hesitate to make decisions they deemed best for young people leaving the campus. When Cora C—— graduated from West Valley in the spring of 1936, Gonser told the board she could possibly live with a family in Lewiston "to work for wages and have the privilege of attending Normal [School]." Mrs. Agnes Paine felt, however, "that Cora would make an excellent nurse and asked Mr. Gonser to make arrangements, if possible, for her to enter the Deaconess Hospital." Supporting her position with action, Mrs. Paine gave Cora "a watch as a graduation gift, which she will find very useful in her new work." Cora entered the Deaconess program with uniforms supplied by Mrs. Paine, enrollment fees from the board's Emergency Fund, and new clothing and glasses from the Educational Trust Fund.[16]

The 1935 Grace Z. Smith bequest improved funding possibilities for post-high school education. Terms of the donor's will specifically empowered the Settlement to use Smith money "for the education of such older children as may desire to pursue their studies and their educational work" but not exclusively for college scholarships. Instead, use of the fund was to be "guided by considerations of a practical character. . . , so that such advanced students shall be enabled to increase their earning ability."[17]

The Board Ladies followed with great interest those who chose other paths. In the spring of 1929 they learned that Katherine E—— had, on leaving the Settlement, gone "to live with Mr. and Mrs. Morgan in Chicago." A year later Charlie Gonser, in Chicago on business, looked in on Katherine and ended up staying with the Morgans. His "delightful report" pleased the board tremendously. Likewise, there was general pleasure at the board's July meeting in 1931, when "Mrs. Paine read a splendid letter from . . . a former Settlement girl who is now married and the mother of a young child."[18]

The Settlement board helped numerous young people find employment. Board minutes show many instances of job placement and referral for the first generation leaving the campus. When Mabel Maley graduated she worked as a cashier at the Crescent Department Store before going on to Cheney Normal School, thanks to some board influence. In at least one instance, Gonser sought a congressional appointment to West Point for a young man, and the Settlement provided funds and encouragement to several youths who went to Alaska in search of employment. As Ira Sisson who left the Settlement in 1933 later put it, "They even checked to see if, when we went out in the world, we were able to make it. They set us up in an occupation to make sure we had a chance."[19] The advent of the Civilian Conservation Corps in the early thirties created one avenue followed by some Settlement boys, and military service called them later in the decade.

Fourteen alumni returned during the Christmas holidays in 1930 and recaptured the fun of sledding on the hill behind the cottages. That Saturday, December 27, "After several hours of coasting, refreshments (wieners, marshmallows and coffee) were prepared around the fire." Five of the girls stayed on for several days. Two years later many of the same people and their friends came again to enjoy "activities centered around coasting on the hill" and the "waffles and coffee [that] were served" afterward.[20]

Sibling groups predominated in the second generation of Settlement residents. Among them were the Graters, Bakers, Taylors, and the Aldrich sisters.

Soon after their widowed mother died in a car-train accident in April 1930, eleven-year-old Bob, eight-year-old Pearle, and five-year-old Glen Grater arrived from Athol, Idaho. One of their aunts had learned of the Hutton Settlement and with the help of a local doctor got them admitted. Again the flexibility of entrance requirements enabled the Graters to remain together; even so they lived in different cottages, and Pearle recalled that they did "not see much of each other." They spent an occasional weekend and summer vacation time with their aunts and uncles in the Spokane area, and all lived at the Settlement until they graduated from West Valley.[21]

Just before school started in 1935, four Baker children moved into the Settlement: Vanita, aged fourteen; David, twelve; Ruth, ten; and Bobby, eight. Their mother had died in 1930, and they lived on a farm east of Colville with their father until he, too, died in late 1934. Two older siblings, including a sister who worked in the office of a Dr. Cunningham in Spokane, had thwarted a plan to parcel the children out among aunts and uncles in Chicago. As Bob Baker later recalled, "My older sister got us into the Settlement through one of the ladies on the board." Vanita and Ruth graduated from West Valley, but David left the Settlement around 1940 and spent the next two years at Boys Town in Nebraska. Bob quit school in his sophomore year, left the Settlement, and went to work in construction.[22] That the Settlement allowed the older Bakers to keep the children together would have pleased Levi Hutton enormously.

Later in the 1930s Jim Taylor and his sister, both born in St. Mary's, Idaho, came to live at the Settlement. Their father died in an automobile accident in 1935 and their mother died in 1937. A year later, a neighbor and an aunt placed the children at the Hutton Settlement. Jim lived first in Cottage Three; his first day there remained a blur: "I think I was crying the whole time." Although his sister stayed at the Settlement through the war and graduated from West Valley, he "did something very foolish, and ran off. I thought I knew more than [everyone else]." After working an apple harvest he returned to school at West Valley, living with the family of a fellow apple picker until he enlisted in the Navy.[23]

The Board Ladies had taken note when he "ran off." Mrs. Ritchie reported that "Jimmy Taylor left the Settlement to attend some affair in the Valley and has not returned." They later learned that "he and another boy were in Oroville, Wn., picking apples."[24]

The Aldrich sisters—Clara and Dorothy—arrived at the Settlement in January 1943, just as the cottages had closed and everyone had moved into the administration building. Their family, living in Sandpoint, Idaho, had virtually disintegrated seven years earlier, sending the girls and two older brothers to the Lewiston Children's Home. Clara, in second grade at the time, later recalled it as a "horrible" place with big dormitories, where "every day I got beat. . . . [and] we were separated." The children "were not allowed to even talk to each other." They stayed three years, then returned to live with their mother until her death at Christmas 1942. Coming in as a young teenager, Clara thought the Hutton Settlement "really was sort of a family. I liked that, and I liked the kids . . . actually, I just loved the place." When she graduated from West Valley in 1948, the board thought her destined for a business course, but she returned to Sandpoint. Dorothy, two years younger, stayed on at the Settlement until she graduated in 1950.[25]

In 1929 one six-year-old arrived at the Settlement alone in time to start first grade at Pasadena School. Sylvia Olsen had lived in Camden, a small town north of Spokane in Stephens County. Her father died when she was two years old; her mother, when she was five. She later recalled:

> I had a brother and two other sisters. . . . we were all separated. . . . one of my sisters
> stayed [in Spokane] with . . . [a family who] . . . came from Norway with my mother.
> . . . my oldest sister stayed with other people, and my brother went and stayed with
> somebody, and I stayed with some people in Spirit Lake [until] they brought me back.
> And I stayed at the Courthouse,

until being transferred to the Hutton Settlement. She had lived the better part of
1929 at the Spokane County Courthouse, in upstairs quarters provided for, as she
said, "women that were in trouble. . . . [though] a nurse in the Courthouse was
always looking out after me."[26]

One Saturday that August, Charlie Gonser came to the courthouse to get her;
she had never seen him before. He took the frightened child to the Settlement as
part of his regular weekly campus visit with employees. She always remembered
her tearful drive and her introduction to the Settlement: on arriving at the administration building, Gonser soon

> sent me on my way over to Cottage Two [alone], and I cried all the way across the
> lawn. . . . the Cottage was full [and] I got there in time to have lunch, and everything;
> the older girls, they always took care of the younger kids, and so I had one girl that
> kind of sponsored me.

She readily made friends and twelve years later graduated from West Valley High
School, where she was a tennis champion.[27]

Levi Hutton had envisioned the Settlement as home for, in the main, full
orphans, and by 1928 they constituted 89 percent of the campus population. During
the next few years their number decreased, however, and the board occasionally
discussed admitting "half orphans," or "boarders" as they would also be known. In
1934 the Financial Advisory Committee discussed again "taking part orphans at
ten dollars a month to tide us over until such time as we can get more full orphans."[28] The Abramson and Dunlap children epitomize sibling groups who
boarded in the 1930s. In many instances half orphans brought with them the
feeling of having been uprooted and abandoned, a feeling that created special problems for them in adjusting to group living.

Anita Abramson and her brother, Lee, were nine-year-old twins, the youngest
of four siblings who moved to the campus in 1935. After their parents' divorce,
their mother had remarried. Anita later related that their stepfather, an itinerant
agricultural worker during the depression, could no longer support the family of
six children, adding

> We were up in the Yakima area picking apples, and hops, and stuff like that, . . .
> and we were just living in a one-room place with a tent on the side for the boys. And
> my grandfather was a doctor up there, and he had heard of Hutton Settlement, so he
> told Mom about it.

She recalled nothing of coming to the Settlement by bus, theorizing that "it was just too traumatic, because I was really attached to my mom"; she did, however, remember feeling homesick, "because I loved my two little [siblings] that were [left] at home." She started life at the Settlement among the younger girls in Cottage One, advancing to Cottage Two when she entered high school. She did not often see her brothers—Lee was in Cottage Three and the older boys, Jim and Al, were in Cottage Four. She left the Settlement during the war to rejoin her family but soon returned to West Valley High School, though not to the Settlement, living and working for a family for room and board.[29]

Kenneth Dunlap moved to the Settlement in 1938, after he, his brother Billie, and two sisters had spent a year "in a children's home in Lewiston." In the depths of the depression, his mother, widow of a Kellogg miner, had placed them there. Ken recalled that his father died at the age of 33, "so my mother was left with [us] kiddos, no skills, and no benefits." She found a job in a hat shop in Spokane; she wanted to be closer to the children so moved them to the Hutton Settlement.[30]

His introduction to the campus remained clearly embedded in his memory:

> You know, . . . it's always traumatic to be rooted out of your home, and all of a sudden end up in a big situation like that. . . . I remember just being terribly lonesome the first week I was there, . . . I went there on a Saturday morning, and they took me to Cottage Three, and all the kids . . . were down in the basement. . . roller skating . . . . Those rooms seemed enormous when I was eight years old, and I remember standing on the staircase, and watching these kids race by. Not one of them stopped to say hello to me or anything, and I guess I don't know what I expected—but they were more for showing off.

Next day at the Millwood Presbyterian Sunday School, the teacher finally introduced him to the other boys.[31]

Ken lived at the Settlement until its retrenchment in 1943 when only full orphans could be accommodated in the administration building. He then lived with a foster family until his mother obtained a better job at the air base and moved with her boys to an apartment in Spokane. While they lived at the Settlement, "Mother was awfully good about coming out a lot. She would come out on the bus and visit with us, and she always was dressed nicely—I remember that." Board minutes have virtually no references to parents of Hutton children; in one notable exception, the Board Ladies read a letter at their January 1941 meeting "from Mrs. Lillian E. Dunlap expressing her deep appreciation of the good care her boys, Billie and Kenneth, are receiving at the Settlement."[32]

Superintendent O. S. Burkholder had arrived in 1930 with abundant energy, ambition, and a flurry of plans for campus activities. His official reports overflowed with accounts of his good works; he appears increasingly to have represented the Settlement in the larger community; and he assumed a larger liaison role with the school district in tandem with the board's education committee. On the campus he tried to instill a professional attitude in the staff, primarily through regular meetings of the matrons. He explained that in those meetings "we are attempting to study our work and employ the best methods of correction that will be the most beneficial to each individual child."[33] Correction stood high among Burkholder's priorities; since corporal punishment was still the order of the day, it may explain why many residents felt no fondness for him.

Burkholder did institute a number of programs on the campus and took a personal role in many of them. He introduced organized athletics: during the 1930 football season he reported that

> we now have two of our older boys coaching two young boys football teams. . . . The enthusiasm is high . . . Bill Honeychurch is coach for boys of Cottage Four, Gordon Windle is coach of Cottage Three. We believe this is good clean fun and splendid training for all concerned.

He also devised letters to award for sports.[34]

More basic was early formation of a cottage council. Four children from each cottage met with the superintendent "on call"; they met three times during January 1931. One of the council's first functions was to "decide on a yell, a song, and colors for the Settlement." Eligibility for the council hinged on willingness to "cooperate with the matron—have interest in all children in the Settlement— make all school grades 80 or above—[have] attitude [of] loyalty." In January 1931 the council members voted to offer trophies to the person in each cottage who made "the greatest advancement [in] . . . Education, Sports and Sportsmanship, Service (Home Work) and General Achievements"; recipients would be judged and selected by the matrons and the superintendent.[35]

Burkholder also started a campus newspaper during his tenure—a four-page mimeographed piece that resembled similar products turned out by small high schools of that era. Although he wrote the editorials, Hutton kids contributed the rest. Heavy on sports, humor, and social events, the first edition devoted half a page to introducing the Settlement Board Ladies, especially the cottage captains. Page one told of current activities of Settlement alumni, most of whom had returned for the sledding reunion during the holidays. Burkholder's first editorial, "The Call of Youth," began somewhat lugubriously: "Have you not heard it said at the funeral of some child: 'He is calling you father and mother'" but finally made the point that today's young people "are calling for council, [sic] advice, sympathetic understanding as they find themselves groping in a confused world."[36]

Although his agenda added attractive programs such as camping trips, sports, and outings, Burkholder did not win the devotion of the Hutton kids. The experience of Mike Mateef offers insight into why. In the spring of 1932, eighteen-year-old Mike ran afoul of him in the wake of rumors of indiscretions allegedly committed by the superintendent as he taught Settlement teenagers to drive. Mateef clearly recalled the events more than six decades later:

I kind of mentioned something like, "Well, this place has sure changed since Mr.
Hutton left." And it wasn't long before [my] suitcase was packed, and . . . [they]
shipped me out. . . . That surprised me, you know. I had no idea. They took me
downtown, and dropped me off.

He went to work in a beer parlor on Monroe Street owned by the Taylis brothers.
He said, "I stayed with them. I slept in the little room downstairs, and then I
worked in the beer parlor" while attending North Central High School. His early
Hutton Settlement sponsor, a Mrs. Alexander, had been drawn to Mike because
he shared her husband's birthday; he had spent many hours in her home. One day
Mrs. Alexander spotted him sweeping the sidewalk in front of the tavern; when
she heard his story, "she took me right [to her house] and I stayed with her . . .
until I graduated."[37]

Mike Mateef's ejection and the superintendent's possible impropriety occurred
while Charles Gonser and the board were preoccupied with the litigation and
financial worries plaguing the Hutton estate. The Board Ladies, always advised of
Settlement admissions and discharges, received the Cottage Four report for April,
which stated simply that Mike "had left the Settlement and was living with an
Aunt." At that same April meeting the board also learned that "Mr. Burkholder is
teaching all children to drive a car before leaving [the] Settlement." Nothing ex-
plains the discrepancies between the two accounts of this singular occurrence.
Although not found in any records, it is firmly rooted in the lore and the memories of all who were on campus in 1932. Whatever the facts, decades later, Esther
Roos, who became the campus nurse soon after the incident, remained "convinced
that there have been no abuses of any kind connected with the operation of the
Hutton Settlement."[38]

Nearly three years later, in January 1935, Waldo Smith moved into the
superintendent's office at the Settlement after eight and a half years overseeing the
Washington State Custodial School in Medical Lake. That school had grown during his tenure even though no other state institution "was forced to operate on
such a low budget"; hence Smith came to the campus with a realistic view of
depression finances.[39]

As he and his wife settled in and were "gradually becoming conversant with
the home life and routine of the Settlement," he encountered "irregularities" that
seemed to test his mettle.

We heard the rapid firing of what we took to be a small caliber gun. We talked to
several of the boys, . . . quite confidentially, and the next morning a 22 revolver and
a full box of shells were found laying on the engineers bed. The gun will be deposited
in the river the first time we drive that way; mean time it is securely locked up.

A month later he confiscated another 22 rifle, an air gun, and a sling shot, because
"there have been too many complaints here at home as well as among the neighbors regarding broken windows etc."[40]

The Smith era was remembered appreciatively by Hutton kids. One plus was the two Smith children, Phyllis and Rosemary. Rosemary, the younger, started Millwood Grade School in the fifth grade, walking with all the Settlement youngsters. She played basketball with them and endeared herself to them over the years by always taking their side: "If any of the kids ever got in trouble, Rosemary . . . [would] go to her mother and dad, boy, and she stuck up for the kids all the time." Mrs. Smith played piano for Sunday School services as long as they continued on campus.[41]

Looking back, Hutton boys credited Waldo Smith for having run a tight ship. Jim Taylor thought him something of a disciplinarian but a fair man. Ken Dunlap "always thought he was a pretty nice guy . . . he was kind to us, . . someone that cared about the children." Bob Baker concurred, saying,

> We all liked him really well. He was real kind. . . . he didn't spank us—well, once in a while I guess he did. . . . he'd come over [to the cottage] and we'd have meetings once a month, and tell stories, and [do] things you wanted to do, and he was a . . . kind, considerate man.[42]

During the staffing problems of the early forties, Smith stepped into the void in the kitchen of Cottage Four when the matron left without warning; he reported, "As there was no relief [matron] available, it was up to me to give the boys a lot of 'fisherman's recipes' for dinner that night." He served bacon and eggs, fried potatoes, bread, butter, jam, "Apple pie (left by matron)" and four gallons of cocoa. With some pride he added, "Not a speck of anything was left and the boys pronounced the occasion a complete success. They all helped with the dinner things and then the evening was wound up by playing cards." Ken Dunlap recalled Smith's use of the bell from Levi Hutton's locomotive; "whenever [we] heard the bell, we had to come and circle around to find out what the latest edict was; it was usually something OK, but they were strict. They kept us in tow."[43]

The daily routine of the Settlement in its second decade mirrored that of its first. Chores and farm work varied little for girls or for boys, and window washing remained their most hated task, though none of the boys relished milking.

> We'd get up at 4:30—4:00, 4:30, and go milk those cows. And in the winter time it was ten below, and you'd be all hunkered up to that cow trying to keep warm. [And] after they closed down [the cottages], then there was only three or four of us to do the manual labor—like the ice plant.

Glen Grater also remembered the ice detail. Levi Hutton had specified an ice machine for the campus. Every morning Glen entered that walk-in freezer in the administration building, removed the three- or four-foot blocks of ice, chopped them in half, loaded them into the horse cart, and made the rounds of the cottages, depositing them from the outside into the kitchens' iceboxes.[44]

The housemothers continued to supervise chores in the cottages. Although their ranks turned over frequently, by and large they left the children with positive memories. Anita Abramson remembered that at Cottage One

> we had the most wonderful Mother Corte, . . . she was a very lovely lady. . . . she did most of the cooking, [and] I remember on Sunday mornings she'd make us great big cinnamon rolls, you know, and oh, they were so good. . . . And she seemed to trust us girls a lot.

Her twin brother, Lee, pursued a career in the ministry and once made his cottage housemother, Mrs. Barkley, the centerpiece of a Mother's Day sermon.[45]

Mrs. Barkley ranked high with most of the twenty or so boys in her charge. Bob Baker thought she "was a real nice lady, but she was a lousy cook." His estimation of Mrs. Barkley did not waver though she, like the other matrons, disciplined the children. He recounted that he and a buddy, Will Warner, went over to the river to swim one afternoon against the rules and "they came looking for us." Mrs. Barkley "sent somebody out to get a switch. . .[from] a great big willow tree over between Three and Four Cottages." The boys she dispatched for the switch "took their knives and put notches in it, so that [as] she was switching us, the switch would break. So pretty soon she doesn't have anything to hit us with. That ended the whipping." The boys had put one over on her, and Baker said, "That's the only spanking I ever remember getting."[46]

Girls from the thirties and forties recalled the continuing tradition of gracious living in the cottages. Anita Abramson said that Mother Corte also "taught us to be ladies, . . . [For example,] if cars were going by and we peeked out the window, she says, 'Now ladies don't do that.' . . she was such a lady herself." Even when the Settlement was reduced to twelve children in the administration building, Mrs. Ritchie maintained social tradition; Clara Aldrich recalled:

> We had a tea for all the people that ran the Settlement from in town, and the board, and everything. And we presided at those teas, and man, we thought that was really uptown. Oh yes, and we had to have the proper manners, and we dressed really nice, and . . . I really liked that. . . . It was a lot more formal than it is today. We were taught the formal way of life, which I really appreciate even to this day.

The boys' cottages, too, stressed the social graces. Baker believed that

> one of the best things that I got out of living at the Hutton Settlement was I learned how to work. You know? And you learned good manners, and actually, you learned how to get along with other people. . . . the social thing is basically one of the best things I remember.

In the cottage dining rooms, table linen and silverware continued to dignify the tables.[47]

The board members who served on cottage committees adhered to Levi Hutton's wish that they have a presence in the cottages and in the lives of the children. Well into her second decade on the committee for Cottage Two, Mrs. Agnes Paine remained a favorite of her girls. Kathryn Metrovich said, "We always had plenty of clothes. Most were hand-me-downs [but] I remember Mrs. Paine taking us to the Crescent basement for our shoes. She was always nice, and tried to please us." She left a deep impression on Sylvia Olsen, who remembered that, when she was in fifth grade, "I wanted to play tennis so bad, and . . . Mrs. Paine saw that I got a tennis racket. . . . Even after I got out of school, I still had that tennis racket." She said further that Mrs. Paine was "a beautiful woman—absolutely beautiful . . . . [She] used to come out and sit in the [cottage] sitting room, and we'd go in and visit with her. . . . when I got out of high school I used to go and see her" in her home in Spokane, "up there by Sacred Heart."[48]

The board continued to guarantee that interested children would have the opportunity for individual music lessons. During her husband's superintendency, Mrs. Smith taught some children, but teachers from off campus came, usually on Saturdays during the school year, and gave forty-five-minute piano lessons. Anita Abramson took lessons, practicing on the piano in Cottage One but soon gave it up. Pearl Hutton Schrader arranged music lessons for Ken Dunlap and Mary Anne Taylor, both of whom stayed with the piano longer; Dunlap's playing remained a happy memory for his cottage mates, but he did most of his practicing on May and Levi Hutton's grand piano in the administration building's reception room, which was otherwise off-limits to the children.[49]

Entertainment and recreation continued to include trips to the circus and Natatorium Park; Friday night film programs in the auditorium gradually waned, but trips to the movies off campus filled the void. Left to their own devices, Hutton kids made their own fun and entertainment. Sledding on the hill in winter, swinging out over the ravine on ropes, sneaking out of the cottages, skating in the cottage basements—all were as popular as they had been to the first generation of Settlement children.

By the midthirties, each cottage boasted a radio in its living room, an addition that greatly enhanced leisure hours. Such staples as "Inner Sanctum," "Jack Armstrong, All-American Boy," and "Charlie McCarthy" were favorites; matrons enjoyed the likes of "One Man's Family"; "Your Hit Parade" topped the Saturday night list for the older girls in Cottage One. Not only did they savor the week's most popular tunes, they used the program to practice their shorthand: they transcribed "all the new songs and everything. That's the way they learned shorthand."[50] Acquisition of record players for the cottages also kept Hutton kids in the mainstream of popular music.

As World War II approached, Settlement boys became enthralled with military aircraft and spent countless hours building model airplanes. In the winter, when no outside farm work took them to the fields, Saturday mornings would find a dozen or so boys from sixth graders through young high schoolers on the top floor of Cottage Four, working on their models. Ken Dunlap recalled, "We built a lot of model airplanes—and that was with balsa wood and tissue paper, and steaming them so [the paper] was all taut." They had great fun and produced some aeronautical works of art. Dunlap laughingly said later, "We always enjoyed those mornings, and I don't know how it was in those days, but I imagine LePage's glue had a lot to do with how happy we were."[51]

Swimming continued to top the summer recreation agenda. Water from the irrigation ditch still filled the pool, although Bob Baker recalled that the staff did "put five gallons of Purex in . . . [and] your eyes got pretty bloodshot" with that amount of bleach. The diving tower was dismantled soon after Clara Scott cracked her first cervical vertebra, having hit the bottom of the pool "doing a sailor's dive." During his years as superintendent, O. S. Burkholder emphasized swimming instruction; he also joined West Valley's vocational agriculture teacher, together with eight of the older boys, to pour a concrete walk along one side of the pool, greatly improving comfort and safety. Most Hutton kids learned to swim, and more than a few earned Red Cross lifesaving certificates.[52]

A majority of Settlement children spent two weeks away from the campus every summer, either with relatives or at summer camp; the rest of the time, farm chores dictated their summer schedules, as they had during Levi Hutton's lifetime. In addition to picking tomatoes and berries, girls helped with the extensive home canning. For example, older girls might skin the blanched tomatoes and cut kernels from the ears of corn shucked by the younger girls; they worked on "the back porch of the cottage . . . [and enjoyed] the camaraderie." Once chores were out of the way, though, the pool beckoned; the spacious porches designed by Harold Whitehouse also helped to mitigate Spokane's oppressive heat. More than a few former residents remembered spending a lot of time "on the sun porch, [where] we'd play cards by the hour." Anita Abramson said that one year, "on the front sun porch, they let the boys come [over] and we girls were teaching them to dance."[53]

With the annual dinner to honor supporters and friends of the Settlement a casualty of the depression, a picnic on the campus for the Rotary Club became the prime social occasion of the summer months. Everyone eagerly anticipated the event that brought Rotarians and their wives (the Women of Rotary), Board Ladies and their husbands, and the Gonser family out from town for games, swimming, and a sumptuous afternoon meal. These affairs were truly community and campuswide efforts.

The menu typical for such gatherings included fried chicken, mashed potatoes, corn, and homemade ice cream. Anita Abramson remembered picnic days as fun, especially making the ice cream in large hand-cranked freezers. Sylvia Olsen detailed further the residents' role in meal preparation:

The kids had to peel the potatoes, and [shuck] the corn. . . . They'd kill the chickens and you'd pluck the chickens—everybody did a little bit of something, [both] the boys and the girls. . . . Each cottage got so many chickens, and you'd pluck them, and clean them, and everything.

After lunch the men and boys usually played a spirited brand of baseball, and later "the kids would go swimming; [sometimes] they'd throw pennies and dimes into the swimming pool—whoever was the fastest to dive would get the money."[54] These events made for a happy, but very long, day for the children and for board members who had pitched in to help.

With help from the wider community, Waldo Smith coordinated a Rotary picnic in his first summer on the campus—July 25, 1935. The Millwood Masonic Temple provided eleven tables and 105 chairs and a Mrs. Andrew Jackson lent knives, forks, and spoons for the 225 places that day. These gatherings grew in popularity, and five years later, the Masonic Temple in Spokane lent all the silverware, and the Millwood Presbyterian Church provided the tables and chairs for 250. In 1941 approximately 375 thronged the campus for picnic day festivities. In what may have been a concession to World War II restrictions, at a special meeting in July 1942, the Board Ladies voted to hold no Rotary picnic.[55]

Spokane Rotarians and the Hutton Settlement had long enjoyed a rewarding and beneficial relationship. Levi Hutton had been a loyal member of the Downtown Rotary Club, and the three men who succeeded him as administrator of the Settlement followed in his footsteps. Over the years, the Women of Rotary devoted enormous amounts of time to sewing and altering clothing at the campus, aided Settlement girls both individually and as a group, and joined with the men in frequently hosting Christmas dinner parties in the city for Settlement children. Rotary men, too, reached out to boys at the Settlement, included them in their occasional father-son banquets, underwrote the cost of summer camp for some, and on occasion paid for transportation for children to visit distant family members.[56]

As the depression wore on and the second generation of Hutton kids left the Settlement, the board members followed closely the course of the lives they had guided on campus. Hilda Lawson entered business school in the fall of 1936 and reportedly "started on her Commercial course and was doing nicely." Mrs. Blackwell told the board that she had visited a recent Settlement graduate "in Lewiston where he is doing radio work," and she also said that another young man had "a good job in California; and Paul Saari doing well at Washington State College." The Board Ladies also followed the progress of Katie Metrovich, who after graduating in 1938 left the Settlement and "worked for my board and room in the city while I attended Kinman's Business School." This was a path that many Settlement girls followed; Pearle Grater worked at the First National Bank and lived with the King Reid family in Spokane for some time. Soon after Sylvia Olsen graduated from

West Valley, Gonser began looking for employment for her and by October she had "a permanent position with the Silver Loaf Baking" company.[57] Meeting minutes show many more instances of Board Ladies offering help and advice.

Many alumni felt later that growing up at the Hutton Settlement during the thirties insulated them somewhat from depression hardships. Compared to their schoolmates, as Bob Baker put it, "We were all poor. . . . [but] we were dressed probably better than 80 [percent] of the kids. . . . We always had plenty to eat, and we always had good clothes." Many locals struggled to get by, but Hutton kids, admitted one, "never knew there was a depression, because we were always taken care of and fed."[58]

For many, realization of any advantage came long after their days on the campus. Most had, as Pearle Grater said, "nothing but good memories of Hutton Settlement," where the privations of the depression were kept at bay. Katie Metrovich echoed her: "Life was good for us, always plenty to eat."[59]

Of course, not all youngsters in the Hutton Settlement's second decade shared a glowing impression of life there. While conceding that they had been safe and cared for, some, especially boarders, would rather have lived at home with a parent. Others such as Jim Taylor left for perceived greener pastures. The board reluctantly continued to dismiss children for behavioral reasons, as in 1942 when the women saw one boy as "rather a disturbing element in Cottage Four" and voted that "his Aunt be requested to make some arrangement to take him" away. After America entered World War II, the Settlement rules about dating seemed too stringent for some of the high school girls. As one remembered, "You couldn't date until you were a senior, and part of the reason so many left in their junior year was because . . . the boys were going off to war, and the girls just decided they wanted to go live with relatives" and have fewer restrictions.[60]

Wartime changes altered life for all in the Settlement's extended family. In 1940, with war on the horizon, the federal government had begun to register aliens. The superintendent had to report a noncitizen "whether he was an employee or one of the child population . . . [and all] over 14 years of age must be finger printed." Waldo Smith told the board, "We have four children that were born in Canada"; only one had to "give his finger prints, but all four were registered."[61] By that time, too, young men from the Settlement had already enlisted for military service or had found employment in war industries such as the Boeing plant in Seattle.

Even before Pearl Harbor, the Army recruiting station in Spokane had sent an officer to the Settlement with a film that "explained the life of the present soldier boy and illustrated all manner of equipment used." Smith reported, "The older boys particularly enjoyed the show." He later shared with the Board Ladies a letter from Leo Billings, a former Settlement resident who had joined the Marine Corps; he wrote "regarding his experiences and also gave considerable 'fatherly advice' to the rest of the boys." Military awareness was heightened in other ways as well. For example, Pearl Hutton Schrader, chair of the entertainment committee, told the board that airmen "from Geiger Field would be glad of invitations to private homes for Thanksgiving dinner. Mr. Gonser said he thought it would be well to have a number eat with the children at the Settlement."[62] Like many other families, the Settlement invited service men into its home during the war.

Following the attack on Pearl Harbor, young men from the Settlement enlisted in increasing numbers, and the campus itself came under consideration for war-related uses. The board met with a Miss Reeves of the Child Welfare League of America to discuss possible evacuation of children from the coast and voted "to co-operate . . . in the event it becomes necessary to evacuate children from that area." In response to a request from a Dr. Ghering for "the use of the Hutton Settlement hospital in case of an emergency" the board voted to offer the hospital for such purpose. Along with most Americans, the Settlement helped in scrap metal drives and filled out forms for ration books; it was a rare board meeting that lacked an announcement of a Settlement purchase of more war bonds.[63]

Like members of countless American families, the Board Ladies and Gonser wrote letters and sent Christmas packages to their boys through the duration of the war; and they grieved for those killed, wounded, or missing in action. Letters they received in return told of improbable chance encounters of former Settlement boys in previously unimaginable foreign locations. Ties to home remained strong for those on active duty; in the spring of 1942 Leo Billings and Curtis Butler sent money "to buy flowers for Mr. Hutton's grave on Father's Day." The board in turn honored the Settlement's young men who served, inscribing their names on a bronze plaque that hangs in the administration building.[64]

The experiences of the Grater siblings illustrate the varied wartime service of Hutton Settlement alumni. Bob, the oldest, served five years in the Marine Corps; enlisting as a Reserve in 1940, he saw active duty in Hawaii, on Saipan among other places in the South Pacific, and in occupied Japan after its surrender. Pearle enlisted in the WAVES, as women in the Navy were then known; she traveled to New York City for basic training at Hunter College and served for the rest of the war as a yeoman at the naval station in San Pedro, California. Glen, the youngest, graduated from West Valley in 1942, where he had been a star player on the championship football team; he enlisted in the Army in May 1943, and with the army engineers built facilities for troops rotating through the Philippines.[65]

Soon after the end of the war, Mrs. Agnes Paine suggested, "inasmuch as Pearle Grater was the only [Settlement] girl who had offered her services to our country in time of war, that we show our appreciation by giving her a piece of Mr. Hutton's silver." The board voted Pearle the berry spoon from that treasured store of silver, which accordingly was "buffed, packed and mailed" to the recently married alumna, now Pearl LaLumia, in Chicago.[66] She never parted with it.

Bob Grater and Dorothy Fuller had married in July 1941, and during the long months that he served overseas, they corresponded almost daily, continuing through his posting to Nagasaki in the wake of the second atomic bomb detonation there. The boy whose prize-winning poem "Christmas Bells" had been read to the Board Ladies in 1934, wrote this to his wife:

> The radios and newspapers weren't lying a bit when they said the atomic bomb layed everything flat. . . . One really cannot realize just how much power that bomb has until you actually see the damage it did. The sand is even melted together like one took wax and heated it. The bricks from the houses and factories are pulverized.

After his tour of duty, unlike some Settlement veterans, Grater returned to Spokane. He and many of his friends continued to look kindly on their childhoods at the Hutton Settlement: whenever his family "passed [the campus], we always drove in and made the loop." At a board auction decades later he bought "a small rocking chair because he had nothing from his own family, and that was at least from his 'home,' so to speak."[67]

The second generation indeed considered the Settlement home, as Levi Hutton had hoped. Had he known this group who had literally carried his dream and legacy worldwide, he would have taken great pride in the accomplishments and the patriotic service of these members of his family.

The Settlement barn and dairy herd, 1925. The farm was Levi Hutton's pride and joy, and for decades it made the Settlement virtually self-sufficient. NMAC photo.

A midtwenties afternoon in the living room of Cottage One. Pianos were fixtures in each cottage. An unidentified housemother stands at the Victrola, and girls engage in two favorite pastimes: reading and playing board games. NMAC photo.

Sunday dinner in Cottage Four, 1925. With table linens, china, and silver in the dining rooms, Settlement children learned proper table manners and other social graces. NMAC photo.

In 1925 girls in Cottage One do their dishwashing chores at counters built in child-size dimensions. NMAC photo.

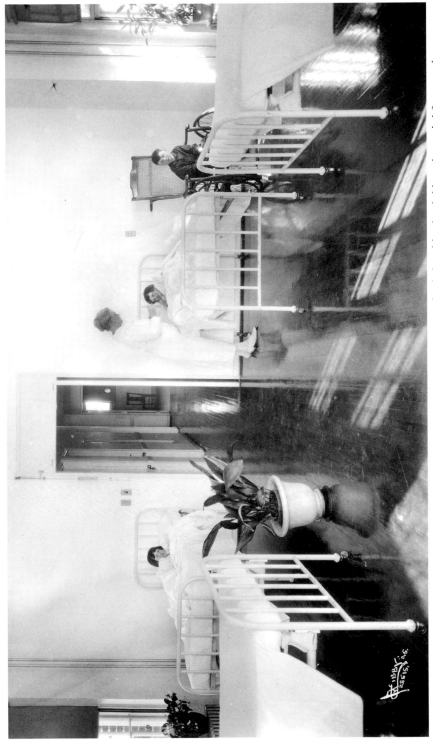

Margaret Martin cares for three children in the infirmary, 1925. "Nursie" Martin was dearly loved by the children she tended for more than a decade. NMAC photo.

Levi Hutton enjoyed hosting visitors to the campus, including Babe Ruth during one off-season in the midtwenties. Meeting the baseball legend was the thrill of a lifetime for Settlement youngsters. Hutton Settlement photo.

Opportunities for play and recreation were important to Levi Hutton. Here he watches some of his boys in the time-honored ritual of choosing sides for a game of baseball. Hutton Settlement photo.

The Hutton Settlement scout troop, ca. 1926. Scouting continues to occupy an important place in the program for boys. NMAC photo.

On the Father's Day following the death of Levi Hutton, the Settlement's Boy Scout troop and Camp Fire Girl bugler led a graveside service of remembrance at Fairmount Cemetery. Over the years, Memorial Day visits to the Hutton plot have lent a sense of heritage to generations of Hutton children. NMAC photo.

Agnes Cowley Paine, first president of the Hutton Settlement Board of Trustees, ca. 1920. Mrs. Paine, a lifelong member of the board, served until 1952. Hutton Settlement photo.

A young and determined Charles Gonser succeeded Levi Hutton as administrator in 1928. NMAC photo.

The City Ramp Garage in 1928. Mr. Hutton had high expectations for the garage, but it became a drain on Settlement finances during the depression. NMAC photo.

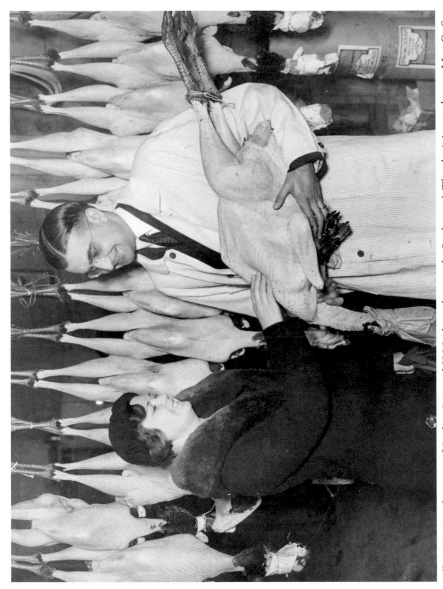

Albert K. Arend, owner of Spokane's A and K Markets, donates the Settlement's Thanksgiving turkeys to Mrs. O. S. Burkholder, wife of the superintendent, ca. 1932. NMAC photo.

The Clark siblings, Ellen, Charles, and Arthur, arriving at the Settlement in October 1933. Photo courtesy of Ellen Clark Bacheller.

A favorite housemother of the 1930s, "Mother" Corte stands in the doorway of Cottage Two with, left to right, Pearle Grater, Julia Napier, Vanita Baker, Gladys Bervar, and Sylvia Olsen. Photo courtesy of the Spokesman-Review.

Charles Clark on "milk duty" one hot summer morning, ca. 1939. Using the Settlement handcart, boys distributed fresh milk to each cottage after the daily milking. Photo courtesy of Ellen Clark Bacheller.

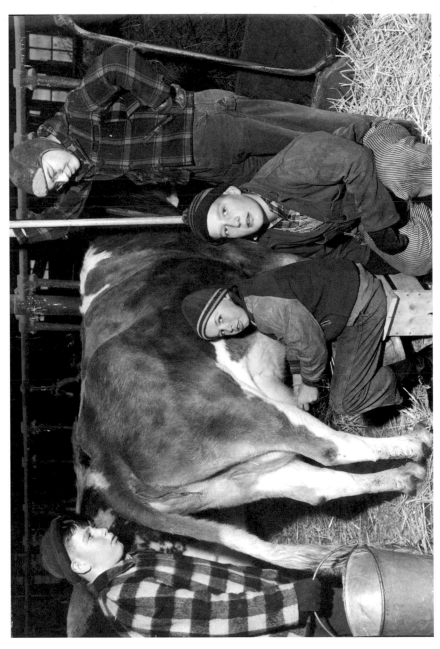

In 1949 the boys still milked the Settlement's dairy herd. Bundled against the November cold are, left to right, Rodney Richardsen, Harry Fisch, Larry Corbett, and Donald Barnes. Photo courtesy of the Spokesman-Review.

7

Wartime Contraction, Postwar Expansion

Τhe board and Charles Gonser had taken the Settlement through trying years of depression and war. After seeing the campus population reduced to a handful of true orphans housed in the administration building, in their postwar stewardship they faced different questions and new hurdles. The war had brought change. During the 1950s, downtown Spokane encountered new conditions and trends, and the Spokane Valley began a gradual shift from rural to suburban and commercial.

Mr. Hutton's chosen stewards had themselves shown adaptability and growth in directing the Settlement. Charles Gonser had earned respect and would serve on numerous statewide committees as state government moved solidly into the realm of child welfare. The coming generation of board members, having come of age with the right to vote as an entitlement rather than a hard-won privilege, possessed more than a little political acumen and became increasingly involved in real estate and affairs of governance. They continued, however, to embody dedication to service. Working together, board and administrator set out to return the Settlement to its prewar size and mission.

As a symbol of dedication and service to the cause of children and the Hutton Settlement, Miriam Ritchie has few peers in board history. Miriam P. Williamson, daughter of an Olympia pioneer and lumberman, married the noted architect Willis A. Ritchie in 1902. One scholar suggests "their marriage may have brought [him] increased financial security because thereafter Ritchie seems to have chosen to reduce his work load."[1] Mrs. Ritchie joined the Ladies' Benevolent Society early on and by 1917 served as treasurer; even after creation of the Hutton Settlement she continued on the LBS board as well the Settlement board. For a short time in 1924, she had served as matron at the Spokane Children's Home when the regular matron abruptly left. She left Spokane in 1934, after her husband's death; the Board Ladies "accepted with regret" her resignation and voted her an honorary member.[2] But ten years later, when she was sixty-four, her former colleagues prevailed upon her to return as superintendent of the Settlement.

From the superintendent's office she reflected the style of the early Board Ladies; her reports resembled letters to friends and radiated pride in the Settlement, even in its diminished wartime state. She told of the children's academic problems and achievements, their health, their social activities, her visits to schools and attendance at scouting and extracurricular programs, and other experiences she knew the board cared about. She viewed the group, now reduced to five girls and five boys, together with the eight adults who lived in the administration building, as family. Her November 1944 communiqué summarized that month's holiday: "Sixteen were seated at the large table for Thanksgiving dinner, the turkey was delicious and dinner perfect. Wish all of you could have been with us to see what a happy family we were."[3]

Miriam Ritchie probably understood the girls at the Settlement more than they realized, but teenagers found her rather remote. One recalled, "Oh, she was so prim and proper." On occasion her small band would refer to the Settlement, with adolescent cheek, as "Mrs. Ritchie's Concentration Camp." Yet, on later reflection Clara Aldrich acknowledged the age factor and allowed that the superintendent wanted the girls to be ladies: "Mrs. Ritchie actually taught me—indirectly, as I grew up" to feel important. Clara once visited Mrs. Ritchie's quarters and thought them beautiful; she said, "I've always been interested in everything, and she had [a piece of furniture] . . . ebony wood. Oh, it was gorgeous. . . . I've never seen anything like it."[4] Miriam Ritchie imparted standards and warmth indirectly, and her reports show more flexibility in dealing with both the boys and the girls than would have been readily apparent to them.

By the summer of 1949, two cottages had opened to accommodate a growing population. Mrs. Ritchie took delight in telling the board, "It begins to seem like old times since our group of children has increased to 27." She resigned as superintendent the following July and by September accepted the invitation to again serve on the board.[5] She rejoined three other charter members: Agnes Cowley Paine, Pearl Hutton Schrader, and Ursula Ruch Sutherland.

The six years of the Ritchie superintendency were a time of considerable change for the board. With closure of the cottages, the cottage committees had become dormant; the superintendent performed the work of the education and entertainment committees; there was less board contact with fewer children. As the campus began to regain population, the board faced increasing turnover among its members. Between 1950 and 1952 both Mrs. Paine and Mrs. Sutherland died; Mrs. Ritchie herself died in 1959; and Mrs. Schrader became increasingly inactive in board affairs.

In December 1956, illness forced Edna Glasgow's resignation from the board. After twenty-one years as recording secretary, her colleagues immediately voted honorary member status for one who epitomized service and board sisterhood. In a landmark election, Lee Nielsen replaced her.[6]

Some practices from the earliest years underwent change or ended, but the more things changed, the more they essentially remained the same. Charter members departed the board, but their successors embraced the Settlement's original home- and family-oriented philosophy and commitment to serve.

Nothing illustrates better the continuing sense of family and caring than the case of Agnes L——. A full orphan, she had come to live at the Settlement in the midtwenties at about the age of ten. The board ladies followed her with great concern because over time it became apparent that she had significant mental disability. When she at last completed grammar school at age eighteen, it was clear that she could not "go any further in her studies. And . . . something must be done about her future." A committee, characterized as "a grieved one," studied the matter, and in March 1933, concluded that "for Agnes' good and safety she be sent to the custodial school as soon as possible." She went to the Lakeland Village facility of Eastern Washington State Hospital at Medical Lake that same month; three Board Ladies visited her soon after. Early in 1934, another committee formed "to see what could be done for Agnes," and the board met in special session "for the purpose of discussing the future of Agnes L——"; the women voted for the committee to continue "along the line of follow-up, reporting on her progress, clothing and needs."[7]

For the next thirty years the women—even those not on the board during her Settlement years—kept track of Agnes. They frequently deposited money at Lakeland Village so she could make incidental purchases and occasionally brought her to Spokane for a day of lunch, entertainment, and shopping, especially at Christmas. Perhaps because they shared the same name, Agnes had struck a special chord with Mrs. Paine, who served on all the committees concerned with the young woman and periodically bought clothing for her. Fulfilling Agnes's 1947 Christmas wish, Mrs. Paine gave her a watch. Several years later, in virtually her last board effort, Mrs. Paine reported that Agnes "was having trouble with her watch"; when the watch proved beyond repair, the board voted that the Hutton Settlement buy her a new one.[8]

World War II had exacerbated the problem of maintaining a twenty-one member board. "The matter of a vacancy on the board" had arisen at meetings fairly often as early as the midthirties. Resignations, coupled with sporadic attendance at meetings and a growing reluctance to accept the presidency, caused no little concern. A bylaw change to address attendance specified that "absence from three consecutive meetings without reasonable excuse, constitutes withdrawal from membership on the Board." In December 1936, at the end of her second term as president, "after considerable persuasion," Pearl Hutton Schrader had consented to continue for another year. She stepped in again to shoulder the burden in 1941 and 1942.[9] But the problem of replenishing the membership ranks persisted.

One recruit of note had accepted board membership in 1935. Margaret Paine Cowles attended her first meeting on May 7—a meeting also attended by her mother. Steeped in the Cowley and Paine family traditions of service, Margaret soon followed in Agnes Cowley Paine's benevolent footsteps. For the next fifty-six years Margaret Cowles sustained a personal link with the Settlement's founding and became well loved by board and Settlement children alike. Her family recalled that she held the first Tuesday morning of every month sacrosanct; she rarely missed a board meeting.[10]

Margaret Paine had, in a sense, grown up with the Hutton Settlement. She had regularly chauffeured her mother to the campus. In addition to summer tutoring, she lent a hand at the Settlement in other ways, as on a morning in July 1927 when she went to the campus "and took the C—— children to Sacred Heart [Hospital] to . . . see their mother." In December of 1930, she married William H. Cowles, Jr., son of the publisher of the Spokane newspaper, the *Spokesman-Review*. The Cowles family played and still plays a leading role in the city's political, social, and economic affairs. Cowles family power and Paine-Cowley family benevolence met in Margaret Cowles. A guest once overheard her father-in-law say to her at a dinner party, "You are so good. I don't know what makes you so good."[11] Her goodness left its imprint on the Hutton Settlement.

In the spring of 1935 Margaret Cowles brought the glimmer of youth to an aging Settlement board as well as a heightened sense of the need for better public relations. An early member of the Spokane Junior League, in the fall of 1936 she hosted two league members on a tour of the campus and reported their wish "to assist in any work which the Board felt was most needed." Three years later, through league channels, she arranged for rotating exhibits from the city's art gallery to be displayed at the Settlement.[12]

The Junior League had sprung from that strain in Progressive Era reform aimed at social betterment and change; founded in 1901 it quickly focused its volunteering efforts on issues of women and children. The Spokane club was admitted to the national Association of Junior Leagues in 1925 and dedicated itself to "promoting volunteerism, developing the potential of women, and improving community through the . . . leadership of trained volunteers."[13] After Margaret Cowles's early liaison effort, over time an unofficial relationship developed between the Hutton Settlement and the Spokane Junior League: within a few decades an outgoing Junior League president might expect to move onto the Hutton Settlement board.

Nominees for board membership had always reflected long-standing friendships, family connections, and fellowship in volunteer associations. As one later member put it, "Like begets like." Board Ladies proposed women with whom they had served in their church parishes, in school groups and Junior League, and in service and cultural organizations. Most new members were well known to a majority of the board who voted them to membership. During the Settlement's first two decades, resignations had been fairly rare. But in the early forties they escalated, often causing multiple board vacancies, and membership replacement reached crisis proportions.[14]

In searching for a solution, the women even considered adding men to the board. In 1944 the members also discussed at length the "matter of a revolving board." Consensus weighed against that idea, in no small part because Mrs. Cazenovia Cowley Weaver reminded them that Levi Hutton had "wish[ed] the board members to serve as long as possible, feeling that the children needed to grow up with the Board . . .[who] should stand in the stead of the child's parents." Mr. Hutton's decree on religious affiliation had also complicated the selection process; for example, in 1943 one nomination was withdrawn, "inasmuch as Mrs. C—is an Episcopalian, and our quota of Episcopalians on the Board is full."[15]

Fortunately for the Settlement, the war and its aftermath had brought new people to Spokane, who became active in its religious, volunteer, and service institutions. From among them, women of accomplishment came to the fore to join younger, longtime residents as potential board members. In the autumn of 1944, with three seats vacant and attendance averaging far less than desirable, the board looked beyond personal circles and created "a Fact-Finding Committee" to investigate qualifications of possible new members and "report back to the Board."[16] After deciding on nominees, the board would dispatch two members to talk with each and invite her onto the board.

The first chair of that fact-finding committee had herself come on the board in 1940. Mae Costello Bright exemplified a new, politically aware Settlement board member. A native of the neighboring town of Mead and granddaughter of a Spokane pioneer, she had graduated from the University of Idaho. She made her mark in politics; as state committeewoman from Spokane County, she attended the 1952 Republican National Convention that nominated Dwight D. Eisenhower. Soon after, she stated her philosophy: "I look upon politics as history in the making. . . . Every woman who loves her country and wants to maintain American ideals is a politician whether she realizes it or not." She had for several years belonged to an organization of politically conservative women known as Pro America and in 1955 was elected its national president.[17] She was a strong and important addition to the Settlement board.

Resignations and recruitment of board members remained a problem through the 1950s. Membership continued to involve prodigious commitment in time and effort. Helen Whitehouse Hamblen, the daughter of the Settlement's architect, joined the board in 1952 and recalled that her new colleagues "were much older" than she and had not fully explained the extent of that commitment; obviously undeterred, she would serve for fifty years. But other women could not carve out the time necessary for a board position. Family and church work were among the demands that prompted resignations and even prevented acceptance of nomination.[18]

Pearl Hutton Schrader had once suggested that "possibly some of the daughters of Board members might be interested in serving," but the idea was tabled. Precedent for mother-daughter combinations existed, beginning with charter members Miss Jennie Dodd and her mother and more recently Agnes Paine and Margaret Cowles. In early 1959, one daughter proposed another—Margaret Cowles nominated Margaret Bean, whose "mother had been a member of the Board and she herself has proved many times her interests in the Settlement." At her first meeting, the new member said she had "the feeling of belonging," and indeed, as well as cementing ties to its origins, Margaret Bean brought to the group expertise and influence in the realm of public relations.[19]

At that time, Miss Bean still reigned as "queen bee" at the *Spokesman-Review,* "the only woman on the staff that had a private office." She wrote a column about happenings in the city. "She was excellent at interviews," any door in town was always open to her, and "all over the city, what Margaret Bean said, went." Her influence stemmed to some extent from her pioneer family heritage. She had maintained important ties, including a long friendship with Jay P. Graves, Spokane's early real estate and streetcar magnate, and his wife, Alice. But her friendship with the Cowles family truly strengthened her hand.[20] It may likely account for Margaret Cowles having induced her to serve on the Settlement board.

On the other hand, both her mother and sister had been Board Ladies, and she had written often about the Settlement. One memorable column alone would have won her lasting praise from the board and Charles Gonser. Written in 1951, when the legislature began seriously to address child welfare standards and regulations, and based on a long interview with Gonser, it reflected perfectly and completely the views he expressed, with which she obviously agreed.

Gonser had just returned from Olympia where he had testified against a proposed regulatory bill that he asserted would put private agencies such as the Settlement "out of business and make children pawns of the state." The state's licensing practice authorized fewer children for the Settlement than it could easily accommodate. Perhaps most odious to Gonser was a provision in the legislation that would require "a graduate social worker in each institution." Margaret Bean's article sketched the Settlement's founding and development, stressed its economic self-sufficiency, and noted that it asked the state only "for the privilege of securing children." The law, Miss Bean wrote, might sound reasonable, but "to those who understand its provisions, it gives dictatorial power to a bureaucracy which is gathering all dependent children under its control." Such overregulation was "one more instance of statism with a bureaucracy telling a community what it can and can't do in operating its institutions, with the Hutton Settlement as a case in point."[21] Gonser and the women on the board agreed completely.

The Settlement was not, of course, the only Spokane institution to protest legislation. Gonser and the board had "no objection to reasonable regulation and welcome[d] inspection by the City and State as to health, safety and sanitation," but through the next two decades they joined with other groups in waging a battle against recurring regulatory proposals they considered excessive.[22] Governor Arthur Langlie had named Gonser to the State Council on Children and Youth in December 1949. Attending the council's statewide meetings increased Gonser's awareness of the politics involved and his influence among child welfare workers.

A special meeting of the Settlement board in October 1950 signaled the approaching regulatory battle. Virginia Fenske of the Washington State Department of Welfare urged the board to weigh in on formulating proposed new legislation governing the licensing of child care facilities, to "take up with our State Representatives any provisions which we think should be in the law."[23] The Settlement did not lack political connections; Helen Hamblen's husband, Herbert, was speaker of the state House of Representatives.

Gonser took the advice and set to work. Five months later he carried to Olympia suggested amendments to the proposed Senate bill for licensing institutions for child care. Characterizing the legislation as aimed at the "fly-by-night type of institution . . . operated from a profit motive," he called for

> the exemption of established, well operated local institutions, such, for example, as the Hutton Settlement in Spokane. . . . Where such an institution is managed by a qualified Board of laymen, or . . . a qualified church organization, there is every reason for establishing an exemption in the bill.[24]

Although it did not become law, this legislation was what sparked Margaret Bean's 1951 column.

Another matter resonated with the board and went to the heart of philosophy—state vouchers for support of children living at the Settlement in 1951. Vouchers had been received for two youngsters whose parents also paid the Settlement a fee for their care; the board voted to return those particular vouchers. The women also instructed Gonser to inform the state that "we do not believe these children should be on the Welfare rolls." Yet Mrs. Ritchie moved to "sign these vouchers, as long as the children have been cared for," which was tantamount to accepting the money, and her motion passed. The record is unclear about what actually happened in this case, but Gonser "sometimes wondered whether or not we should accept any money from the Welfare Department." Independence from state funding would remain a major tenet of the Settlement. As one member of the Financial Advisory Committee later put it, the Settlement was "privately funded—we didn't want public money."[25]

Since early in the twentieth century, the state had indeed been gradually, if indirectly, as Margaret Bean wrote, "gathering all dependent children under its control." After the 1909 White House Conference on the Care of Dependent Children had declared in favor of keeping children with their natural families whenever possible rather than in orphanages, there had followed the nation's first mothers' pension laws, Washington State's in 1913. Changes in the state law during the 1920s broadened coverage, but during that decade, the focus subtly shifted from the mother to the child: pensions came to be seen as a benefit more directly for children than mothers. County courts held jurisdiction over the pensions; gradually they would hire social workers whose visits to inspect recipients' homes approximated regulation and oversight.[26]

The Social Security Act of 1935 not only created a national system of insurance that covered old-age pensions and unemployment, it also included matching funds for states to provide aid to mothers with dependent children. Aid to Dependent Children later expanded to include single fathers and other blood relatives, and placement of children in state-funded foster care would follow.[27] But in the meantime, early in the depression, Governor Clarence Martin had appointed Charles Ernst director of the Washington State Emergency Relief Administration, and in May 1935 Ernst became the first head of the new state Department of Public Welfare. During the next five years he built a highly professional department, "recruiting experienced social workers from private agencies," creating in-service training programs, and "organiz[ing] welfare councils in each community." He encouraged his professional staff to pursue further education, often in the University of Washington's Graduate School of Social Work, which had opened in 1934.[28] The role of the social worker thus accelerated and assumed greater authority, to the consternation of Charles Gonser and the Settlement board.

The Hutton Settlement's quarrel with the state had three prongs: regulation and funding, employment of case workers, and certification (licensing) for the maximum number of children the campus could comfortably accommodate. Board minutes in June 1938 reported, "The Certificate of Approval from the State of Washington will be filed in the office of the Hutton Building."[29] The Board Ladies had acknowledged but ignored most prewar guidelines, proposals, or suggestions received from state welfare officials. But when they sought to reopen the cottages and increase the campus population a few years later, they could no longer ignore or avoid the state.

The board had been invited to join a proposed association that was considering consolidation of child welfare facilities in the Spokane area, possibly using the Hutton Settlement. In 1946 Virginia Fenske offered a state plan that would "change our program entirely—let the other homes take care of the normal, healthy children and fill the Hutton Settlement with . . . sub-normal and delinquent children." The board recoiled from the very thought.[30] Levi Hutton's will and the Deed of Trust formed the Settlement's basic line of defense in struggles to come.

A highlight for the Settlement in 1947 was the reopening in April of Cottage One—completely painted and refurbished, through no small effort by its rejuvenated cottage committee. With the girls having moved out of the administration building, there was room for more boys. Gonser sought certification for additional children. But the state took a hard line; Fenske observed that the Hutton Settlement "had made no provision for a Case Worker, and suggested how . . . [to] obtain one." A second letter drove the point home: the state "could not grant permission to the Settlement to care for more than sixteen children unless a Case Worker were employed."[31]

The board women balked. Their thinking was accurately reflected in Miriam Ritchie's assessment of the Washington State Conference of Social Workers meeting that she attended at the Davenport Hotel that spring. It had made her realize that "the work of the Board is carried out the same as though we had a paid case worker, and problems handled equally as well in every way."[32] In the face of a growing social work bureaucracy, the Hutton Settlement board maintained its old-fashioned approach and traditions inherited from the Ladies' Benevolent Society. On

Mae Bright's return from a child welfare meeting in Seattle, the board minutes record that "much of the talk was about the emotionally disturbed child, but not once did she hear the word 'affection, love or religion' used. [And] the ladies applauded when Mrs. Bright finished."[33]

In July 1947 the board considered the admissions application for a nine-year-old girl "badly in need of a place to live with proper care." Although Gonser pointed out that she would put the Settlement "over our quota as licensed by the Welfare Department," the board women voted to accept her. Virginia Fenske declined an invitation to meet with the board in September. Political pressure, in the form of a letter from the state speaker of the House, Herbert Hamblen, "relative to our application for a permit to care for more children at the Settlement," brought her from Olympia in October to tour the campus with Hamblen and Gonser. By the end of 1949, they had a "certificate of Approval to operate for 40 children" and a promise to "consider the matter of raising the number to 60." Renewing certification became an annual annoyance; the record does not make clear when and how the matter of the required caseworker was resolved, although the 1951 newspaper article by Margaret Bean referred to an exemption "so long as Mr. Gonser lives."[34]

By mid-January 1948, ten girls lived in Cottage One, and Cottage Three had re-opened with thirteen boys. Eighteen months later the population had grown to thirty-two, and the board voted to "get Cottage Four in shape as soon as possible." But the campus population growth stalled. When early in 1949 Community Chest officials proposed closing one of Spokane's children's homes, Gonser assured them of the Settlement's ability and willingness "to care for many more children than we have at present." He also spoke with county officials "in regard to placing children in our institution," but to little effect.[35]

In September 1949, Gonser brought to the board a case that demonstrated the gulf between state and Settlement. A single mother of three children between the ages of eight and twelve "had been receiving aid from the Child Welfare Dept." She garnered a windfall $700 "from the sale of some property in the East and the Welfare Dept refuses [further] aid until this has been spent." The Board Ladies authorized Gonser to investigate and, if "the facts justify the acceptance of these children," to admit them.[36] Two of the children soon did move to the Settlement.

The state would send children to the Settlement, but Levi Hutton's Deed of Trust provided the board a barrier against accepting children whom a physician had not "pronounced normal mentally and physically." Remaining independent from state funding also insured being able to dismiss children who became disruptive or who proved criminally inclined.

Early in World War II, the Settlement had seriously considered housing war orphans from Europe. Gonser and the board revisited that possibility in 1948 but learned from the Associated Lutheran Welfare for the Care of War Orphans that foster care rather than placement in institutions was preferred. Concern for its small population soon turned the board to consider outright promotion of the

Settlement. That October members discussed how to make the public aware of "the facilities of the Settlement and the fact that we can and would be very glad to extend help to many more needy children." They even suggested going "to visit different towns in this vicinity and present[ing] the Hutton Settlement to them." After they rejected that idea, Laura Northrop "moved that a Public Relations Committee study the contacting of out-lying localities and report to the Board."[37] The public relations committee proved essential and enduring.

Over time, two major factors had affected admissions to the Settlement and slowed growth of the campus population. Advances in medicine had both extended life expectancy and improved survival rates for accident victims in the years since the Settlement opened in 1919. Hence, in the 1930s, fewer full orphans came to live in the cottages. Second, in the postwar years a striking increase in applications for child adoptions cut into the rolls of potential Settlement residents. The nation's birthrate soared in the 1940s and 1950s and, as the scholar Elaine Tyler May points out, "Along with the baby boom came an intense and widespread endorsement of pronatalism—the belief in the positive value of having several children." The print media, and gradually television, contributed to "an ideology of domesticity and the nuclear family" as they "romanticized babies [and] glorified motherhood." Childlessness became stigmatized, contributing to growing popularity of adoptions; and the focus of groups such as the Children's Home Society of Washington shifted from residential, custodial care to placement for adoption.[38]

The problem of a low or fluctuating campus population remained a board concern for most of the 1950s. Reopening and closing cottages appeared on innumerable agendas. The years 1955 through 1960 are instructive. January 1955 found eleven girls in Cottage One and seventeen boys split between Cottages Three and Four. Cleaning and refurbishing Cottage Two began that month, and in May the board voted to "open Cottage Two as a Boys' Cottage." By June, a total of forty-nine children lived in the four cottages, and in December, the total reached sixty-four—eighteen girls and forty-six boys. During 1956 the population averaged fifty-seven, with boys in the majority. In 1957, the number dropped unexpectedly; the slide continued through 1958, from forty-two in January to thirty-three in December.[39]

In a special meeting in September 1958, the board reluctantly voted to close Cottage Three but determined that "all furnishing be kept intact, nothing to be removed, and that the Cottage Committee be kept active at all times." The average campus population held steady at twenty-nine through the next year, despite efforts to increase the numbers. The public relations committee proposed contacting service clubs, the press, medical and legal organizations, and the Spokane Council of Churches as well as holding an open house and inviting community leaders to dinner in the cottages. A stalwart on the Financial Advisory Committee, the banker Fred Stanton, suggested "contacting the Trust Officers of banks."[40] In one form or another, the board tried most of the plans to bring in children, and it reestablished familiar connections that had lapsed during the war years.

Optimism and persistence paid off. By midsummer 1960, the population had grown to forty-five, and Gonser suggested that the committee for the closed cottage prepare the building "to open on short notice if necessary." When the total reached fifty-one it did open, and through 1961 the population held steady in the low fifties.[41] Children were coming from juvenile courts throughout eastern Washington and the Idaho panhandle. Most new admissions were wards of the court from needy or dysfunctional families, and true to Levi Hutton's desire, groups of siblings came to the Settlement together.

Meanwhile, the matter of state licensing arose again during the 1955 legislative session. Gonser briefed the board, saying he saw this as the

> same bill they tried to put through . . . in 1951. The Welfare Dept. has made arbitrary rules. . . . A new section makes it impossible to give any needy child (not a blood relative) a home without having a license to do so. This would give the state control over the Hutton Settlement, even though the state contributes nothing to our support. . . . this is a bill to funnel all children into the Welfare Department.[42]

At his urging, the Board Ladies wrote to their legislators, and again Spokane political influence proved effective, postponing the licensing matter for another decade.

Further entanglement with the state came in 1959 with the introduction of a state Senate bill proposing a forty-hour work week. Gonser immediately saw that, "if this law is followed, the Settlement would have to employ three sets of house parents for each cottage." Worrying that the additional cost would mean eliminating the staff nurse, he appealed to Senator David Cowen, a conservative Democrat with whom Gonser and the overwhelmingly Republican board felt comfortable. A Spokane dentist and philanthropist in his own right, Cowan had entered the legislature in 1935 and served longer than anyone before his defeat in 1966. Not until April 1961 would the Wage and Hour bill pass, and its final form included an amendment that exempted children's homes. Gonser happily reported that "Dr. Cowan was especially helpful in assisting with the amendment."[43]

While fending off state moves to regulate, dealing with board vacancies, and refocusing on public relations in order to increase the number of resident children, the women on the board also stayed abreast of a fluctuating real estate market and the Settlement's overall financial health. Members appointed to the Financial Advisory Committee remained closest to the problems, but the entire board weighed proposals Gonser brought for their consideration and decisions.

Always a top priority, the need to maintain confidentiality meant that the board did not distribute written minutes of meetings; each month the secretary read aloud those from the previous meeting. As real estate and finances assumed more time on the agendas, Mae Bright occasionally reminded board members "how very careful [they] should be about mentioning these confidential matters to outsiders."[44] The Settlement's real estate rental income had declined drastically during the depression years, but by the end of World War II, Charles Gonser rejoiced in reporting "every inch of space in the buildings rented, with a long waiting list." The Settlement had paid off the Hutton and Fernwell building mortgages and invested in war bonds.[45] Its economic fortunes continued to rise. Assets totaled more than $1 million in 1948. The following year even its long-held stock in the Hercules Mine, now part of Day Mines, Inc., yielded a dividend of $3,852—the first return in some time. In 1951 the Settlement's income was "the largest in our history": assets had risen to $2,084,723.98.[46] Life was good.

That financial health was a testament to the board's acuity and the shrewdness of Charlie Gonser. Throughout 1944, while authorizing substantial war bond purchases, the Board Ladies had discussed further real estate investment opportunities. Despite high prices, they resolved to "be on the alert for any opening in which we might be interested."[47] Yet when Gonser presented the possibility of buying the New Madison Hotel downtown, the federal government having remodeled and leased it, the board investigated and concurred with the Settlement's Financial Advisory Committee that "it was not the type of investment the Hutton Settlement should place their funds in."[48] A few years later, however, the women approved purchase of the Ashton and the Majestic hotels for the Settlement portfolio.

Buying the latter, a six-story structure built in 1910, was not an unqualified success. Problems developed with the operators of the Majestic, and the Settlement eventually assumed the management itself. At Gonser's announcement, "All the ladies arose and donned aprons, caps and [telephone switchboard] earphones ready to take over all phases of the operation. No hostelry in the city could boast a better equipped snappier looking retinue than Gonser's Majestic Girls."[49] Lee Nielsen injected a far lighter note into meeting minutes than Edna Glasgow ever had. Board members never had to wield a mop or broom, but the Majestic remained a problem during its two decades in the Settlement portfolio.

The Settlement made several substantial investments during the 1950s. One in particular bears noting. In 1955, it acquired the block bounded by Maple, Indiana, Ash, and Nora on the near north side of the Spokane River. "Because of the proposed new bridge, this [was] considered an ideal location" for a new store that the Albertson's supermarket chain wanted the Settlement to build for it. Some board members thought the project too ambitious to undertake, in that it entailed borrowing that far exceeded Levi Hutton's desired debt cap of $5,000. The Financial Advisory Committee considered it a good investment. Once assured that the Maple Avenue bridge would indeed go through as projected, Stanton the banker recommended proceeding, even though he did "not consider it a true Trust investment." The board approved and authorized borrowing up to $50,000, which did not prove necessary. The store opened February 8, 1956.[50]

The success of the supermarket construction project made similar proposals very attractive. Later that year, representatives of the National Cash Register Company approached Gonser about having the Settlement erect a new building for NCR in "a suitable location . . . [with] more space and parking facilities." Two months later the board approved financing for the building to rise at the corner of Indiana and Atlantic, also north of the river. It required a construction loan of some $70,000. To protect the Settlement's tax-exempt status, Old National Bank financed the project, and the Settlement then purchased the contract from the bank.[51]

On completion of the NCR project in early 1958, the Hutton Building lost its oldest continuous tenant; National Cash Register had rented there since 1908. Businesses had begun to move out of downtown or into newer air-conditioned buildings. A survey made that spring showed a steady increase in the number of vacant stores and offices, "although ground floor vacancies seem[ed] to be leveling off." With an eye to restoring the luster of its portfolio's crown jewel, Gonser and the board undertook to update the ground floor of the Hutton Building. They turned to Whitehouse and Price for advice, and by the end of the year the firm had produced architectural drawings for the project. Following the Financial Advisory Committee's recommendation, the board accepted the plans and moved ahead with the modernization, which eventually included a complete retrofit of lighting and a major increase in electrical capacity to allow for air conditioning.[52]

At the end of the decade Stanton spoke to the Financial Advisory Committee "with some concern about the sad state of business in the down town area, [hoping] the Hutton estate would not fail to take advantage of any opportunity to help better the condition." Because Levi Hutton had specified downtown investments, the Settlement's financial moves had helped to stabilize Spokane's central core and to expand business across the river into the near north side. Gonser and the board would soon support Spokane Unlimited in that organization's efforts to foster urban renewal.[53]

With Charlie Gonser's able management, the Settlement had prospered during the fifties. Income rose steadily, keeping pace with new and growing expenses, and on December 31, 1959, assets had increased some $500,000 since 1950 and more than $1 million since the end of the war.[54] In nonfinancial affairs, board and administrator had for a time circumvented state Welfare Department mandates regarding caseworkers, reopened cottages, and increased the number of children on the campus, but the postwar Board ladies drew back somewhat from the parental role that their predecessors had taken.

8
Peace in the Valley:
Change and Continuity on the Campus

he decade of the 1950s popularly bears a reputation as complacent, dull, and conformist, but those ten years of transition ushered in an "astonishing new world of consumerism and prosperity" that totally altered society. A rising postwar marriage rate created a critical housing shortage. The GI Bill that granted educational benefits to veterans also provided home-buying assistance, and thus "made possible the incredible building boom of the late 1940s and 1950s." As industries converted to peacetime pursuits, war workers who had earned more than most ever expected rushed to buy cars, appliances, and most important, houses. To produce affordable housing for this new market, builders pushed out from cities in search of cheap land, and "county governments were happy to welcome them to empty space crying for development." The move to the suburbs was on.[1]

As Interstate 90 sliced its way eastward in the midfifties, it began to transform the rural Spokane Valley into suburbia. By the time the first five-mile section opened in November 1956, ending at Pines Road, many farmhouses bordering the route had succumbed to progress. The valley's smattering of small towns—Dishman, Greenacres, Millwood, Opportunity, Pasadena Park—attracted "realtors [who] bought cheap land, . . and built residence areas as fast as carpenters could nail them together." With prosperity and the freeway came the two-car family, and "the countryside once relegated to the Sunday drive now had the potential to be home." When in 1929 the county had paved Argonne Road from Dishman to Millwood, it had considerably improved local transportation.[2] By comparison, Interstate 90 changed life in the valley enormously and forever.

The population explosion that followed the war put overwhelming burdens on all public services, including schools; the Hutton Settlement, too, felt the effects of growth and change in the valley. Levi Hutton could never have imagined any of this, but much that he had prescribed for the Settlement helped board, administrator, superintendents, and children alike meet the challenges of change.

In January 1955, the Intermountain Mortgage Company sought to buy approximately ninety acres of Settlement land for residential development, offering $1,000 to $1,200 per acre. Charlie Gonser thought selling it would "in no way encroach upon the present operation of the Hutton Settlement," which might be able "to dictate the building restrictions." But after a long and thorough discussion in the Financial Advisory Committee, Fred Stanton moved "not . . . to dispose of any part of the Hutton Settlement holdings at this time." Seconded by another longtime committee member, the investment broker Joel Ferris, the motion carried, and the board followed that recommendation.[3]

Stanton the banker proved to be a fierce defender of the Settlement's interests and traditions. When Intermountain persisted with a second overture, he resolutely opposed it. In February the committee discussed a proposal from a neighbor who wanted to buy a "strip of land from the Settlement for . . . enlarging the landing field for his private plane." Stanton again opposed "selling any land at the Settlement, now or later." Although Charlie Gonser apparently favored a sale, the board sided with the advisory committee, validating Mr. Hutton's decision to create an advisory panel.[4]

The Settlement tried to cooperate with its neighbors when it could. It declined to sign a rezoning petition for an adjacent turkey-raising operator, but when neighbors could not convert to natural gas unless the Settlement also made the change, the board agreed to the conversion. Water supply became an issue in the fifties. In 1917, Levi Hutton had agreed in writing to "always pay four dollars an acre for water rights and [to] pay all maintenance on all laterals." Population growth demanded changes in the valley's water supply, and in the face of criticism of the Settlement's arrangement, the board and advisory committee considered drilling a separate well. The action proved unnecessary: the water district agreed to uphold the Settlement's long-standing agreement.[5]

Two decades had passed since Levi Hutton had taken a major role in campus life, but his legend lived on. As older board members departed, and fewer full orphans lived on campus, links to the Settlement's origins weakened. During her tenure as superintendent, Miriam Ritchie carried the founding board's ideals into the postwar years. On an anniversary of Hutton's death she wrote:

> Before we were seated at dinner, each one was asked to bow their heads in silent prayer and give thanks for the beautiful home and comfort [Mr. Hutton] has provided for us, not only for those who are living at the Settlement, but for those who are to follow in years to come.[6]

Although other superintendents would continue to honor the Huttons, and annual delegations would bring floral tributes to their gravesites, few others could possibly have written such a report.

After Mrs. Ritchie resigned in the summer of 1950, the board turned again to O. S. Burkholder, who had been something of a board favorite during his tenure in the early thirties. After much discussion the women voted to "offer Mr. & Mrs. Burkholder the position at a salary of $500.00 per month with no outside expenses." Returning to the campus in September, Burkholder began again to appear regularly at board meetings, offering recommendations and critiquing Settlement operations. He lobbied for a better on-campus medical staff, judged the campus play equipment inadequate, and called for speedier admissions procedures, but with his comments on pending welfare legislation he may have overstepped. In February 1951, during an intense board discussion of upcoming legislation, the superintendent "said that he felt that we are too much concerned over State laws and suggested that we definitely give [only] passive opposition to the pending Child Welfare Law." Two months later the board met in special session to accept his resignation.[7] Both the board and circumstances had changed in the seventeen years between his stints as superintendent; Burkholder met his match in a more politically astute group of women.

Those women, observing that the Spokane Children's Home had recently closed, instructed Gonser to hire its now available superintendent at Burkholder's salary.[8] Jack Kokeen brought six years of stability to the superintendent's office.

Board members interviewed the Kokeens more or less after they were ensconced at the Settlement, and the group was not disappointed. The children who lived under his leadership and authority viewed him positively. Younger children thought he was nice, but he related better to the older Hutton kids. One who described himself as "a wise-acre teenager at the time," found Jack Kokeen "very fair-minded," a superintendent who "treated the kids pretty well." He recalled also that, although Mrs. Kokeen, a registered nurse, was in poor health, she stepped into active duty in the infirmary "once in a while when the nurse . . . would take time off."[9]

Staffing problems beyond the infirmary once again plagued the Settlement. Kokeen had no illusions. In his first report to the board he wrote:

> Securing good cottage parents is very important and difficult. I think . . . [those in two of the cottages] are fine and are trying to do their very best; they are all past the ideal age for cottage parents but I know that it is nearly impossible to get younger people to take a job of this kind.

Houseparents rather than single matrons now staffed most cottages, and there was continual turnover. Cottage Four for older boys was the most worrisome to the board. Kokeen had identified aging house staff as a leading problem, so a joyful cottage committee happily reported in December 1954 that a younger couple had moved into Cottage Four. The committee had found the pair "very cooperative," and went on to say "the man has fitted up a workshop in the basement and is repairing the furniture, sleds, etc., and wants to set up a hobby shop on the third floor." But the new houseparents departed just three months later.[10]

Their replacements, the Wards, were a considerably older couple, and in August 1955 Mrs. Ward suffered a heart attack. Gonser thought that because Mr. Ward was a cook "he could carry on for a time," but it was not to be. In October, the third set of house parents in less than a year moved into Cottage Four. From the beginning, Mr. and Mrs. Markham "seem[ed] to be working out very well"— so well, in fact, that he would eventually be named superintendent.[11] Markham helped the boys with projects that interested them, as Jack Thurber recalled:

I had my own dark room. When Markham was there, he was kind enough to set it up in a broom closet. My dad was in the photography business, so he got me the chemicals, and the people would bring me their rolls of film and I would develop them and print them. . . . I had an enlarger, I could do eight by tens.[12]

With the Markhams anchoring Cottage Four for the long term, Superintendent Kokeen managed the other frequent house personnel changes with equanimity. Staff and children enjoyed the Kokeen years, and board members more than appreciated the balance and dependability that his tenure brought to the campus. Their regret at his resignation in 1957 was tempered by gratitude for what must rank as one of the smoothest transitions ever in the superintendent's office: Jack Kokeen stayed until his replacement was hired in August and worked with him during a week of orientation.[13]

The board offered O. Lee Howard the superintendency on August 6. The salary was $450 per month, and if Mrs. Howard "did the hospital work" it would be $500. He had come highly recommended from Seattle after thirteen years as assistant superintendent of the Luther Burbank Home for Boys there,[14] but Howard's autocratic methods contrasted sharply with those of his predecessor. One former Cottage Four teenager said,

He just couldn't relate to me. He couldn't relate to anybody, as far as I was concerned...you know how teenagers are, you've got to have a different attitude.... I don't think he trusted anybody, and he knew everything, and no one else could come to him and reason with him.

For their part, the Board Ladies found two of Howard's management practices more than disquieting. Since the day of the Settlement's founding, the children's own funds for discretionary spending had been meticulously handled by the superintendent's office; an account of every nickel and dime spent had been handwritten into ledgers for thirty-five years. When Howard passed this responsibility along to houseparents, the women took great exception, as they did in July 1958 when they reminded him that "house parents have no authority to release children from the Settlement. [I]t rests entirely with the Superintendent and only after he has obtained permission from Mr. Gonser's office." A month later they voted to dismiss him. He had lasted one year.[15]

Jack Kokeen returned as acting superintendent while they searched for a replacement. After three fruitless months, the search committee suggested a temporary plan that "could become permanent" if it proved successful. With few boys then living in Cottage Four, the Markhams could stay there as houseparents while he also assumed the duties of superintendent. As it transpired, Mrs. Markham shouldered many of the additional duties, and six months later the Markhams were officially named superintendent and assistant superintendent. Finally, in January 1960, they moved into the long-closed quarters in the administration building, and new houseparents were hired for Cottage Four. The total campus population remained near fifty-five. But Mrs. Markham's health took a downturn, and the couple resigned in January 1961. Feeling that they had "been fine parents to many children . . . [especially] the older boys," the board tendered them a farewell luncheon in appreciation.[16]

The Markhams had done double duty as houseparents and superintendents for some time with scant increase in compensation. Although salary levels at the Hutton Settlement barely budged, the board added such benefits as medical coverage along with room and board. Social Security regulations changed in 1951, making it possible for Settlement employees to opt for inclusion in that retirement plan. They voted overwhelmingly to do so. At about that same time, houseparents received a 10 percent raise in monthly salaries that then stood at $100 for a single woman and $205 for a couple.[17]

Salary questions reached the board fairly regularly, usually to be handed off to Gonser and the superintendent to solve. Early in 1956 for example, the Board Ladies instructed Gonser and the board president, Marjorie Greene, to work with Kokeen to "arrive at some system of pay raise for the employees at the Settlement." By late 1957 some housemothers earned $135 and some houseparent couples $225. But granting raises to selected employees caused no little discontent. Finally, in 1960, the board voted, on a motion by Mae Bright, that "the By-Laws be changed to allow for a standing committee on salaries" that had been proposed earlier.[18]

One standing committee had functioned since 1920—the committee on admissions and discharges, composed of cottage captains and the administrator. Perhaps it functioned more in committee-of-the-whole fashion because all matters of children's admission to or dismissal from the Settlement came before the entire board for resolution. In evaluating admission applications, as in all other aspects of overseeing the Hutton Settlement, the board adhered to the expectations and provisos of Levi Hutton. Although circumstances that brought them to the Settlement may have changed over time, children "pronounced normal mentally and physically" still came from the Coeur d'Alene mining district and eastern Washington, and they still came with siblings. Among the forty-seven children living there early in 1954, sibling groups accounted for forty of them.[19]

The Settlement continued to ask parents to pay a fee for their children's care, clothing, and housing; the fee in these years ran in the vicinity of $30 a month. But if there was no family or if payment was impossible, the Settlement still accepted no small number of unsubsidized children.

In the fifties, Spokane had a surfeit of children's homes, and the Settlement, though trying to rebuild its campus numbers after the war, tried to avoid competing with other institutions. In 1959, women in the Methodist church in Athol, Idaho, sought to transfer to the Hutton Settlement a teenaged girl then living at the children's home in Lewiston, which had not requested the change. In view of that, the Board Ladies "felt that we should not attempt to remove children from other homes if they are satisfied, but should let the group at Athol know that we are ready to be of service if it can be gracefully cleared through the Lewiston Home." On the other hand, they voted to accept a brother and sister who had lived at Spokane's St. Joseph's Orphanage for six months. Their divorced, working mother said that she had been asked to take them away "inasmuch as her children are not Catholic."[20]

The board women and Gonser felt that Washington's welfare workers did little in referring children to the Settlement during its rebuilding years. Spokane County officials and their counterparts in the Coeur d'Alene mining district proved more helpful, and personal connections also brought applications for admission. Whereas the majority of the campus population in the 1920s and 1930s had been full orphans and children of single parents financially unable to care for them, by 1950, more and more Hutton kids were youngsters whose histories involved family dysfunction, abuse, and parental desertion.[21]

A random sampling of cases reflects the whole spectrum of circumstances that brought children to the Settlement. One 1949 application for two sisters came by way of the Spokane County Welfare Department; anticipating their mother's year-long confinement in a tuberculosis sanitarium, their father sought to place them at the Settlement—it was "impossible for him to look after the girls and also work." The principal of Garfield School in Spokane told Gonser of a boy who had been "shifted around from one [foster] home to another and has not had much of a chance"; the educator, fearing that "sooner or later he may get into trouble," thought that the Settlement might be "just the home the boy needs." While still at the Spokane Children's Home, Jack Kokeen had recommended the Hutton Settlement to a soon-to-be-divorced mother. Her son and daughter were "very fine children," but the boy was "difficult to manage," having been "continuously beaten up" by the father; in Kokeen's opinion, "The children would be much better off at the Settlement than with either of the parents."[22]

Unsuitable or injurious home conditions as well as desertion could result in a child's being made a ward of the court. One group of four brothers, wards of the Spokane County Court for five years, had lived in foster homes before moving to the Settlement; the parents were divorced, the mother "rarely visit[ed] the children," and the "father's whereabouts were unknown."[23] As referrals from courts and welfare departments grew, personal connections brought new admissions as well. A former Settlement housemother, Mrs. Harriet Ashton, advised a widowed friend to place her son there. Again a school principal provided insight: the boy had lived with an aunt in the valley, who "had mistreated and beaten him and he was even afraid to go home after school." Former residents, too, recommended the Settlement to friends and coworkers, and in December 1949 a woman who had lived at the Settlement herself asked to place her daughter there.[24]

Bob Grater, Hutton alumnus from the 1930s, figured in a truly ironic admission story. In July 1961, a single mother talked to Gonser about placing her two children at the Settlement in part because "it would not separate the children."

She lived in Spirit Lake, Idaho, and commuted daily to her waitress job in Spokane. The day after conferring with Gonser, she was injured in a collision on the drive home and died in a Coeur d'Alene hospital. Grater and the woman's brother worked together at the Spokane Glass Company. On learning of the tragedy, Grater extolled the Settlement and contacted Gonser. The brother and his three surviving sisters visited the campus and agreed "that it would be a fine home for the children," who moved into Cottages One and Three in August.[25]

Every application for admission came to the board. Gonser presented long, detailed narrative case histories for each, and the board assessed them and voted for or against acceptance. But during the postwar years of rebuilding the campus population, the board began admitting some children on probation.

One application came from a social worker in Vancouver, Washington, who wrote "asking that we place a problem child in the Settlement," numerous "foster homes hav[ing] been tried without success." A motion not to accept carried easily. At another board meeting, "Miss Sletten, [county] welfare contact worker, appeared and presented a case," which was referred to the admissions committee for further investigation; the Board Ladies rejected outright two other applications that Sletten brought and three of four cases that Gonser himself presented.[26] A worried Spokane grandmother sought to have her grandson admitted to the Settlement; he then lived with his family in California. Thoughtful deliberations followed Gonser's report that the boy had made "friends of dubious characters who have records, although so far [he himself] has none. It appears that he is weak, being easily influenced in the wrong direction." Despite a motion, seconded, to accept the boy on probation, the vote denied admission.[27]

The board accepted far more applications hinging on probation than it rejected, however, and a majority of cases had satisfactory results. One instance that ended well began uncertainly with an application from a Shoshone County welfare official in Idaho for a fourteen-year-old who, he explained, "has caused some trouble but is not a delinquent. . . . [The] father does not contribute to his support and the mother is definitely a bad influence. . . . If [the Settlement does] not take him he will have to go to the State Training School." The board members voted to take him in temporarily; a month later, when the houseparents reported him "adjusting very well," they extended his stay into a six-month probation period.[28]

Another probation success story also originated in Shoshone County with another fourteen-year-old who, together with an older boy, had stolen a car. Welfare supervisors thought the boy, son of divorced parents, was "fundamentally all right . . . [but] should not remain at home as he and his step-father do not get along well." The board voted, pending a "satisfactory character report from his principal," to accept him on probation. He did well at the Settlement; after his first Christmas there, he delighted the board members by writing a rhymed takeoff on "The Night before Christmas" to a civic group as his thanks for its Christmas party for the children. Soon after, when Gonser expressed concern for the boy's health, the women passed Mae Bright's motion to "take things into our own hands at our expense," in short, to send the youth to a doctor for a complete physical checkup.[29]

Although Levi Hutton had declared on founding the Settlement that "no orphan in the Inland Empire will be turned away from this home, no matter what his sect, creed or color may be,"[30] the first nonwhite children appear to have come to the campus in 1953. Records contain virtually no mention of children of color before that time. Gonser presented an application from a native American mother for her two sons, telling the board, "The boys have been in the Indian School at Browning, Montana, and later at Oakesdale, Washington." The Oakesdale principal "gave the boys a good report." On motion of Margaret Cowles the board members voted to accept, pending further investigation: school principals' evaluations almost invariably proved persuasive, and the boys moved to the Settlement in December 1953.[31]

In 1958, another young native American arrived at the Settlement under exceptional circumstances. During the summer, Idaho welfare officials contacted Gonser about a boy who "had been deserted by both parents and seemed to be homeless . . . too old to fit into the Industrial School and too young to fit into the County Poor Farm." Gonser and Marian Marshall, the board president, judged him "a good boy . . . desperately in need"; they agreed to take him on "an emergency and temporary basis," and sent him off to camp at Settlement expense. When they reported to the board, the members agreed to take him on trial and to "try to get Idaho to contribute to his support." On learning that Idaho would not help but that "local merchants [might] contribute some clothing," the Board Ladies voted to "accept any contribution offered but otherwise take care of the boy ourselves." By November the youngster was "amazingly well adjusted and happy," and they voted to accept him on a permanent basis.[32] Board members' instincts usually served children to advantage.

Not all admissions on probation turned out well. That same year after dismissing three girls living on trial in Cottage One, the board women thought it "wise to establish a yard stick for the probationary period." Henceforth the superintendent would report each month "concerning [their] adjustment, until we feel the adjustment is entirely satisfactory."[33] With an eye to maintaining a proper and harmonious home atmosphere on the campus, they exercised their right to dismiss potentially disruptive children.

On the other hand, the board viewed parental removals with misgivings. In one such, they "regretted that the mother . . . insisted on taking her [daughter] from the Settlement, where she was getting along so nicely." The attraction of welfare payments became a growing problem, as in the case of two children removed from the Settlement "so their allotment could be diverted to family living." Once children left the Settlement, they were rarely allowed to return, but there were exceptions. One mother removed her two children when she remarried and later sought to return them when they did not get along with their stepfather; the board voted to accept them back "if the mother agrees to leave them in the Settlement this time."[34] The campus population reflected changes in society; the women on the board, of necessity, became more flexible as they continued to safeguard the best interests of the Settlement children.

Life in the cottages remained remarkably consistent over the years. Corporal punishment had more or less disappeared during the years of retreat into the administration building. Although there was an occasional spanking—one relief housemother in Cottage One used the time-honored willow switch to enforce nap times—Jack Thurber recalled that "we pretty much disciplined ourselves. We really did. We just didn't want to mess up."[35] The morning ritual of sandwich making gave way to the school cafeteria hot lunch, but the 1950s found Hutton kids performing most of the same routine chores as all their predecessors.

There were about 100 chickens to care for, and the boys still gathered the eggs for the girls to wash; when time came for the chickens to appear as Sunday dinner, the boys would "whack their heads off, and . . . the girls had to dip them into hot water and pull the feathers off." Jack Thurber remained unsure about which was the worst job in that division of labor, but he never forgot the furnace chores. Before the conversion to gas, the boys had to haul out the ashes every week and periodically shovel coal, left in a hopper car at the railroad siding, into a truck for delivery to the campus. He recalled, "I didn't mind in the summer, it was fairly nice. But boy, winter was so cold, and [the coal] was frozen, and you had to pick it apart . . . and some of us rode in the open truck on the way back." The Settlement still stored potatoes in the root cellar, and the task of cleaning it out one time burned in his memory. The rotten vegetables smelled so horrible, "I couldn't eat potatoes for years after that."[36]

Saturday mornings in the fifties still meant changing sheets—"one clean flat sheet and one pillowcase every week . . . top sheet was moved to the bottom . . . clean sheet was put on top." Saturday night still meant a bath: "the little girls were bathed by the older girls . . . two at a time" in the raised tubs Levi Hutton had mandated. Pamela Yoho remembered, as a first grader in Cottage One, "The older girls did everything for us," and the housemothers supervised the activities—just as they had in the 1920s.[37]

The Settlement work ethic lived on. Laundry, now decentralized, was done in the cottage basements by each housemother on a wringer-style washing machine. Older youngsters helped and did their own ironing, a practice that taught self-sufficiency.[38]

In restoring campus facilities to prewar condition, the swimming pool ranked low on the list of priorities. Hutton kids went to the public pool in Millwood to swim until 1954, when the older boys helped to resurface the campus pool and repair the plumbing. No longer filled from the irrigation ditch, the pool was still unheated, but it boasted a new diving board and a new cement sidewalk. Board members decided that Settlement kids should again take the lifesaving course taught at West Valley.[39]

Summers had always meant farm work. In the spring of 1950, the state Welfare Department's Virginia Fenske criticized the Settlement for "the lack of pasteurization of the milk"; and on inspecting the barn and dairy operations, the state Department of Agriculture called for corrections. When a majority of the board voted in May to "dispens[e] with the herd and buy all our dairy products," the daily saga of milking the cows and delivering milk to the cottages passed into Settlement history. Carl Olson, the head farmer hired by Levi Hutton in 1917, had retired during the war, leaving the handyman to handle the farm work alone. In March 1954, the board agreed to lease some 100 acres to "a graduate agronomist [who had] spent years in the practice of field-crop production and soil management"; he would take 75 percent of the annual crop, and the Settlement the rest. The Settlement retained the sheds, the barn, the hillside, and the garden parcel for its own use, and haying and field work remained for the Settlement boys to do.[40]

The postwar generation of Hutton kids worked a different farm, but they did do farm work. Before the lease agreement, in 1953 the Settlement planted twenty acres in sugar beets, hoping to realize $100 per acre in its contract with the Missoula Sugar Beet Company. Weeding 1,500-foot rows of sugar beets in the blistering sun topped the boys' most despised chore list that summer; the weeds were brutally hard to pull. On one occasion, after talk of mutiny and running away, the boys staged a sit-down strike. But the labor crisis was averted, and the crew was rewarded with swim sessions and frequent fishing trips. Older girls still picked produce from the garden, and younger ones joined in canning vegetables piled high near the porch, sitting around the piles working, "talking and laughing—more of a fun, social time than a heavy work time." The garden bore abundantly—raspberries, apricots, cherries, tomatoes, cucumbers, squash, and cantaloupes. The Settlement was part of the postwar "fast freeze" phenomenon—by the time every community nationwide offered frozen food lockers for rent, the Settlement had its own freezers, and more than 200 quarts of peas were frozen that year. Two draft horses, chickens, a steer or two, and an estimated thirty or forty hogs remained after the departure of the dairy herd. The hog shed acquired a new cement floor in time for the December butchering of nine hogs for campus use.[41]

The board realized that even after leasing the farm, they would "have to retain one farm man," so Elmer Wicks the handyman stayed on at a $100 monthly salary and continued to live in the administration building. He had come to the Settlement in the early thirties and endeared himself to generations of Hutton kids under his charge. One of them from the 1950s said he "was completely stoical in his supervision. He never berated anyone, he never coddled anyone . . . [he would] point out what had to be done, and you were expected to do it. [He was] very even-handed." Others recalled that he "was a real good guy . . . [who] watched over the kids . . . [and] took them to hockey games, and . . . all over." Some considered him the most positive adult in their lives on the campus: "He was the sweetest person; the little [kids] loved to tag along with Elmer and his dog—he was more relaxed around the kids—we all liked to be with him—he was the most human—the other adults were stuck in their role of authority." During the war, Wicks had worked on civilian construction projects; in one improbable chance encounter, his path crossed that of Bob Grater on an island in the South Pacific.[42]

Dinner tables still reflected Mr. Hutton's wish for a homelike atmosphere, with linens and silver, table manners and saying grace. Food continued plentiful and hearty, and all were expected to clean their plates. Evenings remained structured. Dishes were quickly washed and put away to make time for homework for the high schoolers possibly followed by shooting baskets in the gym; for the younger ones, usually "playing, singing around the piano, being read to, or playing board games such as Monopoly, Sorry, Uncle Wiggly."[43]

Pianos in the cottages became important once more, and lessons again were available. A variety of instruments attracted others—several boys were drawn to the trumpet. Beverly Rickenbauch, who lived at the Settlement from 1947 to 1960, pursued the violin and played in the West Valley Orchestra. Superintendent Kokeen attended one concert and reported approvingly to the board.[44]

Although the fifties brought resumption of Settlement routines, schedules and activities did change with the introduction of television. Television reached Spokane by way of kinescope or microwave transmission from San Francisco during the fifties, and limited reception on the Settlement campus came by way of rabbit ears antennae on small screen black-and-white sets. Cottages did not have sets regularly issued, so houseparents often shared their sets with the children. But with chores and schoolwork, little time remained to watch television—half an hour or so after dinner when they had completed homework.[45]

As they had thirty years earlier, in wintertime Hutton kids took to the hill behind the cottages with sleds. From a high landmark, a tree known as Lonesome Pine, they flew down, usually without mishap; however, on one occasion a not-so-flexible flyer slammed into an immovable object sending a boy to the hospital with a ruptured spleen. Younger children spent time sledding on the small hill or "pulling each other around" in the flat open area near the cottages.[46]

During the fifties the Settlement installed new play equipment on the circle in front of the administration building. This equipment received heavy use from spring through fall; tree climbing was popular among both boys and girls. Autumn leaves brought a favorite activity. Pam Yoho remembered that Elmer Wicks, assisted by the older children, would rake the fallen leaves "into a maze design on the lawn and around the trees or into big piles. The little kids were allowed to run through the maze playing or to jump into the big piles. Elmer would sometimes throw us into the really big piles." Rollerskating continued to be a favorite activity, outdoors, around the circle—on metal-wheeled skates tightened onto shoes with skate keys[47]—or in the cottage basements. Indoor amusements were toys, games, and paper dolls as always. Older boys in Cottage Four participated in one of the decade's crazes with their marathon canasta tournaments that became "pretty intense." After drawing names they launched into something of a round-robin that "went on for weeks," and in the highest tradition of amateur competition, the victor's only prize "just that you won."[48]

Some of those canasta players found old flannel baseball uniforms in a cottage closet. They proved surprisingly comfortable and sparked a Settlement team in the local Babe Ruth League. Hutton boys played league games at several fields in the valley—from Central Valley High to Dishman—and on the Settlement's own turf, where the boys built their own backstop aided by Mr. Markham. They coached and managed the team themselves as well; John Thurber's younger brother, Jim, took the lead in making out "a line up, and decid[ing] who'd play where, and how." In order to field a team, they had to include non-Settlement players, one of whom, a boy named Donovan Beach, rode a motorcycle. Despite the sensation he caused among youngsters not permitted bicycles, the superintendent and board encouraged the team. The baseball experience caused Thurber later to muse

> This is the great thing about the Settlement—you had to use your brain. We became very self-sufficient, especially for sports and things like that. It was a nice thing about it. They gave us kind of a free hand. They didn't clamp down, like some places would, and say, "You don't do this unless—" [or] you don't do this at all.[49]

Suburbanization of the valley brought subtle as well as overt changes. Proliferation of middle-class residential housing had an enormous impact on the schools, forcing creation of a second high school. At West Valley, the affluence of some families, more apparent than real in many cases, created in teens from the Settlement a sense of coming from the "wrong side of the tracks." High school dating seemed to mandate an automobile, a development that limited social opportunity for Hutton kids.[50] No longer were all valley residents in the same boat as they had been during the depression.

The gap between Hutton kids and other students in the public schools was not just social. As the board women took the Settlement into the postwar years, it became apparent that their relationship with the schools had eroded. In 1956 two younger members of the Settlement board—Margaret Cowles and Helen Hamblen—were named to the education committee, and Alice Leonard replaced Miriam Ritchie as chair. When they discovered that some of their children were below standard in reading, Mrs. Cowles urged her colleagues to "become better acquainted with the children and contact the teachers; . . . [and] take more interest in planning." In essence she called for a return to the commitment of her mother's generation of Board Ladies and the practices of her aunt Cazenovia Cowley Weaver, who had long chaired the committee.[51]

An annual board tea for teachers became the social event of the year on campus, and more new books made their way onto Settlement library shelves. With renewed emphasis on education, the board not only encouraged academic achievement among the residents but explored means of sending them on to college. In 1957, the Settlement underwrote Kenny Johnson's first year of premedical studies at the University of Washington, using proceeds from the Grace Z. Smith Fund. Mae Bright took a leading role in the case of Jack Thurber, who graduated from West Valley at the age of sixteen; she thought him "very young for college," and she urged him to apply to small schools. When he was accepted at Whitworth, she talked with his father, who agreed to fund most of the tuition. Saying that he was "a fine boy [who] will make a good citizen," she proposed that "the Settlement cover any deficit in order to keep Jack in college," and the board readily agreed. She proudly reported his progress and good grades the following year.[52]

Motivated in part by this experience, Mrs. Bright spearheaded creation of the L. W. Hutton Award, a scholarship to Whitworth for a deserving West Valley graduating senior. She described the award as open to "the upper 25 [percent] of the Senior Class for moral and spiritual leadership, and pays all tuition and incidental fees for the freshman year" as well as "board and room if it seems necessary."[53]

A long association with the Millwood Presbyterian Church continued into the fifties, and Hutton kids took part in midweek activities as well as Sunday services. High schoolers attended the weekly potluck dinners, and some sang in the church choir, which performed at several places in Spokane. In 1952 the Settlement contributed generously to the church's $300,000 building program; the board also acknowledged its appreciation for "kindnesses to the children of the Settlement."[54]

The larger community continued to take interest in the Settlement, and in the postwar decade invitations to the circus or to picnics at Tillicum Park sponsored by the Spokane *Chronicle* and the like came regularly. A trip to Pullman for a Washington State College football game became an annual event for small groups of teenagers, beginning in 1949 with President C. Clement French's invitation to the game "and a reception at the home of the President afterward."[55]

Like other luxuries, large Christmas celebrations had been curtailed during the war. As the cottages reopened, Christmas trees again went up, and groups such as Spokane's Athletic Round Table and the Rotary Club once more hosted dinner parties at downtown hotels for Settlement residents. The popular campus Christmas pageants resumed, although Pearl Hutton Schrader who had produced them for more than twenty years was unable to continue her role. A resident of Cottage Four, not a board member, picked up the baton. Bythel Nutt, a talented young man who graduated from West Valley in 1957 wrote, directed, and managed the pageants for several years.

Folks in Spokane always enjoyed driving out into the valley, frequently making the loop around the Settlement. One person whose family regularly took this

Sunday drive recalls thinking it "fascinating that kids who didn't have families could live in those neat houses."[56] But by the midfifties, most of the kids in "those neat houses" did have families, families who had placed them there. Some of those youngsters viewed life on the campus in a negative light. Perhaps they felt abandoned or rejected. Likely they felt that the Settlement had usurped their families' role. Restricted in their activities, unable to attend a church of their own denomination, or expected to call housemothers Mom, some were unhappy and resentful. However, most, even those who had chafed at the structured environment, came in time to have a more sanguine view. As one said decades later: "I will always thank my mother for having the foresight to find a safe haven for [my siblings and me]. Were we happy being here? No. We wanted to be home—I wanted to be with my mommy—but it was the best thing that could have happened."[57]

The postwar years presented situations beyond what Levi Hutton might have anticipated in his concept of a home for children. As board members sought to return the campus to its prewar caliber and spirit, they aimed at reinstating that sense of home and family that had guided the Settlement from its founding.

9

The Sixties and Seventies: Challenges on the Campus

A merica's fairly tranquil life of the postwar fifties dissolved into upheaval, turmoil, and controversy during the next two decades. Presidential and political assassinations, investigations of political wrongdoing, and a presidential resignation fueled growing alienation and distrust in America. Revolutions in manners, mores, and music accompanied a new and troublesome drug culture. War in Vietnam sparked tumult that produced divisiveness and a youth rebellion at home. Light-years away from the counterculture of San Francisco's Haight-Ashbury and radical turbulence in the streets and on college campuses nationwide, Spokane felt only mild reverberations of the social turmoil that stamped the sixties and seventies. The era's styles and fads did reach the valley's young people, however, and circumstances that brought children to the Settlement paralleled changes in the family and society in general. Superintendents and houseparents continued to come and go on the campus, and for the first time in more than thirty years, a new administrator took the reins of the Hutton Settlement.

In planning the Settlement, Levi Hutton had stipulated that "there must be a man Superintendent, one that is big enough to handle an institution like this."[1] After the departure of Jack Kokeen, five years of constant turnover and uncertainty had followed as Charlie Gonser and the Board Ladies searched for a man big enough for the job. Gonser had often cooperated with the Spokane County Juvenile Court in placing children at the Settlement. One evening in the spring of 1961 he telephoned a young probation officer who had made a strong impression on him and asked if he would be interested in the job of Settlement superintendent, which again was vacant. In due course, twenty-eight-year-old Robert K. Revel accepted the position.[2]

Revel sensed board reservations about his ability to switch from court work and criminal procedures involving delinquents to working "with dependent, neglected orphan and half-orphan children in a family relationship." He also thought, after initial interviews, that the women were "more interested in meeting my wife, to see how she would fit the picture than they were in me." His perceptions were correct; according to one board member, "They interviewed together, yes. And it's important, especially for the superintendent on campus to have a wife who is cooperative."[3] Dorothy Revel had never heard of the Hutton Settlement until

Gonser had phoned, but deciding to move there was not difficult: "Not for me. When the board ladies asked me—I was very quiet in those days, . . . they said, 'Now Dorothy, how do you feel about it?' And I said, 'Well, you know, wherever my husband's happy, I'll be happy.' And that impressed them."[4]

In hiring them, board members had indeed viewed the Revels as a team. On campus there was palpable excitement when the couple moved into the administration building with their daughters, Darla and Valerie, aged nine and six. Confined to the infirmary at the time, then twelve-year-old Dana Finley later said, "I was sitting in the hospital bed with mumps, watching through the window, and I saw the Revels arrive on their first day. . . that was exciting. . . . they looked young. In fact, they . . . were *very* young." The Revels' presence soon conveyed a sense of security. Dana observed them again, walking arm in arm across the campus and recalled: "Mr. Revel was not an affectionate man. And so to see him with his arm around Mrs. Revel really, really made an impression. So when I say that we felt secure—yeah. The world was OK, because . . . [we had] Mother/Father figures." The new superintendent's quarters were always open to the children, recalled Revel, and "I was young enough that I could participate in sports with them, and organize activities and games, and swim with them, and be involved with them."[5]

As for father or mother figures, Bob Revel himself had known neither. He was born in Pueblo, Colorado, on June 14, 1933. Four years later, authorities found him "in a third rate hotel room, abandoned, in Missoula, Montana. . . . [and sent him] to the Montana state orphanage in Twin Bridges." He stayed there until he was almost fourteen, when he ran away. He recalled, "I've basically been out on my own ever since." He lived for several years with a farm family in Alberton, Montana, and with a teacher in town during his senior year at Alberton High School. The autumn after their graduation in 1951, he and his high school sweetheart, Dorothy Murray, were married. He worked in railroading and timber in Montana and Idaho before they moved to Cheney, where Bob enrolled at Eastern Washington College of Education.[6]

In lieu of fulfilling a cadet teaching requirement, he served as a student trainee at the Spokane County Juvenile Court. After that four-month training stint, he was hired as a probation officer and stayed with the court until Charles Gonser's phone call six years later.[7]

The early months at the Settlement were difficult. On the campus, the new superintendent found "no such things as social workers. . . .[or] recreation people. No counselors. . . . no secretary. I did all of the secretarial work as well as the counseling," along with running all the other campus operations. In the wake of the temporary and stopgap arrangements of the late 1950s, "the state of morale was not real good" either. He had to prove himself to the staff, all of whom were much older than he, to assure them "with his direction and leadership that the ship was going to run smoothly."[8]

He had walked into a staffing crisis in April; Cottage Four's houseparents had just been dismissed. It may have had an unrealistic view of the difficulty involved in houseparenting, but the board knew that "every effort should be made to employ younger people when the occasion arises." Revel moved quickly to address other problems inherent in staffing. By midsummer he had clarified salary policy, secured raises for some staff, and sought increases for the others. He established an unprecedented five-day work week schedule for all, which the board accepted in October.[9]

The new superintendent wielded a new broom. He found much to sweep out, including "outmoded equipment and odds and ends which are of no value" in attics and basements. In surveying buildings and grounds, he thought the old, unused fruit dryer would make an excellent garage, and the board agreed to have it converted to shelter employees' cars. The board more than appreciated his initiative, not least his change in purchasing procedures that placed all requests with the superintendent and took authorization for purchases off the board's monthly agendas.[10]

His new approach extended to the children at the Settlement, and he tapped funding sources known to him through his work at the court. He also used "Sunday school money . . . [to buy nicer] clothing for the children who were graduating from 8th grade and for two children who had no financial help beyond what the Settlement provided." After the Board Ladies reimbursed nearly $200 he had spent himself, he asked them to create a fund he could draw on for such uses in the future.[11] No other superintendent had ever suggested the like, not even O. S. Burkholder.

Revel started the Settlement moving with the times on all fronts and, at the end of five months, proposed what would prove to be a lasting legacy. He approached the board with plans for starting a 4-H club at the Settlement. The women encouraged him to go ahead, and from then on successor boards enthusiastically supported what became one of the most successful programs on the campus.[12]

Revel introduced other programs as well, and it pleased the board that "he makes it possible for the children to participate in activities which are of particular interest to the individual child, just as [regular] parents would do." Given the background of his own childhood, however, and with his professional experience with at-risk youth, he did not come close to indulging or coddling the Hutton kids. Almost without exception, those who lived at the Settlement in the early sixties said he "ran a tight ship" or "ruled with an iron hand." Both Revels espoused a demanding work ethic equal to that of the Settlement's first decade, and both worked longer and harder than anyone else on the campus.[13]

The Settlement farm had become financially unviable. Major crop production had been discontinued during the war, leasing out acreage had proved unsuccessful afterward, state health regulations had compelled elimination of the dairy herd, and other livestock was sold. Despite its orchards, gardens, and poultry, the Settlement was not self-sufficient by the sixties, so the Revels shopped at the nearby Safeway store. They would fill up to a dozen shopping carts, "load the Settlement station wagon up with all those groceries," and deliver them to the cottages. One practice from the past—canning produce, either homegrown, purchased, or donated—continued awhile longer, though somewhat altered: Revel now took the abundance of pears, apples, beans, and peas that the Settlement residents harvested to the Spokane Valley Cannery for processing, but there was still canning in the cottages. He and the older boys went on trips down along the Snake River in the Settlement's truck and returned with loads of peaches. They would "pull up in front of the gym, lay newspapers out on the floor of the gym and spread all these peaches out, and then the canning would start." The long-time Board Ladies Margaret Cowles and Harriet McElroy usually headed a board group that pitched in to help.[14] State regulations, however, soon put an end to home canning.

Dorothy Revel could not bear to waste anything from the Settlement garden. Lois Riddell, housemother to the older boys in Cottage Four, described a summer routine reminiscent of past decades:

> We had the biggest garden you've ever seen, and Mrs. Revel and I would stand out here in the middle of the road selling plums, and corn—we sold everything down [on] Upriver Drive. . . . Mrs. Revel canned and froze everything. . . . And the little boys—the little children took care of the radishes, and onions, and lettuces, and the bigger boys took care of the bigger garden with the corn, the potatoes, and all that.

Her husband, Russell, added that Cottage Four "had eighteen boys at that time, and Mom and I would make twenty. And there was 20 rows down there of corn and potatoes." They assigned each person a row, themselves included, and the boys "couldn't leave the campus on a Friday night if their row wasn't weeded."[15]

By the late 1970s, however, production had dwindled to a point that would have amazed and perhaps dismayed Levi Hutton. The poultry enterprise continued virtually unchanged into the seventies, and neither the boys nor the girls enjoyed their roles in preparing chickens for the freezer any more than their predecessors had. But absent farm chores there was enthusiasm for the 4-H club. When the Revels proposed the year-round campus program, they considered raising cattle, hogs, or horses, but settled on sheep, because as Dorothy said, "You can raise a lamb and sell it within four months. And of course, we had our own breeding, too." It was to "be a self-supporting, self-sustaining project." The Spokane Valley Lions Club donated $200 to buy lambs and breeding ewes to get them started. Bob said he "planted about 40 acres in alfalfa, and we raised our own hay to support the livestock program." When they sold lambs at the Junior Livestock Show and the Interstate Fair, all proceeds went back into the program.[16]

Teas honoring teachers in West Valley schools were major campus social events. In November 1957 as Zula Weiss pours, the board president Marjorie Greene stands to the left of Superintendent Jack Kokeen and Mrs. Kokeen. The board's longtime recording secretary, Edna Glasgow, is third from the right. Photo courtesy of the Spokesman-Review.

Bythel Nutt at the keyboard in Cottage Four shares the bench with Jim Thurber; gathered around, left to right: John Thurber, Richard Overhauser, Lawrence Wiegele, Garry Overhauser, Jim Stockton, and David Bucknel, ca. 1954. Photo courtesy of John Thurber.

Clad in wool flannel uniforms found in a cottage attic, the Settlement baseball team, ca. 1956. Standing, left to right: Jim Thurber, Richard Overhauser, unidentified, Garry Overhauser, John Thurber, John David Nutt, unidentified, and a nonresident, Donovan Beach. Kneeling: Peewee Miller, and Superintendent Markham, flanked by the Brooks brothers. Photo courtesy of John Thurber.

Jim Thurber takes a flying leap off the diving board, ca. 1956. The campus pool was a favorite spot on Spokane's hot summer days. Photo courtesy of John Thurber.

Boys in Cottage Four in the midst of a marathon canasta tournament, ca. 1956. Clockwise from left: Tom Page, Bythel Nutt, Jim Thurber, and Steve Lebeouf. Photo courtesy of John Thurber.

The Revel family brought youth and vigor to the campus. Left to right are Dorothy, Darla, Bob, and Valerie, ca. 1961. Photo courtesy of Dorothy Revel.

Robert Revel with his friend and mentor, Charles Gonser, who visited the campus in the mid-seventies after retiring as administrator. Hutton Settlement photo.

Bob Revel and Russ Riddell, a houseparent, with the Settlement's Pony League team, 1964. NMAC photo.

Bob Revel and Settlement youngsters in the barnyard working to ready lambs for a stock show in the early days of the 4-H program. NMAC photo.

Diane Hunt and Dennis McLellan were winners at the Junior Livestock Show in 1966. Hutton Settlement photo.

158

The Settlement swimming pool, May 1969. Built in 1923 at a cost of $2,000, the swimming pool has been renovated and upgraded several times. Hutton Settlement photo.

In search of heritage, Settlement groups make occasional trips to Idaho's Coeur d'Alene mining district. In 1968 they visited the now defunct Hercules Mine at Burke and the Bunker Hill smelter in Kellogg, where they are shown heading back to the tour bus. Photo courtesy of the Spokesman-Review.

The Settlement hosted a meeting of the Washington Conference of Child-Caring Institutions in June 1964. Left to right: Robert Revel, Mrs. Margaret Cowles, Charles Gonser, and Robert Hart of the state Department of Public Assistance. NMAC photo.

The Settlement built this award-winning structure specifically for IBM; completed in November 1964, it remained a major Settlement holding at century's end. NMAC photo.

Charles A. Gonser, Hutton Settlement administrator, 1928-70, ca. 1965. Hutton Settlement photo.

Margaret Bean, influential Spokesman-Review *columnist, ca. 1963. Daughter of a founding Board Lady, she herself joined the Settlement board in 1959. Photo courtesy of the* Spokesman-Review.

The board president Jessie Satre and Elmer Wicks on "Elmer's Day," marking the 1972 retirement of the longtime campus maintenance man. Wicks was a true and trusted friend of Settlement youngsters. Photo courtesy of the Spokesman-Review.

The houseparents Russell and Lois Riddell stand with two of their Cottage Three boys, Brian Anderson and Mark Burnett, in 1974. NMAC photo.

Spokane's Downtown Rotary Club befriended the Settlement from its beginnings. In 1976 Rotarian Roger Barth presented new tennis rackets to Nancy Hoyle and Cletis Hydrick while Bob Revel looked on. Photo courtesy of the Spokesman-Review.

Fifty years after Babe Ruth visited the campus, the Philadelphia Phillies shortstop Kevin Stocker, nephew of a board member, Marilyn Stocker, came to sign autographs. He and Futton children met in front of a photo of Ruth. Photo courtesy of the Spokesman-Review.

Dishwashing crew at work in a cottage, ca. 1974. Even after commercial dishwashers were installed, residents still cleaned up after meals as their predecessors had since 1919. NMAC photo.

Dorothy Revel loved the 4-H club and its lambing project. She recalled its beginnings:

> My husband and some of the boys—maybe the girls—went out to this old farm and
> bought some old-age ewes, so we started with old-age ewes, and they'd drag the
> kids in and out of the barn—it was a lot of fun. We didn't worry about anything. . .
> [I] had a lot of children in my 4-H club. They could all be in it if they wanted to be
> . . . They weren't forced to be in it, and some loved it.

Her work with the club won the admiration of the board members, who stood in awe of her frequent all-night vigils in the barn at lambing time.[17] Both Revels' enthusiasm inspired the youngsters. Raising and preparing a lamb for showing required the children's commitment and months of hard work before and after school, in addition to their regular chores. Hutton 4-H members won countless ribbons and trophies at the stock shows. By that time, some lambs were almost pets, and selling them could be a wrenching experience.[18]

The club had started slowly, financed with the likes of a bake sale that netted $33 in 1962. In the spring of 1966, the flock of sheep totaled eighty-two, including thirty-two lambs. There were thoughts of disbanding the club or trying "to find an outside 4-H leader" after the Revels left the campus, but one of the alumni stepped in. Dick Hamilton, just returned from four years in the Air Force and married to a former Settlement girl, Diane Hunt, who had raised champion lambs, took over in time for the Interstate Fair in September 1972. Lambs were still a part of Settlement life at the end of the century.[19]

The board could not have been more pleased with the young Revels. The women thought they were "wonderful with all the children who were in 4-H" and pleased that they took an active interest in the children's progress in school. Revel not only brought youth and stability to the Settlement, through his court connections, he also increased the resident population. Forty-seven children had greeted him when he arrived on the campus in April 1961. By early 1964 the number had nearly doubled, and the board president, Margaret Cowles, commented, "Mr. Revel's ability to cope with some difficult cases helped make this possible."[20] Board members soon began to view Revel as a successor to Charles Gonser, who turned sixty-seven years old in June 1964. Following several months of discussion, on May 4, 1965, they voted to offer Revel the post of assistant administrator when "a satisfactory replacement for Superintendent . . . is found," but finding his replacement took another eighteen months. They interviewed a number of applicants "but none seem[ed] to have Mr. Revel's qualifications." Finally, in December 1966, Clair McKie, a member of the staff of Lakeland Village at Eastern Washington State Hospital in Medical Lake, accepted their job offer.[21] The McKies and their three children moved to the campus soon after, and Robert K. Revel assumed new duties in the Settlement's downtown office on January 2, 1967.

But stability eluded the Settlement. After six months, McKie resigned. A houseparent served as interim superintendent until the board hired William D. Johnson in May 1968. After five months of disorder and confusion on the campus, the women dismissed Johnson, and the general sense of unease enveloped the staff. In June 1969, Roy Schermer came to the superintendency highly recommended by the Spokane County Juvenile Court Probation Office. Eight months later the board received word that "Mr. Schermer is resigning as superintendent. His wife is not happy with her life there."[22]

The tenure of Walter Burnett also proved shorter than the board hoped; hired in July 1970, he lasted until March 1971. Robert Rodgers took the post in July, and in October he, too, gave notice, citing his wife's physical inability "to stand the work and personal involvement with the children." Their departure forced a return to makeshift arrangements on the campus; between July and December 1972, Revel divided his time, spending mornings on the campus and afternoons in the downtown office.[23]

The superintendent's responsibilities covered a broad spectrum—from overseeing buildings and grounds and lambs and gardens, through staff hiring and oversight, to supervising and interacting with the children. The half decade of frequent resignations had forced the board into wholesale evaluation of the situation, especially the matter of salary. The Revels had been hired in 1961 at an annual salary of $5,400, plus the considerable advantage of room and board. George Whitaker took the position in December 1972 for substantially more—$9,600, which would increase to $10,200 should he perform satisfactorily for three months. Whitaker stayed until midsummer 1975. When they undertook to replace him, the Board Ladies sought a person with a background in the counseling field, offering a salary of $13,500 while requiring a master's degree "or its equivalent in experience."[24] The position now carried the title of resident director. In May 1976, the board hired John Blackburn and soon delighted in the Blackburns' work with the children, even suggesting that "a job should be created for [Mrs. Blackburn] making use of her special talent on a regular salary basis." Saying he was "not comfortable as resident director and would prefer to . . . work with the children as a counselor," Blackburn resigned in October.[25]

The long period of uncertainty and makeshift arrangements ended in April 1977. A more realistic compensation package—$14,000 annually with an increase to $15,000 after six months—secured the services of Samuel P. Skogsbergh as resident director.[26] When Sam, his wife Patty, their eleven-year-old son, Jeff, and eight-year-old daughter, Julie, moved into the administration building, they brought fifteen years of stability and improvement to the Hutton Settlement.

A native of Minnesota, Skogsbergh had followed graduation from Augsberg College with graduate work in sociology at the University of Minnesota. In the latter he emphasized work with delinquent youth, and it was a short step from the classroom to pioneering work at a conservation camp located in northern

Minnesota, north of the Iron Range. There he dealt initially with hard-core young offenders, and during his twenty-one years he introduced forestry projects and activities similar to those of the Outward Bound program. His interest in forestry and love of the outdoors stemmed from student summers spent working in the woods of Washington and the Coeur d'Alenes.[27]

Cottages had closed and reopened to accommodate a fluctuating number of children during two decades of staff turnover. Under Revel's superintendency, the campus population had surged initially, reaching seventy-one by the end of 1964. By the time he moved to the downtown Settlement office as assistant administrator in January 1967, the numbers were dwindling, and the year ended with a total of forty-six children on campus. By the end of the seventies, the four cottages housed only twenty-seven—eleven girls and sixteen boys.[28]

In admitting new residents through the years, the Board Ladies always honored Levi Hutton's desire to keep siblings together, but his hopes for a high percentage of full orphans had proved impossible to realize. As Revel drew on his juvenile court background, the women of the board came to accept more at-risk children. Admissions during the sixties included such cases as the girl who "was a run-away from [Spokane's] Galland Hall, complaining that she was unable to get along with the adults," and a thirteen-year-old who had "had a brush with the juvenile authorities . . . but Mr. Revel thought he would have no trouble." In the midsixties, convinced that the houseparents could cope, Revel recommended admitting a troubled second grader from a dysfunctional family who was "proud of being a tough guy."[29]

On the other hand, the board continued to be selective and regularly rejected applications. Rejections included those of two girls referred from Pierce and King counties. One "will be delinquent unless given proper care now. . . . [but] her qualifications do not seem to fit," and the other, with behavioral and medical problems, "is too old for the Settlement."[30] Board members and administrator did not consider the Settlement a treatment center, and they dismissed children they felt unequipped to handle. In 1969, for example, they sent away a boy who had become defiant and "had too great an influence on the other boys and some of the girls"; they learned later that things had "settled down considerably since [he] left."[31]

As the population dropped in the midseventies, Revel sought clarification of Hutton's words, "Normal children" in the Deed of Trust. The attorney Herbert Hamblen recommended that board members should simply employ their usual "good practical common sense . . . in evaluating an application."[32] This they continued to do. Applications reflected societal changes in the sixties and seventies— a growing divorce rate, increasing dysfunction in families, greater economic stress, growth of illegal drug use—but by and large, circumstances leading to admissions during the two decades differed little from those of the forties and fifties. Early in 1967 the board admitted two children whose father had died and whose mother abandoned them. In the summer of 1972 the board voted to accept three children whose grandmother applied on their behalf; the mother was "emotionally unstable and . . . the father has developed a drinking problem."[33]

By the midseventies, the Settlement population included a growing number of at-risk and troubled children, and the staff now included a person who, the board insisted, was to "be referred to as a counselor and not a case-worker." Yet there was no clear policy on "how to cope with a child who disobeys, swears, and refuses to cooperate with adults." Each case on campus received board consideration, from the boy dismissed because he was out of control at school and causing many problems to the occasional youngster caught shoplifting or using drugs. Revel asked the juvenile court judge "to put in writing what disciplinary actions can be taken by Staff in the control of the children."[34]

By the late seventies, a number of referrals had come from the Spokane Center for Youth Services, thirteen- and fourteen-year-olds from "families in conflict." Events of the wider world brought a query from Lutheran Family Services about Cambodian and Vietnamese children; the board agreed to handle any such cases through regular admissions channels.[35]

Although a few children came alone to the Settlement between 1960 and 1980, such as nine-year-old Joy Brady, sent from Chicago to relatives in western Washington after her mother's death, siblings predominated during the period. Family groups included the Finley sisters, the Hoyles, Hamiltons, Hunts, Hydricks, and Croffs.

Thirteen-year-old Bambi McMillan, the Settlement's lone full orphan, had arrived in 1960. She was among the group to greet the Revels the following spring, and that summer she went with them on their family vacation trip to Denver. One of many memorable Hutton girls of the era, Bambi took part in the 4-H lamb project; she graduated from West Valley in 1965 and returned to her hometown of Kelso to be near her brother's family.[36] Some residents thought that, unlike youngsters on campus who came from single-parent, deprived, indifferent, or abusive homes, Bambi "was really the lucky one, because she knew that when her parents [died] they loved her." As one former resident said, "You sort of interpret as a child, when you're [at the Settlement], 'You don't love me, and that's why I'm here. Because otherwise, I'd be with you.'"[37] The wistfulness of that observation echoed across generations of Hutton kids.

Dorothy Revel had helped ameliorate such feelings. From the start, she had endeared herself to the children and staff alike, and despite high praise for all her work, her greatest contribution to the Settlement may have been a subtle one. For many of the residents, she softened her husband's stern and disciplined administration. Brooking no nonsense herself, she nonetheless transmitted a sense of caring that contrasted with his brusque, if not gruff, style. Although he had brought structure and security to their lives, more than a few Settlement boys would have agreed with Dick Hamilton who had arrived in 1959:

> It's probably no secret that [Revel] is a pretty strong personality, and was a very authorita[rian] figure to the boys, and a role model in that sense. I don't think that it would be accurate to say that the kids were intimidated, or afraid of him, or anything like that . . . you knew better than to mess with him. You were not going to win.... But in the course of . . . helping him with one project or another, there was a lot of interaction, and . . . respect is probably the definitive term for his relations with the boys. I don't think he [was] somebody you would go to in a moment of vulnerability. . . . [But he] made the kids feel that things were under control, and made them feel secure.[38]

Joy Brady, who arrived the same year as Dick Hamilton, recalled that "Dorothy Revel was a jewel," but she had nothing positive to say about the superintendent himself. Tere Hoyle, another Cottage One resident, admitted, "At the time, I could not stand Mr. Revel," but she added, "As time's gone on I've actually become pretty good friends with them, and I admire him immensely." Dana Finley credited Mrs. Revel with being "certainly more involved with us than [he] . . . but you know, girls need a Mom. They need that interaction"; Mr. Revel remained distant and overprotective of the girls.[39]

Revel took a dim view of Settlement boys and girls fraternizing. "One time he got upset, and put an imaginary line across the entire campus. The boys had to stay on one side, and the girls had to stay on the other." As the sixties sexual revolution came into full swing, he seemed determined to keep them apart, one way or the other. Yet Tere Hoyle recalled, "Sometimes we'd just go out behind the cottage and meet the boys out there."

> In the summer time we'd lay out under the trees and play cards, and—I remember the boys getting bull snakes out of the fields and . . . . terrorizing the girls. And I remember sitting out there watching the thunder storms roll in . . . and we'd . . . just watch the lightening. . . I don't remember it being a big deal . . . [Revel] knew there were boyfriends and girlfriends out there.

Older girls did feel restrained in dating, however; it involved a boy's having to present a driver's license and proof of insurance in an interview with Revel. With so formidable a requirement, "It really wasn't worth going out on a date!" "Dating was zero . . . real dating?—the boys didn't like the hassle."[40]

Both Revels supported the children's school activities. Like other parents, they went to football and basketball games and encouraged participation in school sports programs: "The coaches knew who we were, and that . . . we were glad our children were in this," recalled Dorothy. When her husband's promotion to the downtown office came, "It was difficult for both of us to leave the children." The couple had wanted to "make a small dent in their lives," to be family to the Hutton kids and "show them . . . there are people that do care."[41]

Life on the campus mirrored that of earlier decades, minus the most grueling farm work. Boys continued to gather eggs and girls washed them until December

1971, when state health regulations forbade that practice. Revel announced that "all the laying hens will be killed soon and eggs will be purchased from a distributor."[42] Twenty-one years after eliminating the dairy herd, the Settlement ended its poultry operations. Only the garden remained of Levi Hutton's farm that had been both his joy and pride.

Bells still heralded the start of the day in the cottages and sent residents to meet school buses bound for West Valley schools. Household chores such as cleaning and dishwashing continued, however, as did summer work in the garden followed by swimming in the pool. Everyone had laundry duty, but on their assigned days the girls would go down to the cottage basement and listen to Elvis Presley records while they worked. Settlement life still included homework, playing on the terrace, endless card and board games, and television—three channels viewed on small black-and-white sets.[43] Boys still took part in varsity sports at West Valley High School; in 1968, Hutton kids made up one-fourth of its championship wrestling team. Girls made their mark as cheerleaders; cheerleading "was a big deal . . . to be a cheerleader . . . validated that we [were] OK people out there" at the Settlement.[44]

Sneaking out at night and smoking the odd clandestine cigarette continued along with other age-old mischief making in the sixties and seventies. "We'd just sneak out because we could do it." On one memorable Halloween, some enterprising older boys picked up Dorothy Revel's Volkswagen Beetle and carried it into the gymnasium. For all his stern reputation, "Mr. Revel got a chuckle out of it," as he occasionally did other escapades. The fast-flowing irrigation ditch was the site of another incident that Revel recalled with amusement decades later.

> I wake up at three o'clock in the morning, and I hear all this giggling and laughing, and I thought, well what's going on now? So I go outside, and here's Bambi [and three others] . . . here they are in their nightgowns, walking up and down this ice-cold ditch in the middle of the night, and when I finally got to the bottom of it, they were trying to catch colds so they could stay home from school.

Needless to say, the boys had to return the VW to its accustomed parking place, and the girls no doubt caught the school bus next morning.[45]

Youthful high jinks were part of the era, but there was also youthful rebellion on the Settlement campus. Everywhere else, young people were resisting authority and breaking rules. But Bob Revel "always took a strong position, and every child knew it, that regardless of the circumstances—it made absolutely no difference to me—the teacher was always right, period." Besides supporting school authorities, he held the line against girls using heavy makeup and wearing miniskirts or two-piece swim suits, "and the boys better get a haircut or he'd give them an RK special with the bowl on their heads!"[46]

The sixties posed problems for Settlement teens beyond the length of their hair. Limited in what they could do on weekends, they could not "hang out" at shopping malls or teen gathering places, and consequently, some felt segregated from the social mainstream. Life remained structured. The Settlement provided the basics, which families might augment beyond any fee paid; children's own funds were tightly held in their individual accounts; and the Hutton van was the approved means of transportation. One common recollection was that two or three days before school started "we'd all go in the van, and we'd all go shopping for school clothes." Some, but not all, thought that "as far as dress and that type of thing—we were right up to date," bell-bottoms, tie-dyes, and all.[47] More than one chafed at the financial restrictions and thought "how wonderful if I was to have a little money of my own." In the 1970s, the board finally began to address the matter of spending money and Revel began holding "fruitful student 'rap' sessions" in the cottages to hear the teens' views on allowances, vacation policies, and the like.[48]

Disciplinary tools during that period were grounding and extra work. Revel "believed . . . that you were not going to raise children properly unless you taught them how to work, and what the work ethic was all about." Grounding meant "you could not go past the front steps of the cottage. . . . You could not go out on the playground." Sneaking out at night carried the grounding penalty.[49] "You don't know how many times I sat down in front of Bob Revel's desk," recalled Tere Hoyle. "My junior year I think I was grounded three out of four weeks, every month. . . it isn't so much what he would say—it's the look he would give you. You'd just [groan], 'Oh God. You'd think I'd learn.' " Into the seventies, when his office was downtown, "You knew you were in trouble if you had to talk to Mr. Revel. . . . you knew you were in trouble if he came out to see you. . . . you would shake," boys as well as girls.[50]

As they had in earlier decades, houseparents also took a disciplinary role in the sixties and seventies. Although corporal punishment had ended, Cletis Hydrick, a seven-year-old full orphan who came to the Settlement with his two brothers on September 1, 1970, learned otherwise. He recalled their arrival in Cottage Two: "The first thing that happened was our house parent . . . took us down into the basement, and . . . three or four kids got spankings down there as we stood along the wall watching. . . [we] just watched, to see what can happen. So that's the first memory that I have of living out there." The impressionable youngsters witnessed the spankings, administered with a paddle, and found the cautionary lesson effective.[51]

For the most part, however, cottage discipline was not spanking but setting and enforcing strict rules. One housemother was labeled a drill sergeant by girls in Cottage One. Many residents thought houseparents distant and uncaring: "There was no love. No hugs. No compassion. It just wasn't done." Houseparents seemed to be "just there to do a job. It was, 'You're here to eat, you're here to do your chores, then you can go play. . . . and then I'll do my crossword puzzle.' " Of course, there were notable exceptions such as Lois and Russell Riddell, who brought warmth and stability to the boys' cottages.[52]

The Riddells had known Bob Revel at the state hospital in Medical Lake, where Russ was night maintenance supervisor and Bob worked while going to school in Cheney. Revel convinced them to join the Settlement staff in 1963, and they became mainstays on the campus, working well with the children and other staff. Board members, too, considered them outstanding.[53]

They served the Settlement in any number of capacities. Russell assumed Elmer Wicks's duties after Wicks retired in 1972, and Lois became relief cook for the cottages and administration building; they filled in as houseparents in Cottage Four; they served in Cottage Three as houseparents for several years; and in their last year at the Settlement, 1977, he became campus engineer and she the cook for the administration building.[54] As housemother Lois Riddell rose at 4:30 to start breakfast for her boys. She recalled that "we rang first bell, [which] meant to get up. Second bell meant to be clean, and your teeth brushed and your hair combed, third bell meant your beds are made, and come down for breakfast." Her husband stayed upstairs in the cottage supervising showers and grooming and the tidying of quarters. "We'd go to the door when they went to school and tell them all goodbye, and then I'd start peeling potatoes," said Lois, who spent her day cooking and putting the cottage in order. "Sunday I had a roast, you know—I'd put it in the oven early before they'd go to Church. I made pies on Sunday . . . just like you would at home." Russ agreed, "It was just like living at home, only on a bigger scale."[55]

For each boy's birthday Lois baked a cake of his choice. Each chose the flavor of ice cream to go with it (the Riddells "didn't buy gifts, because with the money we were making we couldn't"). Both Riddells kept strict standards, and she admitted to occasionally putting a boy "over my checkered lap," to drive home a point. Russ took another approach; once consulting with Revel about a troublesome boy, he suggested putting the miscreant in the chicken house and making him "wash the windows with a toothbrush." Younger boys benefited from Lois's care:

> When they came home from school—I'd always be in the kitchen, and I'd be waiting for them. They'd have coloring books or whatever—we'd sit and visit—talk about school—and if I had to get after them, I always said, "Discipline is love, and if we didn't love you, we wouldn't make you mind."[56]

Norma Elsey's three years in Cottage One had a far different tone from that of her predecessor the drill sergeant. Nancy Hoyle, a late 1960s arrival at the Settlement, said that when Elsey came in the summer of 1976 "it was a welcome change—we were all excited for it." Only six girls lived there then, and Mrs. Elsey would often, on impulse,

> get a cab, and put all of us girls in it, and we would go have lunch, or dinner, or do something at Perkins [restaurant]. She was wealthier, so she spoiled us that way, but would also let you know that she cared about you—that you were special. I don't know if she told every child that they were special, or what, but I know that she made me feel that way. She loved us.

Mrs. Elsey took part in her girls' lives beyond the cottage. She attended teacher conferences at the elementary schools; and for one Halloween party, she "portrayed a fortune teller." She left the staff in 1979; two years later she donated a charitable gift annuity to the Settlement. It involved her half interest in real estate in Honolulu, now a hotel parking lot, that devolved to the Settlement on her death.[57]

In replacing her, the Settlement broke fifty years of tradition by naming Mr. and Mrs. Gus Watts houseparents for Cottage One rather than a housemother. Superintendent Skogsbergh reported on the Wattses' first meal there—"The girls all sang, 'It's So Nice to Have a Man Around the House.' . . . a real ego trip for Gus who thoroughly enjoyed it."[58]

During the sixties and seventies, the board members did not reestablish the close personal involvement that their prewar counterparts had had with Settlement children; however, they knew the children and their needs, especially in regard to medical and dental care. They underwrote numerous orthodontia programs. They insisted that Hutton kids receive the best care: for example, in 1965 they spurned the suggestion that a boy's surgery be done "by a class of Interns under the supervision of an experienced doctor" and voted instead to have it "performed by a surgeon of our choice." They monitored the mundane as well, such as polio booster shots. Increased operating costs forced closure of the campus infirmary in 1978, a measure the Board Ladies regretted particularly because for fifty years it had been a haven for generations of Hutton kids.[59]

The board tradition of encouraging talent and providing music lessons continued. Piano lessons remained a staple offering; rented band instruments made possible participation in the school band. The guitar, which virtually symbolized the sixties, became the musical instrument of choice on the campus. Four boys wanted to take guitar lessons so badly that they offered to get jobs to pay for them. Joy Brady's few years of piano lessons ended when she found a broken guitar in a cottage basement. Elmer Wicks abetted her in repairing and painting it, and with her purple guitar she was on her way to a music career that would take her nationwide as the opening act for such headliners as Seals and Croft and John Denver.[60]

Some earlier Settlement routine had changed, but in leisure hours and vacation time, the children still enjoyed the usual movies, hockey and baseball games, Ice Capades, the circus, Riverfront Park, and summer picnics. On May 4, 1968, all the children, several board members, and campus staff toured the Coeur d'Alene mining district; meeting Henry Day, son of the Hercules partner who had discovered the mine, gave the Settlement group a new sense of heritage. The tour was repeated in June 1976. Spokane's Expo '74, a singular event, drew Hutton kids at least twice, including one trip with the board that members had thought worthwhile and enjoyable for everyone. Halloween parties came to mark autumn on the campus; a crowd of 230 attended the celebration in 1966. Board members often came in costume, and as late as 1979 two of them, Ruth Jensen and Marion Phillips, ran a popular bingo game. Christmas remained the high point of the year. Community groups such as the Athletic Round Table continued to host holiday dinners at downtown hotels, complete with Santa Claus; one sixties girl said she "looked forward to that night all year long. It made me feel so special." The annual campus Christmas program resumed its former importance during the seventies. In 1978 a Whitworth College student directed the children in a play, and board members donated "materials, costumes, cookies and enthusiasm" in support.[61] When Patty Skogsbergh took over, she returned the Christmas productions to their fondly remembered greatness.

The seventies closed on a Settlement much changed by the preceding twenty years. Indeed, the world was a different place: The Age of Aquarius had come and gone, "The Beverly Hillbillies" had added cornball levity to television, and "All in the Family" had brought previously taboo topics and language to the small screen. War in Vietnam had altered the nation in ways that Levi Hutton and his generation could never have imagined. Administrator and board were more sophisticated and professional; on campus there were fewer orphans and more children with troubled backgrounds than ever before. The mainstays of the Settlement farm life had succumbed to regulatory and economic forces. Through it all, the Hutton Settlement had continued to manifest the spirit of half a century of caring.

10
Taxing Times:
Administration, Real Estate,
Finances, and the IRS

During the 1960s and 1970s, the nation's postwar economic boom ground slowly into the doldrums; Spokane's downtown real estate values suffered decline; and a mid-1970s oil crisis drove prices up and forced the cost of living ever higher. The Hutton Settlement found itself engaged with both state and federal governments even as it sought to maintain complete independence, and the board faced Charles Gonser's retirement. The rise of a new women's movement also marked those years.

There were multiple vacancies on the Settlement board as there had been in the 1930s and 1940s. New and younger women replaced the old guard, bringing new expertise and assertiveness to the group and a gradual change in the collective mindset. Characteristics of the nineteenth-century board inherited from the Ladies' Benevolent Society began to diminish. The death of Myrtle Osgood in 1962 severed the last link to boards that had served under Levi Hutton, who had himself nominated her for membership. To replace Mrs. Osgood, the women elected Wanda Cowles, wife of Margaret Paine Cowles's son, James.[1] With a master's degree in education from Stanford and several years of teaching experience, Wanda Cowles was the first of a new generation of Board Ladies with professional experience, notably in education and home economics—the fields that, together with nursing, most welcomed women at the time.

A spate of resignations came in 1966, including that of Mae Bright who, on her death in 1970, left a bequest to the Settlement that became basic funding for the scholarship that bears her name. Three resignations in 1968 were followed by two in 1970, including Margaret Bean's, which severed another tie to the founding board. As before, nominees included women whom members had known in their churches, school groups, Junior League, and other service and cultural organizations. Many new members still had ties to the pioneer Inland Northwest, but by the early seventies, recent arrivals in the region came forth to serve. Professional experience became a desirable criterion, and the board became what one member called "this great patchwork quilt of talent."[2]

A new, more professional approach appeared early in work of the education committee and two of its chairs—Wanda Cowles and her successor, Marion Phillips. Both experienced teachers, these newcomers to the board could fully understand teachers' concerns, comments, and evaluations; they began to look for root causes of learning problems and underachievement reported in the Settlement's children. Even before joining the board, Wanda Cowles had tutored Settlement children, and soon after assignment to the education committee she began to study their school records and make recommendations to improve performances. Efforts paid off, with better grades in fall semester 1963; at the high school level, "Diane Hunt again made the Honor Roll and quite a few others just barely missed."[3]

As chair of the committee, Wanda Cowles continued to tutor on campus and kept the board apprised of such matters as "problems involved in counseling graduating seniors about their continuing education."[4] She and her committee urged their colleagues to adapt policies to the changing times, to put Hutton kids on a par with their peers at school. Early in 1968, they asked the board to consider "an allowance system for the children" and a year later "to consider ways in which the children could earn money; and learn the value of money and money management." Not until spring semester 1971 did the board agree to give seniors "the opportunity of working part time in the school employment program . . . as a trial only." In March 1972, the education committee, now renamed student affairs, again considered "ways to give all the young people more responsibility in handling their own affairs, to prepare them for the time they will be completely on their own after leaving our care." They recommended that residents "be allowed, if they so desire[,] to apply for specific jobs that come up on campus . . . over and above the usual work assignments" and to receive an hourly wage. In a true departure from traditional policy, the board accepted the plan.[5]

With work on the Settlement farm a thing of the past, except for the garden, the seventies demanded new and different summer activities. In 1972 five Settlement boys spent August in a program funded by Washington Water Power that combined hard physical work, counseling, and recreation for boys over the age of fifteen and paid them the minimum wage. Off-campus employment gradually took hold. In midsummer 1974, older boys in Cottage Four were employed, but "the younger boys in that Cottage [were] complaining that they have nothing to do." Chores followed by sessions in the swimming pool were soon supplemented with weekly summer sports events or trips, and younger Hutton kids could participate in craft sessions conducted by a Fort Wright College student three afternoons a week. The valley branch library offered story hours and gave book selection advice. Camping became frequent when Sam Skogsbergh became resident director.[6] This new focus required additional staffing. In 1972, the board had hired a counselor. Three years later the education-turned-student-affairs-turned-student-activities committee urged hiring "part time staff to work on campus with the children this summer," and in 1976, the staff included a recreation graduate with "firm plans for the summer campus activity program."[7]

Wanda Cowles left the board in 1974, but within a year, the education committee, now chaired by Marion Phillips, had gained two other new members, Nancy

Henry and Carol Wendle—both with teaching experience. Clearly in tune with student needs and social change, this group proposed policy changes for off-campus employment and spearheaded on-campus programs in drug education and personal development, the latter a euphemism for sex education. They urged increased use of volunteer tutors and in-service training for staff. In addressing the student wage situation, they recommended that high school juniors and seniors save 75 percent of their on- and off-campus earnings and younger children 85 percent of theirs. The board voted to adopt the changes.[8]

By 1977, Hutton kids received weekly allowances—those in grade school, up to fifty cents; in junior high, seventy-five cents; and in high school, one to two dollars.[9] The committee continued its yeoman service in the children's behalf, and the arrival of Sam Skogsbergh in 1977 gave them a kindred spirit in the administration building.

The board may have been ahead of the curve in moving to pay for campus jobs. In 1977, a New York state court ruled on the work that could be required of children in homes such as the Settlement. It stated that "children can do nothing beyond three feet of their bed unless they are paid." For child care institutions around the nation, insurance and liability became major concerns. A case in point was a boys ranch in Nebraska that added an insurance clause "to cover emotional damage to a resident."[10] The Settlement board was operating in complicated spheres.

Longtime members not only applauded the abilities and expertise of the newcomers but also joined in their efforts to keep the Settlement in step with the era. Although never ceding responsibility or authority, they had relied heavily on Charles Gonser's recommendations and judgment. He, in turn, had continued Mr. Hutton's exclusion of the board women from financial planning. Although most members would agree that he "had taken the Settlement through a time when money was very scarce, . . . and we have Mr. Gonser to thank for the fact that . . . the Hutton Settlement [exists] today—because of his very tight rein and watching of every penny," by the late sixties, there were the beginnings of board dissatisfaction with the situation. His practice of informing the women of fiscal matters as faits accomplis—telling what was happening and what was being done—seemed outmoded to incoming members accustomed to a role in setting policy.[11]

In 1969, an ad hoc board group convened at Evelyn Morgan's house to establish a budget. No written record exists of this quasi-rebellion, but those present never forgot that unprecedented meeting. The women "were very anxious that they have part in some of the things being decided and done." In retrospect, that "budget meeting was really something, because none of us knew anything about the finance end of it, or the budget, or anything else." They resorted to numerous phone calls to Gonser in the downtown office as they worked to fashion a budget; looking to the long term, they also created a budget committee.[12]

The full board considered this tentative budget in special session in October 1970. That first budget committee had focused on salaries, operations, maintenance, education expenses, clothing allowances, and the like. The board took no action; it considered the committee's budget a guideline and, always practical, knew that "total figures will have to be revised downward." Bob Revel, who had now taken the Settlement's financial reins, was there and asked the women "not to infringe on the responsibilities of people employed in the downtown office." He later saw that meeting as a watershed event before which the Board Ladies had not set policy, but "after that time, absolutely" they did.[13] New enterprise and initiative had emerged. The budget committee became an assignment for members with financial expertise.

Another committee soon utilized the talents and experience of those with home economics backgrounds. Corine Brown, a graduate of the University of Minnesota, had a career as a hospital dietitian prior to coming on the board in 1968. She and Catherine Hyslop headed efforts to update the cottage kitchens and bring current practices to Settlement food services. When, for health reasons, dishwashers were installed in the early seventies they planned the kitchen remodeling and "set up standards for house cleaning and menus" as well. They held monthly meetings with the housemothers "furnished them with recipes, discussed their problems with them, and tried to help them with menus."[14]

Bob Revel had found no social workers when he took the superintendent's job in 1961, a fact that reflected the board and Gonser's long-standing aversion to hiring case workers and the long-running battle against state licensing. As Gonser's assistant and then successor, Revel and the board gradually came to add qualified counselors and social work professionals to the campus staff, but the Settlement never wavered in its opposition to state licensing. It had always conformed to certification requirements and complied with all health and safety regulations, but as Revel later put it, "We consider those licensing laws as regulations that impede our ability to program the way we want to program."[15]

Early in 1965, the Department of Public Assistance (formerly the Department of Welfare) issued a report on child caring agencies that contained recommendations that Gonser said would adversely affect the Settlement if included in upcoming legislation. The board immediately authorized him to "spend as much time in Olympia as necessary to bring about the defeat of the legislation." He kept the board apprised of events, Mae Bright urged contacting legislators, and she presented the board's position before a legislative subcommittee in Olympia. When House Bill 167 finally came to committee in the fall of 1966, Gonser's influence was evident in a paragraph that exempted any nonprofit organization that neither sought nor accepted state or federal funds, had been in existence five years or longer, and was administered under adequate control by a qualified board of laymen complying with all regulations relating to health, safety, and fire. The Hutton Settlement being the only such entity, that exemption received immediate board endorsement and no little legislative scrutiny.[16]

In fact, in final form, the exemption, lodged in subsection (k) of Substitute House Bill 167, came under fire as rendering the bill unconstitutional, thus giving the governor cause to veto the entire legislation. But challenges did not prevent passage ultimately, and the Settlement's exemption from state licensing was written into law.[17] The long fight against licensing that had erupted three times in the fifties and again in the midsixties was over at last.

Charles Gonser must surely have considered this victory a high point in his long tenure as Settlement administrator. Gonser had devoted his entire adult life to the Hutton Settlement. Since 1928 he had acted as Levi Hutton's chief steward and set the agenda for the board's consideration. One board member said, "If he suggested something, we immediately thought that was just fine." The journalist Dorothy Powers, who covered every postwar aspect of Spokane's business life during Gonser's administration, said that, in a time when men of "the establishment ran Spokane," Gonser was

> admired for his financial abilities. . . . He was, I would guess, [a member of] every male's club in town, and on lots of downtown committees, usually for civic reasons or patriotic reasons. . . . He was very much admired by other men downtown, and they'd all say, "Ask Charlie about that," and he knew it—whatever you asked him about.

A longtime friend and colleague, Ed McWilliams, concurred: "There were not very many areas of Spokane in which he didn't fit. He was active in business, he was active in Boy Scouts, he was active in the United Way . . . He was head of the Building Owners and Managers Association for many, many terms."[18]

He had been the Settlement's presence in the Downtown Rotary Club for forty years. The board appreciated the public face of the man of whom one said, "you can't use the word dynamic, . . . he represented Hutton Settlement throughout the community by his quiet manner." Reflecting the influence of Levi Hutton, Gonser once served as potentate of the El Katif Shrine, and the board cherished the fact that he was "totally dedicated to the memory [of Mr. Hutton] and wanted to do exactly what the deed of trust said."[19]

But the women remembered Charlie Gonser most fondly as the Hutton Settlement family man. "Everybody liked Charles Gonser. . . . He was a gentleman in every sense of the word. . . . very warm, and always interested . . . he got to know the board members and their spouses." The Board Ladies knew him as a caring person with a quiet wit who remembered anniversaries and other significant events and milestones, a man who would provide solace during a husband's final illness. "He was almost like an uncle to all of us, or a grandpa, or Cousin, or something. There was a very family feeling."[20] Retiring from an important business position would be one thing, retiring from a family would be wrenching.

Margaret Cowles had been on the board for twenty-seven years when, with serendipitous timing, the board elected her president in 1962. The Hutton Settlement had never had a true pension system, nor had the board given much thought to retirement plans. With her long association, her considerable influence, and the historical perspective she brought, she was the ideal person to lead the board into those uncharted waters.

Equitable retirement for longtime employees had always interested Mrs. Cowles. Ten years earlier, she had addressed the case of a man nearing the end of his 36-year tenure in moving to pension him, "guaranteeing him $100.00 per month for the rest of his life." In December 1962, under her leadership, the board offered "a pension for life, prorated on the length of [service] . . . and salary received" to Max Crosby, who had worked in the Settlement's downtown buildings since 1927. [21] But it was Gonser's case that presented Mrs. Cowles's greatest challenge. He turned sixty-five the year she became board president, and as her board colleague Evelyn Morgan recalled,

> We had a meeting . . . to develop a retirement [plan]. Here was this dear man, Mr. Gonser, and we didn't have anything for him. And so Margaret Cowles said, "Now, we've got to do this before Charlie gets hit by a truck." . . . She felt that we had to protect him—in other words, she . . . inspired it.

The women had always had difficulty in getting Gonser to take well-deserved vacations and even in getting him to accept salary increases, so they knew his retirement would not be easy.[22]

The board executive committee seriously pondered the Settlement's future without Charles Gonser in September of 1963, when its members met at Mrs. Cowles's home to consider future management and organization plans. Gonser, like Mr. Hutton himself, managed both the downtown office and the campus with a minimal staff. The full board soon discussed plans to hire more office help and someone to learn the Settlement's business details from Gonser. A former board president, Marge Greene, said the members "owed Mrs. Cowles a vote of thanks for attending [at last] to Settlement problems which have been bothering Presidents for ten years."[23]

Before leaving the city that November, Mrs. Cowles again assembled the executive committee at her home to discuss establishing an annuity for Gonser. She had obtained the services of a professional financial planner and had several discussions with bankers on the Financial Advisory Committee and with Gonser himself. On her return she hosted the December board meeting, which, among other things, dealt with plans for Christmas on the campus and at which the members unanimously elected her to a third term as president. When Gonser left the meeting they stayed on in executive session to discuss a retirement plan for him. The women voted that "the Hutton Settlement, Inc. finance its own retirement plan for Mr. Gonser based on a minimum of $500 a month for life" with lifetime survivor benefits for Mrs. Gonser. The plan would go into effect "upon Mr. Gonser's retirement at an undetermined future date."[24] He learned of the board's action when he read the minutes of the executive session. To Mrs. Cowles he wrote:

One point that is not entirely clear is whether or not the Board would wish me to remain or whether they would prefer that I retire at some future date, to be decided by the board.

Many times, a long-time employee is "tolerated" and continued in employment . . . when possibly it might be advantageous to the firm to retire [him]. . . . Whatever is done at any time should be done with first consideration to the best interests of the [Settlement]. I will be pleased to abide by whatever decision you make in this regard.[25]

In 1968, the year after Robert Revel left the campus to become assistant administrator, the seventy-one-year-old Gonser raised the retirement question again in a letter to Virginia Osborn, board president. "If I'm not needed I would not wish to remain," he wrote. "Possibly the time has arrived for me to step aside." Whatever the board members decide "will be entirely satisfactory to me."

It has been a genuine privilege to me to have had a small part in our wonderful work. It has had its challenges and its very dark days and many bright ones. But with the whole-hearted interest and support of a wonderful board of Trustees and other interested people, the future of The Hutton Settlement, founded by the late L. W. Hutton, is assured.[26]

Meanwhile, in the autumn of 1967 the board had feted Gonser with a gala dinner party to mark his fifty years with the Settlement. Margaret Cowles, historian, raconteuse, and herself a Settlement legend, acted as toastmistress. At her entertaining best that evening, she recalled Gonser's diligence and many talents.

Ringling Bros. Barnum & Bailey [should] have a head line act—"Charles the Great"— who can keep his ear to the ground, nose to the grindstone, shoulder to the wheel, finger on the pulse, feet on the ground, head in the clouds—all at the same time as keeping right on the ball.

She recounted the growth of Settlement real estate holdings under his stewardship and noted that "frugality and careful planning, never sharp dealing or extravagance[,] marked the financial plans of the man we honor." After citing the many "nights and days, Saturdays and Sundays Mr. Gonser has spent on the Settlement worries and pleasures," she turned to his "working with a board of 21 women for 50 years," a feat that amounted to "63,000 women hours" of meetings. For a man who relished cigars, he was a marvel: in all those meeting not once had he lighted up.[27]

Recalling his years as Gonser's assistant, Bob Revel said that at "five o'clock every afternoon when the office shut down, and Saturday mornings . . . we'd spend an hour together, just visiting." Gonser shared Settlement history, his own ideas and hopes for the future, and "what to look out for." Even after he retired on July 1, 1970, he would come down at 5:00 from the office the board had arranged for him next door to the boardroom on the fourth floor of the Hutton Building, and the practice continued. Transfer of authority did not end his influence. Gonser continued to represent the Settlement on the City Ramp Garage board, in the

Taxpayers Association, and in Spokane Unlimited as that group moved forward with planning for the city's world's fair.[28]

By the midsixties, Fred Stanton's son, Philip, had returned to Spokane with a Stanford law degree and joined his father in Washington Trust Bank. He recalled, "I took over the management of the bank from my father, and shortly after that they asked me to join the [Settlement's financial] advisory committee." Like his father, he had a regard for the Settlement that went beyond finances. He appreciated the Board Ladies' values and

> wonderful care of the children. I was always impressed when people like Mrs. Cowles
> . . . would actually go out and spend their time at the Settlement. They were very
> caring and loving people, and it really made a difference, in my judgment, . . . [to]
> a lot of young people out there.[29]

Other men on the committee shared his concern for the children; Gonser kept them informed about money matters and life on the campus as well.

Although local elections brought in new mayors and county commissioners whose attendance was sporadic, one new county commissioner reportedly said of his first meeting, after having missed several, "If he had known what he was missing he would have come long before." The advisory committee's work could be enjoyable as well as serious. The members were always an independent lot, but Stanton felt that "when Charlie Gonser recommended something, unless you firmly disagreed with it, that you really weren't too vocal." Stanton's long tenure brought stability to committee membership as bank personnel also began to rotate through the roster more frequently. As he put it, with bank mergers and consolidation, Spokane became "more of a branch city": most of its banks became branch offices, leaving Washington Trust the only major locally owned one. Absentee ownership meant frequent reassignment of banking officers and a "constant change of representatives . . . [that became] rather a serious matter for the subjects discussed in the monthly meetings are all of a very confidential nature."[30]

Levi Hutton's faith in the viability of downtown real estate would have been shaken severely by the suburban malls that were taking a drastic toll on Spokane's retail establishments by the 1960s. Rental prospects grew bleaker for downtown office buildings when additional construction downtown and in the outlying areas added competition for tenants. The Settlement's founder would have approved Gonser and the board's early affiliation with Spokane Unlimited, which sought to stem declining income and property values; the organization's ultimate accomplishment would be Expo '74, the city's highly successful world's fair. As its historian, William Youngs, wrote, the business community's

> efforts eventually merged with attempts by city planners to beautify downtown Spokane. The new urban center that would emerge during the 1970s grew out of dissatisfaction with the decaying city core of the 1960s. At first progress was slow, but from adversity would eventually come new life for the city and its river.

The Hutton Settlement's heavily vested interest in the city's core guaranteed continuing financial contributions to Spokane Unlimited.[31]

Together with Edmund F. (Ned) Cunningham, the Settlement's longtime property manager,[32] Gonser monitored with some dismay the income from Settlement real estate in the sixties. The City Ramp Garage, Mr. Hutton's dubious anchor for downtown business, finally had become profitable during the war and finally yielded a profit. But early sixties gasoline price wars drove the garage income down, and in July 1962 Gonser reported that receipts "are still down . . . reflecting a general business slump." Five years later, despite a new competitor, he could say, "Ramp Garage receipts are up; so far the Parkade has not hurt us"; garage business and profits increased throughout that year. Profits remained middling in 1971, and in March 1972 inquiries came regarding purchase of the garage. The Old National Bank Corporation owned 50 percent of the garage, the Settlement 25 percent, and heirs of August Paulsen 25 percent. The Financial Advisory Committee recommended that the Settlement sell, the other owners agreed, and on June 5, 1973, the board voted the first divestment of an endowment property. The Settlement received $153,333 from Mr. Hutton's original $75,000 investment—some consolation for the anguish and near financial disaster the garage had wrought for some forty years. Proceeds for the sale were to "be kept separate in order to maintain its identity as endowment."[33]

Meanwhile, the Hutton and Fernwell buildings were also causing concern. In 1961, because the Fernwell's "age and floor plan make it impossible to remodel," the board voted to explore a possible sale. Within two years Gonser reported that "old tenants are slowly leaving and the building is not modern enough to attract new ones."[34] In 1966, the future of the Fernwell Building again came up for board consideration. By the end of the year, mirroring general downtown decline, it had a 60 percent vacancy rate and again the options were "to close everything above the street floor, keeping up appearances, or tear it down to the street floor." During its seventy-seven years, it had returned more than $1 million to the Settlement, but in March 1967, the board voted "to close the upper five floors. . . and leave it standing in good condition." Within three months the tenants above street level had moved to the Hutton Building. Although the Financial Advisory Committee urged Gonser "to carefully cultivate" buyers, there was little interest in the Fernwell until 1974 when the effects of the world's fair could be felt in the city.[35] The Inter Mountain Investment Corporation made an offer, which the advisory committee approved. In October, on motion of Mrs. Cowles, the board accepted the offer of $275,000. In marking the passage of its second endowment property from Settlement hands, the board accepted Catherine Hyslop's heritage-inspired motion to "retain the original abstract [of title] for its historic value and give [the new owners] a copy with the portions pertinent to the Fernwell Building."[36]

As for the Hutton Building, since 1917, the Settlement board had held its meetings there. Mr. Hutton's office had evolved into Settlement headquarters, and early in 1964 the once ornate dining room of May and Levi Huttons' apartment had been converted for use as a boardroom. The building had great significance, although it had become, as Bob Revel put it, "an older, Class B building." In 1966 the board approved spending $85,000 for "two operator-less elevators . . . not to modernize the building but to make a necessary replacement." But the women knew that a decision had to come. Selling the crown jewel in its portfolio would be "heart-wrenching. But it seemed like the practical thing to do."[37]

Agents for a potential buyer contacted Revel in October 1970. A year later the building's vacancy rate stood at 27 percent, "with prospects of large vacancies in the future" should state offices move out. The Settlement launched a round of feasibility studies and appraisals, and by August of 1972, although in no hurry, the board began seriously to discuss selling the Hutton Building. By the time of Expo '74, the vacancy rate had improved. In November 1977, in the fair's lingering afterglow, Revel reported 98 percent occupancy and a good return on the investment, adding, "If there are serious thoughts on the sale of the building the time is right just now." After eighteen months of discussion, in April 1979, the Financial Advisory Committee recommended selling "the Hutton Building and other properties in the block, if possible, . . . to one owner and not in separate pieces." Fittingly, Margaret Cowles moved at the next board meeting to accept the recommendation. Setting a minimum price of $1.2 million, the Settlement soon advertised the property for sale.[38]

Wayne Guthrie, a Spokane developer, among other interested parties, made an offer of $1,125,000 in June 1979. After further negotiation, Herbert Hamblen, the Settlement's attorney and longtime friend, approved a contract calling for a $500,000 down payment and a note for the balance at 10 percent interest. Philip Stanton and the rest of the Financial Advisory Committee recommended acceptance. In action heavy with symbolism, the board accepted the Guthrie offer on the motion of Helen Whitehouse Hamblen, who, other than Margaret Cowles, had the board's longest ties to the Hutton Building.[39] The sale closed in September, marking divestiture of the last of the original endowment.

Even as they agonized over selling the endowment properties, new ventures in real estate came before the Board Ladies during the sixties and seventies. In the summer of 1962, Gonser piqued their interest with a report that IBM Corporation envisioned a new building in Spokane on 8th Avenue between Washington and Stevens. IBM had approached parties potentially interested in "buying the property, building according to specification, and renting [to IBM] on a long term lease." Gonser estimated the cost at approximately $420,000. The women voted to explore the matter.[40]

Later that month, the Financial Advisory Committee endorsed the plan to pursue a contract with IBM. Because the site, situated on South Hill between the city's two major hospitals and just outside its downtown commercial core, was then owned by the city, Mayor Neal Fosseen abstained from voting. Swiftly the women voted to proceed "with latitude for Mr. Gonser to negotiate the terms of the lease," and within two weeks IBM awarded the contract to the Hutton Settlement.[41]

The Settlement had entered into a similar venture with the Albertson's grocery chain in the 1950s, but the IBM project did not go so smoothly. After purchasing the land, hiring the Seattle architectural firm of Kirk, Wallace and McKinley, and paying for the topographical survey and initial excavation,[42] Gonser and the board learned of possible cost overruns. They authorized amending the original agreement from $420,000 to $450,000 in April 1963, but the low bid from general contractors came in higher than anticipated in July. As details requiring board action mounted, the women voted Gonser power of attorney to expedite matters. By October the building had emerged above ground, and Gonser "urged the Board members to turn in off Stevens and observe the progress. They are about four days behind schedule."[43]

But the May 1, 1964 target date for completion had begun to slip. Water encountered in excavation remained a problem, delays mounted, and construction ran farther behind. August came and went, though the board and Financial Advisory Committee toured the unfinished structure that month and agreed that it "should be a source of pride for the City as well as the Settlement."[44] The next date set for occupancy also passed, but finally, in November 1964, IBM moved in and "invited the Trustees and their husbands to attend a demonstration of the computer." The project had cost $560,000, necessitating renegotiation of the lease, which IBM signed a year later. All parties were well satisfied, however: Kirk, Wallace and McKinley had created not the familiar IBM glass box but a building in the Northwest style. It won a 1965 award from the Seattle Chapter of the American Institute of Architects.[45]

About thirteen years later Robert Revel responded to IBM's need to expand by beginning a second building adjacent to the first. By mid-1978, final documents had been signed, but the Settlement was short of funds for completion of the project. During this period of "soul searching and adept reasoning on the Board's part," when the women were already seeing the wisdom of selling the beloved Hutton Building, the Settlement's stewards experienced frustration and "major problems" yet persevered. Jessie Satre, board president, noted in December 1979: "As Mr. Revel admittedly enjoys challenges, he must have had a great deal of pleasure from working with IBM. A building that was to have been completed a year ago is just now ready for occupancy."[46]

Sale of endowment properties and the IBM construction projects stand out as the major real estate dealings of the sixties and seventies, but board and administrators continued to manage and monitor the other portfolio holdings as well. As they did in January 1963, the Board Ladies periodically made tours, "to personally inspect each property" owned by the Settlement. They saw the sale or razing of some older buildings, including demolition of the long-burdensome Majestic Hotel;

and they acquired other new property beyond the downtown core, including the East Town Shopping Center. Following the advice of Gonser and then Revel, the recommendations of the Financial Advisory Committee, and the charge given in Mr. Hutton's will and the Deed of Trust, in a fifty-year period the women had parlayed the original endowment into total assets of $2,034,317.22.[47] Levi Hutton would have been proud and perhaps a bit astonished at the Board Ladies' financial savvy and business acumen.

Beginning with the initial term of Agnes Cowley Paine, the Hutton Settlement board had benefited from outstanding presidential leadership, the right person in office at the right time. As in the past, ability came to the fore in 1971 when the board elected Catherine Hyslop during another crucial period in the Settlement's history. She brought political astuteness, superior organizational skills, and forceful conviction to bear when circumstances called for all three.

Born in Bridgeport, Washington, Catherine Cornehl majored in home economics at Washington State College and in 1938 married a classmate, Thomas Hyslop. While raising their four children in Spokane she "was very active in Scouting—both Girls and Boys—and Music Club—my children were involved in music—band mothers, PTA, all the usual things." As a national officer of Alpha Gamma Delta sorority, she visited chapters "across the country . . .[on] campuses when they were having struggles—real struggles" during the 1960s social upheavals. An unabashed Republican, she served the party as both precinct and state committeewoman and managed the Spokane County campaign of John Spellman in his successful 1980 run for governor.[48]

Catherine Hyslop joined the Hutton Settlement board in 1966. Assigned to the administration building committee, she immediately saw the need for changes. As its chair the next year, she made a thorough study of the building "and was rather appalled at how barren it was." At a time before the board asserted itself in financial matters, her committee's response to her suggestions for improvements that would cost $1,000 was, "Oh, Mr. Gonser will never let you spend the money!" She replied, "Well, I'm going to ask. All he can do is say no." When she presented her list at the next board meeting, the members approved funding it. Indeed, she gradually made her colleagues see the need to allocate funds for updating the whole campus. A guardian of Settlement interests, in the summer of 1969 she spoke forcefully against a West Valley School District attempt to build a middle school on twenty acres of the campus.[49] Her organizational talent came into play early, and board minutes throughout the late sixties show her growing influence.

Within the committee system she pushed the importance of organization and formulated a rational flow chart with clear lines of authority flowing from the board. As president in the early seventies, she ran "a very tight meeting," delegated through committees, and had high expectations. With vision and drive she urged procedural changes "to make the Hutton Settlement less cumbersome to administer and better able to serve needs of the children." Speaking to the latter, the board finally added a phone in each cottage in 1972. During her three terms as president, she laid the foundation for annual board evaluation and goal-setting meetings, for written staff job descriptions, and orientation procedures for new board members.[50]

Mrs. Hyslop took pride in having initiated recognition parties for the Settlement staff, which evolved from a Valentine dessert to show them that "we loved them" into country club luncheons. In inaugurating the annual achievement dinners, she had several goals consistent with Mr. Hutton's desire that the board involve themselves in the lives of the children.

> I wanted the children to go out for dinner and learn how to act. I wanted them to learn that you dress up . . . and behave in a certain manner. I wanted them to have self-pride in anything they had accomplished, and [know] that we were aware of it.
> . . . We established the Mae Bright Scholarship Cup for the achievement dinner
> . . . We wanted to honor Mr. Gonser, and gave a citizenship award in his name.

The first achievement dinner was held at the Stockyards Inn in May 1971; the theme was railroading to reflect Levi Hutton's early life; Robert Brown, husband of the board's Corine Brown, was toastmaster; and the world-class track star Gerry Lindgren was featured speaker.[51]

Catherine Hyslop's presidency coincided with campus staffing dilemmas and real estate and financial matters in a time of urban decline. As a member of the Financial Advisory Committee, Philip Stanton said of her performance:

> I really admired her for . . . [getting] the board members to really understand what was going on, so there [would be] a good flow of information and decision making between the board and the administrator. . . I think she was very strong in that regard—a very capable lady.[52]

She first assumed office six months after Robert Revel moved into the administrator's office. These two pragmatic, dedicated, and tough-minded people did not always agree, but they forged a strong partnership to combat the greatest threat to the Settlement since the early legal challenges to Mr. Hutton's will: the IRS. Throughout its existence, the board and administrator had steered clear of government as far as possible. Levi Hutton had been permitted to claim Settlement children as dependents in the early twenties; the Settlement had been ruled exempt from federal income taxes in 1937; and a 1951 Internal Revenue Service law had prompted sale of Settlement investments other than real estate, including government bonds.[53] But the Tax Reform Act of 1969, aimed at a few large foundations perceived as abusing their nonprofit status to avoid taxation, caught the Hutton Settlement in a web of unintended consequences.

With overwhelming support from the Spokane community and help from its congressional delegation, the board surmounted the first hurdle erected by the new law—proving the Settlement's right to exist as a 501 C3 tax-exempt organization.

The second challenge was determining whether the Settlement was a public charity, a private foundation, or a private operating foundation. The new law imposed federal excise taxes and draconian rules of income distribution on both foundation categories but a lesser burden on public charities. Should the board choose to operate the Settlement as a private foundation, tax structure and income distribution would insure its gradual liquidation. As Revel told the board, "It is up to us to decide which of the three we are."[54] After months of debate and consultation with attorneys and accountants, the board elected to seek status as a public charity by showing that the Settlement was responsive to the general public.

Herbert Hamblen spelled out the situation in stating the case:

> There are two main requirements. One is that Hutton Settlement, Inc., normally receive ten percent of its support [income] from governmental and public sources, and, secondly, that it be organized and operated so as to attract new and additional public or governmental support on a continuing basis. Hutton Settlement has met the ten percent support limitations. . . . Furthermore, Hutton Settlement was organized and has operated to attract continuing public support.

Somewhat surprisingly, he noted that in fifty years of operation, the Settlement had "received substantial public funds through Juvenile Courts and State agencies dealing with needy and dependent children" who are wards of the court. Income from sale of endowment buildings and from endowment funds originally contributed by the general public could be applied toward the 10 percent requirement of support from public or governmental sources. Hamblen cited the impeccable credentials and stewardship of board members and Financial Advisory Committee and noted, "finally, Hutton Settlement has always made available its facilities to the general public."[55]

Acting on Hamblen's advice, the board and Revel submitted documentation to the IRS in support of their claim to public charity status. The package included supporting letters from the mayor, the Spokane County Board of Commissioners, the superintendent of the West Valley School District, judges of the Superior Courts of Spokane and Whitman counties, and, perhaps most impressive of all, a collection of responses from former residents. The Settlement had sent 100 questionnaires to alumni asking them about the quality of their Settlement experience; within a month 72 percent had been returned, many former residents expressing alarm that the Settlement might be in jeopardy.[56]

In addition to this convincing documentation, Congressman Tom Foley interceded, as did Senator Warren Magnuson, who made the point that in caring for hundreds of children at its own expense the Settlement had "saved the State of Washington thousands of dollars." In return, the Settlement received a Valentine from the IRS; on February 14, 1972, came official word of its public charity status.[57]

As one board member said, "That IRS thing really threw us into a tizzy," but by counting bequests already received that year, Revel and the board met the 10 percent quota for 1972. It soon became clear, however, that they must move actively into fundraising, a prospect the women decried. Catherine Hyslop summed up their feelings, saying becoming a charity had "indeed required a change of view in a beloved conservative private organization of 54 years."[58]

Tradition and public perception hindered early fundraising efforts. All board members received "a precise statement for public quotation" regarding the need to solicit support. Some people in the larger community harbored the "general feeling that the Hutton Settlement doesn't really need the money." A few saw nothing wrong with accepting government funds, and one even suggested that the Settlement seek help from the government because of its charity status.[59]

The 10 percent requirement grew more burdensome. In the spring of 1979, Revel met in Washington, D.C., with the state's two senators, Congressman Foley, and a member of the Joint Committee on Taxation to discuss basing the 10 percent on net rather than gross income. The matter went to the House Ways and Means Committee for study, and later that summer Foley came home to Spokane and toured the campus as part of renewed attempts to secure relief.[60]

All efforts failed. At century's end, the Settlement still had to raise from the public each year a sum based on gross revenue averages of the previous four years, even though those annual gross revenues included every public donation received. Failure to meet this test of public support for two consecutive years would result in the Settlement's being reclassified as a private foundation with all the tax and income distribution burdens that would carry.[61]

Many former residents—from Chester Rouse of the early twenties to Bambi McMillan of the sixties—rallied with gifts. Formation of an alumni group in the summer of 1975 assured continuing alumni support. Board members made contributions, as they had in past years. In 1977, for example, Edith Whitney and her husband, Howard, donated generously to the endowment fund; she always fostered campus landscaping and beautification with her own time, money, and labor, and their gift planted seeds of the Settlement camping fund that bears her name.[62]

Despite their ample experience with fundraising in their churches, PTA, and other organizations, the Board Ladies shied away from traditional soliciting for the Settlement. Marilyn Stocker, who joined the board in 1978, said, "I had raised funds for Junior League. . . . So I was not looking to raise funds."[63] Instead, the women turned to the public relations committee and to tried-and-true PR events from the Settlement's past, to which they added a few new twists. Originally, only the need to increase the campus population had driven public relations efforts. There had been teas on the campus, strategic ties with Rotary and other civic groups, and a photographic slide show to present the Hutton Settlement story to numerous organizations. Individual board members had carried the word, as Virginia Osborn did in speaking before the Spokane Council of Churches. In the midsixties the board reinstated summer picnics for groups such as judges and juvenile authorities, legislators, and both downtown and valley Rotarians. By 1968, Gonser and Revel were making radio and television appearances "telling the story of the Settlement."[64]

Now, goaded by the IRS requirement of public funding, the board offered the administration building dining room to groups for meetings to be followed by a campus tour that gave "a lot of people an opportunity to see the facilities who have never done so." The board also hosted a campus tour and dinner for chamber of commerce members and their wives. Other instances of outreach followed. Catherine Hyslop recalled that, among other things, the IRS challenge led to creation of a Settlement newsletter: "We had to have the public know more about us. . . . I wanted something to go out to the public . . . [and] we needed to get in touch with our alumni." So the board women, doing most of the writing and other work, produced a sheet that, on reflection, "was not very good," but it soon improved.[65]

In 1976, Bob Revel established the Century Club, a donor category for people contributing more than $100; the strategy proved successful and enduring. The board appreciated its financial returns as well as the fact that it appeared "to be a splendid public relations tool." When Henry Day, with his Hercules Mine connections, received a solicitation he congratulated Revel on the concept and promised future support. In 1979 individual contributions of some 100 club members averaged nearly $200.[66] The board had by then come to believe that fundraising required professionals, and in the spring of 1978 it hired Don Dagman as public relations director. With a background in marketing, he initiated the production of informational brochures that were mailed in large numbers. That September, Patsy Gottschalk joined the staff as community relations liaison; she developed the newsletter into the very professional semiannual *Tower Topics* that keeps alumni and the community at large apprised of Settlement happenings.[67]

Although the Board Ladies had been forced into fundraising, their efforts succeeded. Ruth Jensen, president in 1978, said they had "done pretty well. . . . you're worried every year that you may not make it, [but] about the end of the year something comes in that puts you over the top." Indeed, that July they received a challenge grant of $3,400 for a new campus van, and in December, three anonymous donors met the challenge, the Settlement met its IRS quota, and the Hutton kids rode into the new year in a new vehicle.[68]

The sixties and seventies witnessed a sea change in Settlement affairs. Administrative change had come for the first time since Mr. Hutton's death, and the campus staff slowly became professionally oriented. Economic and political forces had forced board decisions and actions previously beyond considering. The board acquired a new assertiveness; it utilized its pool of individual talent to move the Settlement forward even as it remained committed to mandates in the Deed of Trust. Through everything, the spirit of sisterhood and dedication to the Settlement remained constant.

At the end of her term, each president always thanked the board for help and cooperation in meeting the goals of the past year; none put it better than Betty

Corliss in 1976: "My deepest thanks goes to each Board Member who performed her duties faithfully. Not once did you ladies say 'no' when asked to serve on a committee. What joy you are! And the children—let us never forget them and the hurtful loads they carry." One member of that era recalled, "The basic goal was always to try to make this place a real home for those children, and to make it as happy as we can, and to carry out Levi's basic thoughts and purposes." Younger members found among their senior colleagues "some tremendous role models" who lent leadership at critical times; however, one of those role models later said, "I think I've . . . gained more than I've given."[69]

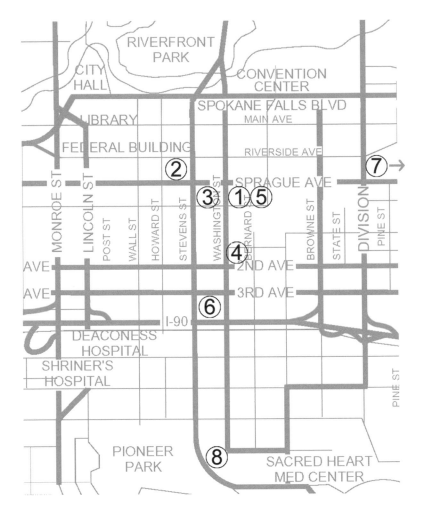

DOWNTOWN SPOKANE

11

Honoring the Past, Facing the Future

*L*evi Hutton's Deed of Trust had guided the Settlement board through six decades. It remained the bedrock reference for decisions and action as the century's last twenty years grew increasingly contentious and complex. Both the need to meet the IRS public support test and changes in welfare policy kept the board entangled with government rules and regulations. The 1980s and 1990s brought new personnel, financial growth, capital improvements, and enhanced campus programs to the Settlement and both joy and heartache to the board women as they monitored the fortunes of the children entrusted to them.

Another round of multiple retirements and resignations hit the board in the 1990s. Electing younger, professionally accomplished members was important but problematic. As greater professional opportunity opened for women, some members left the board after short service in order to resume careers. Lifetime tenure and the cyclical nature of board turnover produced something of a generation gap and a perpetual shortage of forty-five- to sixty-year-olds. Before 1980, most members had raised their families before joining the board; as youth became a priority, the addition of mothers with small children altered board dynamics somewhat.

The board's postmeeting luncheon was a tradition of at least thirty years' standing. After adjourning their official first-Tuesday board meetings, the women reassembled in the Tea Room of the Crescent Department Store. In these sessions, with administrator absent, they discussed Settlement affairs openly and off the record. The gatherings also strengthened bonds of friendship and sisterhood. Younger members found it difficult to move on for lunch with the group. A senior member recalled that "they had to get home to their children and things," so the unofficial group "kind of disbanded, and it was too bad." Another longtime member thought that the lunches gave the board women an opportunity to get to know each other better and to balance the work with fun.[1] Those informal meetings at the Crescent ended by the time the store closed in the nineties.

Service on the Settlement board requires a time commitment virtually impossible for a full-time career woman. The first hint had come in 1972; Millie Smith (Mrs. Del Cary Smith), on the board since 1965, found it impossible to continue and resigned because of "the demands of my work as a substitute teacher in District 81."[2] Nancy Henry and Carol Wendle, two of the first young mothers to join the board in the midseventies, reflected on the situation at century's end.

Henry said, "We've lost several very good board members to careers and work." Two in particular, she noted, left in the mid-1990s for administrative posts in higher education. They were able, experienced volunteers who had been Junior League presidents, "very conscientious and . . . rather than not doing their part, they chose to resign." Board membership demands so much time, said Wendle, that it is imperative to accommodate careerwomen and young mothers. She remembered that the Settlement had been "very sensitive to me, and to my children, and schedules, and babysitters." Board women with small children, Henry said, "are a breath of fresh air" and have contributions to make to the work—"if [only] we don't scare them to death or burn them out." [3]

The office of board president can at times approximate a full-time job. Long tenure and lack of a board middle generation made it increasingly difficult to secure candidates for that post. By the midnineties, most longtime members had served two consecutive terms, some three, and the younger women were not yet ready to assume that responsibility. After serving in 1987 and 1988, Marion Phillips had thought, "Boy, I'm through, that was it." But ten years later the nominating committee pleaded with her to accept the presidency again, and her sense of duty prevailed for one more term. Sharon Cortner, elected to the board in 1995, succeeded her in 1999, served three years, and was followed by two presidents who had joined the board in 1997. Throughout this time, newer members had been catalysts for change. They had requested a five-year moratorium before being asked to stand for president, giving them time to serve on such committees as finance, education, and personnel. Bylaw changes accepted in 2002 substituted the post of president-elect for second vice-president, creating a previously lacking line of succession.[4]

Although it could move with the times, change had never come easily for the Hutton Settlement board. So strong is the bond with the past that the cottage committees' original charge to "keep a record of the furnishings and condition of the cottage" still drives an annual inventory of everything in all cottages, to the chagrin of both committee members and campus staff, who find it intrusive. With Edna Glasgow's election to the job in 1935, recording secretaries began routinely to sign their own names to the minutes, but board rosters and Settlement letterhead continued to list members by their husbands' names until the nineties and meetings relaxed enough to permit coffee to be served.[5]

Given the need for confidentiality in business dealings, board meeting minutes had never circulated; the secretary read them at the following meeting for additions and corrections. In the autumn of 1985 the board finally considered mailing them to members, but long discussion "indicated that the group did not wish to have the minutes distributed outside of the Hutton Settlement office." Continuing pressure came from women accustomed to the practice of other organizations, and in 1992 the full board conceded, with the stipulation that "financial information be deleted from the minutes when they are mailed . . . and that members sign and return the minutes after they have been read." In the midnineties the proviso on returning minutes was dropped.[6]

Levi Hutton and the founding trustees had taken a prudent and sage approach to legal matters, but they did not anticipate the litigious bent that developed in society toward the end of the twentieth century. This penchant for lawsuits forced their successors to reassess their vulnerability to litigation, both frivolous and reasonable. In December 1989 they accepted a bylaw revision that included a new article on indemnity. It held that the private property of trustees, officers, and employees of the Hutton Settlement were not subject to payment of corporate debts and liabilities and that

> the Corporation shall indemnify any and all persons who may serve or who have served at any time as Trustees, Officers, or employees . . . against any and all claims, liabilities, expenses and costs . . . in connection with any proceeding to which she/ he may be made a party, or . . . become involved [in] by reason of being or having been a Trustee, Officer, or employee . . . except in such cases where the Trustee, Officer, or Director is adjudged guilty of willful misconduct in the performance of duties to the Corporation.[7]

A like amendment to the Settlement's Articles of Incorporation was filed in the secretary of state's office in May 1997; it included two new articles that spoke to liability. One of them specified indemnification as required by the Washington Nonprofit Corporation Act and the Washington Business Corporation Act, two laws that had clarified and strengthened the position of volunteer boards in Washington State.[8]

By the end of the century, as the younger echelon moved into the presidency and brought new ideas, other changes followed. Members finally received a board manual in 2000, under Sharon Cortner's leadership; it covered every aspect of Settlement operations and included documents that securely rooted the present in the past. This codification of responsibilities and procedures aided orientation of new members and served as a ready reference for all; previously, the board had "kind of [gone] with the flow." Younger members suggested other departures and new directions that might have been unsettling in the short term but not disruptive of board cohesiveness. No member recalls less-than-harmonious deliberations, and one attributes this equanimity to their "all working for the same thing . . . the children—and I guess maybe most of us are mothers, just trying to be peacemakers. . . . you know how it goes—'we'll work this out.'"[9]

A change that the board women found both unsettling and painful cut one of their strongest ties to Levi Hutton. They had maintained their offices in the Hutton Building since selling it in 1979. Faced with higher rent and the new owner's plans for renovating, they reluctantly moved the Settlement offices to the Old National Bank Building in November 1986. No one found the move more wrenching than Margaret Cowles, who reportedly assured her colleagues that "she explained the move to Mr. Hutton as she lovingly carried his picture to the new office."[10]

Board membership had never been predicated on financial connections or fundraising ability. By the mid-1990s, however, the IRS requirement that 10 percent of Settlement gross income be derived from public support had made an interest in fundraising a desirable quality in prospective members. Rather than hold fundraising events, however, the board chose to inform the public about "what Hutton Settlement does, and to . . . [explain] that it depends upon its benefactors to continue." As one member said, this strategy resulted in "some very generous bequests from people that we don't even know."[11]

After ten years of operating as a public charity under IRS rules, the Settlement revisited the entire matter. Robert Revel turned again to political allies, and after meetings in Washington, D.C., in April 1980 he presented the board women with alternatives. The Hutton Settlement could remain a public charity, become a private foundation (and cope with punitive tax burdens), or "turn our program over to DSHS and accept Federal funding." The last option was anathema. The Settlement accountant advised that the status quo was the best course. The board voted to continue as a public charity, but Revel continued to work for either complete exemption from the tax law or alleviation of the gross income ruling. After several years Congressman Tom Foley reluctantly advised surrendering to political reality, hence the Settlement continued to show that 10 percent of its annual gross income came from the public. Confronted with a shortfall of some $15,000 in December 1994, for the first time the board solicited donations; a return of envelopes enclosed in the year-end issue of *Tower Topics* produced more than the amount needed.[12]

The 1981 charitable gift annuity of Norma Elsey was the first donation of that sort. The following year the Settlement accepted the $450,000 George Riddle estate in a living trust agreement that yielded Riddle $12,000 a year. In administering the trust, Bob Revel established a close and caring relationship that endured through Riddle's declining years. Former residents included the Settlement in their own estate planning, as did one of the Trounce siblings from the 1920s, whose will designated a $10,000 gift "in grateful remembrance of Mr. Hutton."[13]

On June 4, 1985, the board received word of a surprising and substantial bequest from one of the "people that we don't even know." A Spokane businessman, Orville Cox, left the Settlement virtually his entire estate, valued at more than $2,250,000. Born soon after the historic flight at Kitty Hawk, North Carolina in 1903, Cox proudly bore the name of the younger Wright brother; he had worked for Standard Oil for a time, acquired considerable real estate in Spokane, and then retired to manage those properties. His attorney related that Cox "was pleased to leave a substantial estate to a charitable organization which [is] such great benefit to the Spokane area." When it received final distribution of the estate in the autumn of 1987, the Hutton Settlement's total assets reached $9,038,847.[14]

Fred Stanton, ca. 1950. The banker
was a longtime member of the
Financial Advisory Committee and
staunch protector of Settlement
interests. Photo courtesy of Washington
Trust Bank.

Philip Stanton, ca. 1975. He succeeded
his father on the Settlement's Financial
Advisory Committee in the mid-sixties and
still served in 2003. Photo courtesy of
Washington Trust Bank.

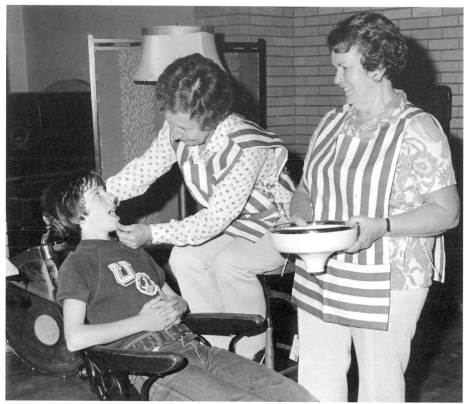

Ruth Jensen, Catherine Hyslop, and Brian Rice, a Settlement resident, dramatize the function of the Settlement's old dental chair, which was a top attraction at a 1980 auction of antiques and collectibles. Hutton Settlement photo.

Robert K. Revel, Hutton Settlement administrator, 1970-95, ca. 1986. Hutton Settlement photo.

After forty-seven years, the Settlement office moved from the Hutton Building at Christmastime 1986. Margaret Cowles carried the founder's portrait to its new home. Hutton Settlement photo.

Herbert Hamblen, ca. 1985. A devoted friend and champion of the Settlement, for several decades the attorney donated time to guide it through legal thickets and political snarls. Photo courtesy of the Spokesman-Review.

The 4-H lambs could become pets, and parting with them, difficult. Jimmy Metreveli once planned to take his lamb and go AWOL from the campus. Hutton Settlement photo.

Mike Butler and a 1930s Settlement alumnus, Bob Baker, met at the 1993 Junior Livestock Show. Hutton Settlement photo.

As resident director, Sam Skogsbergh made camping a favorite activity. Settlement youngsters are shown here at a lakeside campsite in 1995. Hutton Settlement photo.

The Board Lady Helen Hamblen observed window replacements in 1996. She had often accompanied her father, the architect Harold Whitehouse, to the campus during installation of the originals in 1918. Hutton Settlement photo.

"Baby Jane" Wiese Anderson (on the left). The first child to enter the Settlement when it opened in 1919 visits with Dorothy and Bob Revel at the 75th anniversary reunion. Hutton Settlement photo.

Michael Butler, Hutton Settlement administrator since 1995. Hutton Settlement photo.

When Michael Butler assumed the administrator's responsibilities, he inherited oversight of Settlement 4-H activities and became a stock show regular. Hutton Settlement photo.

Tom Hyslop, loyal WSU Cougar, always backed the Settlement's 4-H activities. At the Junior Livestock Show in May 1996, he sat at the board lunch table with Lani Ellingsen, to his left, and opposite him, right to left, Marion Phillips, Maxine Kopczynski, and Carol Wendle. Hutton Settlement photo.

Settlement runners rest on their laurels after a good showing in the Coulee Dam run in 1996. Hutton Settlement photo.

The Settlement hosted Congressman George Nethercutt (in jacket) at a campus picnic in 1996. Shown here with Marion Phillips, Catherine Hyslop (back to camera), and Mike Butler, Nethercutt donated a flag that had flown over the Capitol in Washington, D.C., occasioning an impressive campus flag ceremony. Hutton Settlement photo.

Jo Ann Nielsen, a past president of the board, and her husband, Ben, at the 1996 Achievement Dinner honoring the children's accomplishments. Hutton Settlement photo.

After retiring in 1992, Sam and Patty Skogsbergh had time to enjoy such things as a trip to the Oregon coast, where they are shown here. Photo courtesy of the Skogsberghs.

Today's resident director, Mary Jo Lyonnais, joined the campus staff as a counselor in 1979 and was named director in 1992. Hutton Settlement photo.

Margie Hemming and the boys' caseworker David Milliken share a light moment in the secretary's office, ca. 1999. Hutton Settlement photo.

After they leave the school bus every afternoon, Hutton kids make a beeline for Margie Hemming's office to find out "what's up," ca. 1999. Hutton Settlement photo.

By the 1990s inner tubes had replaced Flexible Flyers for hours of winter fun. Hutton Settlement photo.

In 1996 Sharon Cortner organized a summer sewing group on campus; here she stands on the right with a fellow home economist and Board Lady, Corine Brown, and four young quilters. Hutton Settlement photo.

Settlement Christmas programs created lasting memories for Hutton residents. Four youngsters prepare for performances in the mid-nineties. Hutton Settlement photo.

Settlement residents stay abreast of recreational and sports trends. Here a group assumes a karate stance under the watchful eye of the instructor. Hutton Settlement photo.

Everything was up-to-date in Cottage Four at century's end, and residents' homework was aided by computers. Hutton Settlement photo.

Despite the Cox acquisitions, major property concerns arose in the mideighties. In October 1983, IBM notified Revel that when its lease expired the company would leave the building the Settlement had constructed for it in two stages during the sixties and seventies. Built specifically for IBM the property proved hard to re-let; interim leases and subleases were negotiated between 1985 and 1988. In November 1990, Revel reported no income from the building for two years. At the time, a 22 percent vacancy rate prevailed in downtown commercial property, and the Financial Advisory Committee advised the board "to sell or otherwise occupy the IBM Building." In April 1993, Itronix, Inc., a Spokane manufacturer of ruggedized hand-held computers and detection devices, signed a five-year lease with renewal options.[15]

Addition of the twelve Cox properties to the Settlement portfolio meant more numerous and detailed reports of real estate dealings on board agendas and required that Revel spend even more time on property matters. As complexities increased, the board embarked on a course of long-range planning. The five-ten-year planning committee, chaired by Catherine Hyslop, weighed whether to use the services of a professional management firm, to continue with in-house management, or to try a combination of the two. In October 1994, the board voted to employ a management firm, and the following spring Revel began changing over to "property management by the firm of Kiemle and Hagood, as directed by the board."[16]

In fact, a hybrid arrangement evolved. With the administrator's oversight, Kiemle-Hagood serves as a leasing agent and manages the Settlement's full-service leases. Under such leases, the firm contracts out and oversees all maintenance and repairs in a building, thus freeing the administrator from time-consuming detail. The administrator himself continues to negotiate land leases and building leases in which the lessee assumes all maintenance, taxes, and insurance.[17]

Over the years, the Settlement Deed of Trust had been subject to legal interpretation, as when the board sought to expand real estate holdings beyond the downtown business core. The board's 1994 long-range planning committee sought another interpretation of the Deed of Trust as it related to investments. Whereas Mr. Hutton had specified real estate investments for his private corporation, the Settlement as a public charity was no longer so limited. The committee dissolved in January 1995, and in his February financial report to the board Revel included for the first time the category of Stock Portfolio, then valued at $60,617.50. In essence, the board now administered a charitable trust for the benefit of the children living at the Settlement and as such operated under the "prudent man rule," a statute authorizing a fiduciary

> to acquire and retain every kind of property, real, personal or mixed, and every kind of investment specifically including but not by way of limitation, debentures and other corporate obligations, and stocks, preferred or common, which men of prudence, discretion and intelligence acquire for their own account.

The board continued its policy of maintaining a cash reserve of at least $500,000 to cover a one-year operating budget for the campus; this 1990s interpretation of the Deed of Trust allowed diversity in assets and flexibility in their management.[18]

Executive committee members had long attended Financial Advisory Committee meetings, but after taking the initiative and forming a budget committee in 1969, the board women took increasing interest in financial operations. Meanwhile, as Spokane banks were absorbed by larger regional banks, their officers became more remote from local interests and less committed to serving on the Financial Advisory Committee. As early as 1983, difficulty securing a quorum sent Margaret Cowles to search the bylaws for the committee's meeting requirements. By 1987 the problem was so severe that the board sought legal grounds for selecting advisers other than the "presidents of three of the principal banks in the City" mandated in the Deed of Trust.[19] These two trends met in the early nineties and became the catalyst for a significant change in the Settlement's committee structure.

In 1993 the board voted to reform the Financial Advisory Committee into two separate bodies. Accordingly, the bylaw revision of 1995 created both a Financial Consulting Committee of bankers and elected officials and a board finance committee, the latter to "have general supervision of the financial affairs" of the Settlement, confer with the Financial Consulting Committee when appropriate, and prepare the annual budget. The Financial Consulting Committee seldom met, but the administrator asked advice from individual members in making investment and real estate decisions.[20]

In 1919 Levi Hutton said he intended the Settlement to last 250 years, established mandates to keep it strong financially, and left its future to a twenty-seven member board of trustees. Eighty years later, nearly a third of the way to his goal, his faith and foresight had proved themselves. By December 31, 1999, the value of the Settlement's net assets stood at $12,137,430.[21]

Board and administrator together had managed the Settlement's in-city holdings judiciously, and in 1988, they completed a five-year capital improvement program of renovating and redecorating the campus buildings. In their stewardship of the Spokane Valley property, they remained alert to threats of encroachment. They rebuffed developers who continued to covet the acreage and neighbors who wanted to buy small parcels to enlarge their own homesites; they denied requests for easements and a proposal to build a nine-hole private golf course. In the late nineties a neighbor did encroach on half an acre of Settlement property, setting off a round of negotiations to determine equitable compensation. The incident also led the board to order a complete survey of property lines, installation of adequate signage along the boundaries, and investment in an enlarged and updated security system.[22]

The greatest threat to property came from county plans to build a road through the heart of the campus. When West Valley School District 143 had sought to buy twenty acres for a middle school in 1969, ensuing board debates had shown rare disagreement with the Financial Advisory Committee's advice to sell. Those in favor of the sale had pointed to a plan to extend Wellesley Avenue as a four-lane highway through Settlement property, which they contended would lessen the land's value in the future.[23] The women declined to sell. But twenty years later a similar situation arose.

Early warning came in 1986. The county proposed to change the agricultural zoning to commercial in the area encompassing the Settlement and "to develop a new arterial through the campus near the Administration Building." Although nothing came of that idea, two years later, developers again sought a zone change in order to build a convenience store at the corner of Argonne Road and Upriver Drive, and the regional committee studying ways to relieve traffic congestion officially recommended building a four-lane road through the campus. Bob Revel and others succeeded in thwarting the rezone. The following spring the Spokane County Library system signed a letter of intent to buy the land at the intersection in question but lacked sufficient funds. Because a library would be an asset for Settlement and valley children alike and because it would also protect against commercial intrusion, the board reviewed the legalities of the situation and voted to "provide $10,000 to the Spokane County Library as a restricted gift for the acquisition of the site." The library that rose on that corner held public meetings when planning resumed for the future of the surrounding area. Board members attended some of these meetings, including a divisive one in the summer of 1993 at which the citizens traffic advisory committee voted six to five to include Settlement land "as part of a 'study corridor'" for a major arterial.[24]

In searching for means to combat this latest threat, board members looked back to 1972 when the six acres containing cottages and administration building had been placed on the state and national registers of historic places. Now they launched efforts to include the rest of the acreage in the designations, and by November 1993, both state and federal preservation groups had "conceptually approved." At a valley traffic-planning meeting early that month, Kit Garrett, the local historic preservation officer, presented the case for removing the campus from the road plan that became known as the Argonne Road bypass. The issue moved to the county commissioners. Revel and the board president, Jo Ann Nielsen, planned to meet with Commissioner Skip Chilberg, who wanted to broker a compromise, but on May 3, 1994, with Chilberg dissenting, the commissioners voted to accept the plan that would bisect the campus.[25]

The Washington State Advisory Council on Historic Preservation met in Spokane on May 20, and even though the chair of the county commission, Steve Hasson, sat on the Settlement's Financial Advisory Committee, he spoke strongly against extending the original six-acre historic designation. Despite his objection, the council approved the extension; its decision was forwarded to the National Park Service with the recommendation that the entire Settlement be included on the national register. Any plans for an arterial through the campus would now be subject to a federal review process. Mrs. Nielsen said later that the elevated roadway running close to the cottages "would have been a nightmare." As it happened, anticipated traffic congestion developed away from Argonne Road, following building growth and suburban sprawl farther east.[26]

Jo Ann Nielsen was elected to the Settlement board in 1984. A native of Montana, she graduated from Montana State College in 1958, and with a graduate degree in nursing she later taught in its School of Nursing in Billings. She and the architect Benson Nielsen met there, married in September 1963, and moved to Spokane a year later. While raising their two sons she volunteered widely in the community; Hamblen Park Presbyterian Church benefited from her many talents, as did Ferris High School, where she continued to volunteer several years after the boys had graduated. Her great strength, ability, empathy, and nurse's diagnostic approach to problems served the Settlement well during her three terms as president and afterward. "Of all the members on the board," a colleague later said, "Jo Ann Nielsen is our mainstay."[27]

The Argonne Road bypass struggle marked her presidential terms. Three other events of considerable magnitude occurred as well—the decision to replace all the windows in campus buildings, the Settlement's Diamond Jubilee celebration, and the retirement of Robert Revel.

Fundraising for the window project and installation carried over into Carol Wendle's term, but budgeting and planning were well under way in the autumn of 1995. When campus heating costs soared in the early eighties the board considered window replacement, but the cost had seemed astronomical. A decade later, however, the deteriorating condition of seventy-five-year-old window casements and frames demanded action. The board selected double-hung windows manufactured by the Pella Company to match the original windows. "Made of wood, clad with aluminum," they did not conflict with preservation guidelines; Spokane's Historic Preservation Office praised the board for taking "the historic significance of the Hutton Settlement" into account in planning.[28]

The Pella Company donated $23,550 to the $350,000 project, and the company-related Kuyper Foundation, another $5,000. Seed money from a recent $100,000 bequest from May Gibson, who had lived at the Settlement from 1926 to 1931, initiated fundraising on a scale never before considered by the board. The pursuit of grants netted $100,000 from Spokane's Comstock Foundation, and mail solicitation produced gratifying returns. *Tower Topics* reported on the "Window of Opportunity" fund drive in the spring of 1996: "Contributions ranging from five to thousands of dollars poured in, each gift as important as the next. . . . In just three months, enough money was raised to . . . begin scheduling installation for later this spring." One $20,000 gift had come from a Minnesota friend of Sam and Patty Skogsbergh. Former Settlement residents responded generously to replace windows that as children they had so hated to wash, and in an inspired move, Bob Revel convinced Jim Taylor to buy the window he had frequently sneaked out through in the 1940s.[29]

Window replacement, undoubtedly the largest single renovation of campus buildings to date, proceeded one building at a time, reaching the administration building in mid-June 1996. A celebration to dedicate the windows took place on September 8. In her president's report for that year, Carol Wendle praised the "approximately 170 donors [who] generously contributed to this vital project" and cited one board member in particular, Regina Manser, and Bob Revel as "invaluable in fund raising efforts."[30]

Milestones in Settlement history had been celebrated publicly since November 1969 when an estimated 1,500 to 2,000 guests attended an open house to commemorate the Settlement's founding fifty years before. Community supporters sent flowers that day, and the El Katif Shriners band provided entertainment. The Crescent Department Store had heralded the event with a window display of mining and other artifacts related to Levi Hutton's early years. In July 1979, the board staged a weekend of events to mark the sixtieth anniversary. On Saturday there were games, picture taking, and a barbecue for alumni and friends; a public open house followed on Sunday afternoon. The two-day format was used ten years later to observe the seventieth as well, and board members were admonished to "wear their reunion t-shirts on both days [with] either white pants or a white skirt." Sam Skogsbergh called it a remarkable event highlighted by a wealth of intergenerational sharing. Hutton kids had pitched in to help with "general 'sprucing up' . . . and the Settlement never looked lovelier!" The children were rewarded with a pizza party later.[31]

The Diamond Jubilee in 1995, a major and emotional two-day affair, drew on the earlier celebrations. On Saturday, former residents from every decade were among several hundred guests welcomed by President Nielsen; each came "with different memories and for different reasons" but united by a common bond— "We have all been drawn together because of L. W. Hutton's dream." She added,

> Somewhere Mr. Hutton is smiling today. He is smiling because these very buildings are standing just as he had dreamed they would and that they continue to provide shelter, sustenance, love, and nurturing just as he had hoped. He is smiling because his Masonic brothers are present . . . and he is smiling because his children have come home, safe and sound, for a family reunion.

The Masonic brothers opened the 1918 cornerstone that day and replaced it along with a copper box containing late-twentieth-century artifacts and statements from Levi's children present that day, including the first, Baby Jane Wiese.[32]

In December 1986, President Donna Greenough had formed a task force to address the next change of administrators. That ad hoc committee included Margaret Cowles and Evelyn Morgan, both board members when Charles Gonser reached retirement age; not surprisingly at its initial meeting the group noted that

Bob Revel would be eligible to retire within ten years. After two subsequent task force meetings, the board accepted its recommendation to hire "an assistant administrator who will concentrate efforts on campus administration." The executive search firm engaged at the urging of the personnel committee quickly encountered traditional board parsimony in the matter of salary for the new position and advised offering a minimum of $35,000 annually. By November 1987, applicants had been winnowed to two who interviewed that month. In December Michael Butler was hired at a salary of $39,000 and the agreement that he could act as consultant to the agency he would be leaving in Cowlitz County.[33]

Michael Butler was born in Longview, Washington, in 1950. After graduating from R. A. Long High School there, he went on to the city's Lower Columbia Community College. He then worked in the local paper mill for about a year until, as he put it, he realized that he did not want to carry a lunch bucket all his life. He enrolled at Portland State University and completed a degree in sociology in 1973. He immediately went to work as a counselor at the Toutle River Boys Ranch, in the shadow of Mount St. Helens.[34]

Butler said that in this entry-level position he had done everything from admission and supervision to being "watchman": he "would counsel boys. . . . go pick them up when . . . they'd run away," and just do whatever was needed. The program of the boys ranch centered on reforestation—planting trees, building trails, fighting forest fires, and the like—and boys were placed there by the juvenile court. Within four years, the board promoted him to executive director, making him at age twenty-seven, by his estimation, the youngest head of a delinquent child care agency. State oversight took him frequently to Olympia. The most exceptional trip came in early 1981. The eruption of Mount St. Helens destroyed the boys ranch; securing federal emergency funds to rebuild depended on an operating contract with the state, but Butler had to fight to retain state funding for a facility that no longer existed and that he "was operating . . . out of a motel."[35]

Butler's experience in the financial arena along with his professional success at the boys ranch impressed the Settlement board. Implicit in his hiring was that he would succeed Robert Revel. In the meantime, he worked with campus administration, staff, and programs.[36]

Even before the board had decided to bring in an assistant administrator, the pension committee had worked countless hours with legal counsel and two members of the Financial Advisory Committee to craft a retirement plan for Revel, which the board accepted in January 1984. Simply put, the Board Ladies had created a tax-sheltered annuity for him that protected Dorothy Revel too. President Marilyn Stocker spoke for all: "We are so glad that this plan has been implemented. It has been long overdue." Euphoria evaporated with the 1986 Tax Reform Law; it forced the Settlement to drop the annuity in 1989. The pension committee reconvened in June 1991; after considering the cost of available plans and in light of the Settlement's current financial position and obligation to maintain operating reserves, its members recommended "that no retirement plan be adopted by the Hutton Settlement Board of Trustees at this time." The board accepted the recommendation, postponing further the matter of an equitable retirement package for Revel.[37]

Early in 1994, Revel set July 1, 1995, as the date for his retirement and requested that a committee work with him for the next year "to ensure that an orderly transition takes place." Negotiating a retirement agreement with him became the task of the personnel committee; not until six months after he formally retired could the committee report that "the retirement offer made to Mr. Revel has been accepted, finalizing the work that began in 1983." The board approved this package as well as a contract for him to act as a consultant to the Settlement. In retirement he continued to oversee some construction projects and the lease of property in Hawaii; he and Dorothy continued to direct the Hutton 4-H club. The Revel era at the Settlement ended in the spring of 1997, when he did not renew the consulting contract. He and Dorothy severed connections with 4-H and the sheep program; the flock was liquidated, with plans to resume the program in the future but to buy rather than breed the Settlement's own animals.[38]

Bob and Dorothy Revel's contributions to the Settlement were enormous and varied, but their focus was always on the children. Board members expressed admiration for their hard work and devotion, which were epitomized in the lamb enterprise and stock shows. Margaret Cowles said, "Twice a year at ring-side, there they are—Bob with his rancher's hat on and Dorothy with her hands full of blue ribbons." Carol Wilson recalled going to the Junior Livestock Show soon after joining the board,

> When I got there, a judge had just made a rather critical comment to one of the Hutton children. . . . [Revel] put his arm around the child and said exactly the words of support and encouragement you would hope all fathers would say, and pretty soon, a smile replaced the tears.

The women respected his astute handling of Settlement business affairs but identified his "greatest gift" as "his genuine love for the children." His successor cited his commitment to Levi Hutton's dreams for the children; Butler doubted that Mr. Hutton would see the Settlement in 1995 as "any different than what he planned" and credited Revel's caring administration for sustaining that vision.[39]

The board appointed Michael Butler administrator designee in July 1994 and formally voted him administrator effective July 1, 1995. He had spent seven and a half years in a dichotomous role: an assistant administrator who had no authority in the downtown office and was excluded from real estate and property matters unrelated to valley operations, he had tried to do as the board wanted and "concentrate efforts on campus administration."[40] But his had been an awkward situation that made a muddled flow chart.

Butler had operated in something of a limbo between Revel and the resident director, Sam Skogsbergh. Revel had perpetuated Charles Gonser's philosophy, albeit with less aversion to social workers. During his tenure, the Settlement had gradually expanded programs, and by the mid-1980s, the board was amenable to augmenting those and adding professionally trained staff. The Cox bequest made upgrading financially possible.[41]

In Sam Skogsbergh the Settlement had a trained, experienced resident director and a true gem. The longtime campus secretary said, "Everyone loved Sam.... He was quiet and more subdued, and would [play] a practical joke on you, and not smile. . . he had a . . . dry sense of humor"; everyone agreed that "he was wonderful." His popular camping and fishing trips for Hutton kids became legendary. He had arrived in 1977, declared hiring and retaining good personnel to be essential, and in the spring of 1979 added a girls counselor, twenty-four-year-old Mary Jo Lyonnais, who soon proved herself invaluable to board, staff, and children alike.[42]

A Spokane native, Mary Jo was one of eight Catholic siblings raised in St. Aloysius parish near Gonzaga University. In 1972 she graduated from Marycliff High School, a parochial school for girls. She began preparation for a career in social work at Spokane Community College and moved on to Eastern Washington University, where her studies became compelling and exciting for her and tapped into her great compassion and empathy. Her own family having been rent by divorce, she knew that dysfunction "affected every one of the children differently," and now she was "studying things that [she had] been through." She enjoyed her student practicum at Catholic Family Charities, working with adoptions, foster care, counseling, and home visitations. She had never heard of the Hutton Settlement when she responded to an ad for a counselor that Skogsbergh had placed in the newspaper.[43]

She joined the boys counselor on campus to deal with individual needs of children and a wide range of other matters; but counselors' duties were demanding, and their resignations were frequent. In February 1983, the sudden death of boys counselor Steve Mason rocked the Settlement; in his memory the older children planted a golden locust tree to which the board affixed a plaque so that "he will be remembered as being special." Mason was a rare person; six months later his position was still vacant, awaiting someone "willing to give on a twenty-four hour basis and who will look after the place when left second-in-command." In August, Skogsbergh hired Bob Cabeza and said, "He shows a great deal of enthusiasm and doesn't seem to be afraid of long hours and hard work."[44]

In 1987, the board added a recreation director to the campus staff, noting that "his presence is allowing the counselors more case work and individual time with the children." Such terms as *case work,* long associated with social workers and formerly anathema to the board, began to appear in meeting minutes and reports when new ways of working with the children took hold on the campus. The following spring Skogsbergh reported that seven children had "attended the self esteem seminar on March 19th" and that "a behavior modification type of program" was developed for a boy who had long been considered a problem. One of Mike Butler's first actions was to purchase a staff training course on "how to talk so kids will listen and listen so kids will talk." Campus employees, including houseparents, received it gladly. Patsy Gottschalk, editor of *Tower Topics* and self-described jack-of-all-trades, introduced a "Life Skills Program" on campus in which children learned such fundamentals as planning social events and personal shopping. A further change saw Hutton children making use of counseling services offered by Spokane's Community Mental Health Center. Sam Skogsbergh retired July 1, 1992, after fifteen years; he had seen many improvements at the Settlement, but he was still concerned about "the difficulty of hiring good staff to work with the children."[45]

In replacing Skogsbergh, the board chose to ignore Levi Hutton's belief that the post required a man. The women promoted Mary Jo Lyonnais, giving a $26,000 annual salary and changing her title to campus life director. Kay Stipe, president then, acknowledged the "hurdle" of Revel's bias against a woman superintendent; any such board concern went unrecorded. In the thirteen years since her arrival on campus, a number of male counselors had come and gone but Lyonnais had stayed, done her work, and earned a master's degree in social work too. The first woman to direct the campus since Miriam Ritchie sounded very much like her World War II counterpart: "This Thanksgiving we bow our heads and give thanks to God for Levi Hutton, for building such a safe and wonderful home that the Hutton Settlement is for so many children and staff."[46]

When the board women created the post of assistant resident director in 1987 and appointed Lyonnais, she had continued on with her counseling duties. When she became director, she kept her counseling role, even though she stressed the need for on-campus counseling that was increasingly "apparent in the children that currently come to Hutton Settlement." As finances allowed, the board began to add staff, but still she retained her duties as girls counselor. Early in 1993 Butler hired a director of education to oversee such activities as the tutoring program, which in the autumn of 1994 brought twenty-six enthusiastic Gonzaga University students to work with the children. Learning disabilities and behavioral problems such as anger management received attention both on and off the campus. By the midnineties, universities in the region were placing a growing number of practicum students at the Settlement, thereby improving the ratio of children to profession-ally oriented adults on the campus.[47]

The infusion of income from the Cox properties allowed the board to offer Settlement employees better salary and benefit packages, ongoing staff training, and funding to pursue advanced degrees. It had always given monetary Christmas gifts to each worker, and since the early eighties, the personnel committee had sought to give regular salary increases. By the midnineties that committee estab-lished annual cost-of-living adjustments and merit increases. As director, Lyonnais tried to hire well-educated staff who wanted to be at the Settlement and who came with "plans and activities for the children, . . [and] perspective that I didn't have at that young age." By century's end, besides clerical and grounds workers, the campus staff included houseparents, three counselor-case managers and an activities-education director as well as the resident director. As the boys case manager put it, the structure was now in place for "providing the love and nurturing [to let] the children know that we care."[48]

Society had changed over the decades, and so had the family circumstances of children who came to the Hutton Settlement. In working with deprived, neglected, and sometimes abused youngsters who frequently acted out their hurt through defiance, disrespect, and other adverse behavior, the Settlement staff now dealt with problems related to such phenomena as fetal alcohol syndrome and attention deficit disorder and to growing parental use of methamphetamines, crack cocaine, and other illegal drugs. The board, complying with its mandate to accommodate "normal children, mentally and physically, who for some cause are deprived of the advantages of family life," based its early 1990s admissions on a legal interpretation of Mr. Hutton's intent that defined *normal* in a layman's sense rather than on a narrow, technical, medical definition. As the use of such prescription drugs as Ritalin and antidepressants more than doubled among children and adolescents nationwide between 1987 and 1996, the board set limits on what the Settlement could or could not handle in a child's behavior and turned away youngsters who required more than the Settlement could provide.[49]

Although some children did receive prescription medications, the Hutton Settlement was never a clinical treatment center. The staff began to focus on maintaining children's ties with their own families, knowing that regardless of family problems and a parent's actions, "the child still loves that parent." At the same time, they also worked to help the children comprehend that the adult conduct that may have led to their living at the Settlement was not normal parenting behavior.[50]

David Milliken, boys case manager, said that the Settlement aimed to help children build relationships and develop personally. His job meant being available virtually twenty-four hours a day to be the "liaison between the child and the school, the child and the family, the child and the cottage."

> I'm pretty much the advocate there of the child. . . . And along with that, [and] providing these children guidance counseling, I also deal with discipline measures . . . [and] some administrative duties. . . . But for the most part, it's just being that advocate for them—whether it's in Court, whether it's at school, whether it's here at Hutton Settlement.

As Levi Hutton had hoped, his home remained a *home* for children even as its staff became professional.[51]

Houseparents were integral to the program of building relationships. By the 1990s houseparents welcomed new residents on their arrival, helped them get settled, and involved them in some activity related to their main interest—a soccer lover would soon be on a team, for example. Things had changed since the 1930s, when Mr. Gonser would bring new children to campus, assign them to a cottage, and leave them to adjust whenever and however they might. But the Settlement's values remained constant. Houseparents, in short, practiced sound family management, "teaching kids what's important through discipline—teaching them personal responsibility—teaching them [to make] the right choices," in the expectation that they will "come away learning that, 'OK, I know what a healthy family looks like.'"[52]

Mike Butler, the first Settlement administrator to have had experience with another child care agency, moved the campus staff in this new direction that also increased the emphasis on individual counseling. But Sam Skogsbergh had laid the groundwork for this change. He emphasized good family management in the cottages and reinforced it in regular meetings, despite frequent turnover in houseparents. The board rule against hiring houseparents with children was abandoned in 1979; Ted and Lynn Marshall brought a new dimension in family relationship building to the residents of Cottage Two, for, as Skogsbergh reported, "Mrs. Marshall is expecting in February[,] which will provide the girls and the Settlement a unique experience." The resident director hoped "this whole 'adventure' will work out alright. Ted seems very calm about the matter but somebody has to worry." The baby came early and forced a longer hospital stay than usual, but the family was fine and the girls in the cottage were "excited about the baby and took turns going to Sacred Heart Hospital to visit."[53]

The Marshalls' baby was the vanguard of a new group of cottage children; some, in a sense were second-generation Hutton kids, born to houseparents who had themselves lived at the Settlement. In 1988, Nancy Hoyle Skillman returned to the campus along with her husband, Rod, and eighteen-month-old daughter, Kayla, where they served in Cottage Two. That year Teri Barsness Hanson returned with her husband, Tim, and their toddler and took over in Cottage Three. Skogsbergh relished the stability and high level of energy these families brought. In 1992, another alum and his wife, Ron and Kerri Barsness, were named houseparents in Cottage One; two other former residents, Cletis and Pam Croff Hydrick, replaced the Hansons in Cottage Three. Both the Skillmans and Hydricks added children to the campus population in 1993—Christa Jo Skillman, born in March, and Haley Winona Hydrick, in April.[54]

Board members cherished the concept of family on the campus. In 1988 the women had delighted in the fact that two alumnae had "rejoined our Hutton family." Three years earlier a "surrogate Auntie and Grandma" board committee had arranged the Hydricks' wedding reception in the administration building auditorium, and when Cletis reported for basic training in the Air Force, board members welcomed Pam back to live on campus for the duration of his training. He later served at McChord Air Force Base near Tacoma, and Pam completed her Associate of Arts degree in human services at Tacoma Community College. When they returned to Spokane she finished a degree in social work at Eastern Washington University, doing her practicum at the Hutton Settlement. She was named girls counselor in 1995 and remained in that post after they moved from the campus.[55]

Houseparenting, like case managing, is a twenty-four-hour-a-day commitment, five days a week. Housefathers held jobs off campus, so the Settlement salary went to the housemother, but by the mideighties, in recognition of their contribution, housefathers received payment equal to half the mother's salary. Cletis Hydrick's schedule in a typical day resembled the one that Russell Riddell had earlier kept in Cottage Three; but after he saw the boys off to school in the morning Cletis left for an office in downtown Spokane and returned that evening to a household of about fifteen little boys. He outlined his routine:

> I get home around 6:00, and then eat dinner with the kids and do chores. . . . get dinner done and cleaned up, watch a little television or go outside, depending on the weather, and then at 7:00 [enforce] study hour until 8:00. . . . All the Cottages have study hour at the same time. . . . They study 'til eight, and take their showers 8:00-8:30, and then they have until 9:00 to have a snack and watch TV.

A nine o'clock bedtime for younger and ten o'clock for older children ended a very full day. Scheduling of days off depended on the availability of relief houseparents.[56]

The number of houseparent offspring increased through the nineties, and the older ones did their share of house chores just like Hutton kids themselves. Some Settlement rules impinged—such as the no-pet policy—but for the most part both houseparents and their children viewed life on campus positively. Their families lived in separate quarters, but Kayla Skillman, who grew up in Cottage Two, noted the advantage of having eight other girls under the roof, "If I ever got bored, then I'd have someone to play with, and if I needed to talk to someone, then I could talk to someone. Someone more my age." On the other hand, it meant sharing her parents: "But then, some other times . . . [I] didn't get as much time with my mom and dad as I could have."[57]

Her mother agreed, saying that living at Hutton Settlement was "good for my kids": they grew up knowing that people "come from different situations," which meant that her "children are wonderfully rounded. [Their] social skills are above and beyond all the kids in their age [group] just from living with so many kids." She never had to put her youngsters in day care. "Hutton isn't work, it's like our lives, so you get swallowed up by Hutton." Immersion in the Settlement left limited time for friends and relatives beyond the campus. Pam Hydrick cited the houseparents' dilemma of wanting to treat Settlement children "exactly like your own" but failing, and "trying in the cottage, to have fairness. But sometimes the children don't see it that way." These factors contributed to the Hydricks' and Skillmans' decision to move from the campus by the end of the nineties, along with the desire to allow their own children greater freedom—freedom for such things as learning to drive.[58]

Nancy Skillman credits the Skogsberghs with making possible the family-fo-
cused environment that prevailed at the Settlement in the year 2000; as a teenager
there in 1977, she had seen things change when they arrived from Minnesota.

> They loved the kids. They loved the Settlement. Sam loved his job. It was important to
> him. It was important to Patty. . . . I still see [them] today, and they still send my kids
> birthday cards. I remember when I first started working out there, Kayla was . . . a
> year and a half, and she would go over to Patty and just play in the kitchen. Patty—
> she was like the perfect Grandma. Just wonderful.[59]

Sam Skogsbergh also smoothed the way for campus programs by hiring Margie
Hemming as the first full-time campus secretary in 1982. There had been a part-
time position for ten years, but beginning with Hemming, the secretary became
pivotal to every campus operation and a major factor in campus life.

A native of Charlotte, North Carolina, Margie Hemming came to Spokane in
December of 1980, by way of Fairfield, California, and Adak, Alaska; her husband
had recently retired from the navy and was returning home. She worked a short
time for a Spokane insurance company, but after her job was eliminated in the
economic downturn of the early eighties, she answered a newspaper ad for "Secretary with bookkeeping experience," phoned, talked with the resident director, and
agreed to come out for an interview. Seeing the campus for the first time, she
remembered being surprised that none of the buildings looked like "Little Orphan
Annie's house." She and Skogsbergh liked each other immediately, and she got
the job.[60]

Consensus holds that her "office is the main place that everything happens,"
and Margie Hemming wore many hats besides that of secretary-bookkeeper. David
Milliken said that when the bus drivers drop off the children at the ad building
after school "the kids . . . come into the office. . . . They want to talk with Margie,
our secretary, and check the mail . . . they want to see what's going on." For everyone who lives or works on campus, the secretary's office is where to "find out what
[you] need to know. And so it's the hub of everything."[61]

Asked to describe a typical day, she said,

> You know, each day is really different depending on what time of year it is. . . . The
> secretary here has to be somebody that can do ten things at one time. . . . The
> children come home from school, they're asking you questions, the phone is ringing,
> you've got all these papers on your desk . . . and it can get very harried, and so you
> have to learn to maintain your control . . . [but] you do not have the opportunity to get
> bored, because there's always something to do.

She handles a myriad of forms relating to new residents as she works with counselors on referrals and applications. When newcomers arrive, "I am pretty much the
first person they deal with, . . . [I] bring them into the reception room, and they
meet with the counselors" and houseparents, who take them to their assigned

cottages. The office computer expedites her tracking expenditures for food, clothing, allowances, school fees, medical, dental, and activities—in short, everything that is spent on the children.[62]

The Hutton Settlement children themselves entered the computer age in 1983 thanks to three 1960s alums. Charles and Dana Finley Miller, who had married on leaving the Settlement, donated two computers and software programs for math and reading. Dick Hamilton both pleased and greatly relieved the non-computer-oriented board when he "agreed to come out to teach the children how to use the computer." Computer use in the schools had increased, and the Hutton kids were excited to have equipment available at home. The board bought additional software, and in 1988 added two "state-of-the-art Apple II computers." Not until 1998 did each cottage finally have a computer and a printer, the computers on loan from the West Valley School District and the printers bought with specially designated donations.[63]

In 1984 the Board Ladies set a goal "to get to know our children better." By virtue of voting on admissions they knew all the Hutton kids in the abstract, but individual involvement with them varied. On-campus staff replaced the women of the education committee in teacher conferences and academic advising, eliminating one of the strongest traditional board ties with the children. The education committee continued to review the children's progress in school, however, to encourage remedial measures where needed and private lessons for any child who showed talent and interest in a particular area. Cottage committees still redecorated and kept the houses in good repair and the pianos tuned; they were welcome at staff meetings where discussion kept them abreast of children's activities, needs, and desires. Other established committee functions that brought board and children together included directing such things as the biennial tea for West Valley teachers, providing lunch at the Junior Livestock Show, helping stage the campus picnic each summer, and assisting with the Christmas programs.[64]

A long-planned landmark board event on campus took place on June 7, 1980. Spurred in part by the need to meet the IRS public support test, the women staged an auction of Settlement antiques and collectibles amassed over six decades. Oversight and planning rested with the administration building committee, but the auction literally involved everyone—the Skogsberghs, houseparents, children, and the entire board. Cottage committees combed attics for memorabilia to add to campus furniture and implements and to articles genteelly scavenged from the Hutton Building. Items in the auction catalog ranged from artwork, a wooden butter churn, books, silver, and linens from the Hutton home to a stereopticon with thirteen cards and a fifty-five-inch xylophone. The Peerless Harvard dental chair from the old infirmary tempted Settlement alumni who came to bid. Board women spent enormous amounts of time and effort on the auction, but they considered it very fruitful. Run by professional auctioneers and well attended, it produced net receipts of $25,490.73 and the public relations bonus of bringing many people to the campus for the first time.[65]

Board members continued to follow the fortunes of former residents, and summertime reunions maintained ties with alumni from decades past. The board took great interest in the jobs that these young people pursued and occasionally bent the rules to allow those bound for college or vocational training to live on campus over the summer. The Gulf War once more put Hutton young men in harm's way in 1991; board members wrote to them while they were gone and in tribute to their service wrapped 200 yards of yellow ribbon in bows around the trees bordering the campus lane. When David Smith, a Hutton kid of the eighties, returned from Saudi Arabia, a welcoming party greeted him at the airport, and the board hosted a dinner party in his honor.[66]

In 1987, Robert Baker, a resident during the depression years, donated $10,000 to establish an alumni scholarship fund for post-high school education. The funds, invested in tax-exempt stocks, bonds, and mutual funds, grew; in 1989, Baker gave another $10,000 and challenged the board to match it. On December 31, 1999, the scholarship fund totaled $275,992.95. Anyone who had graduated from West Valley High School while living at the Settlement was eligible to apply. A board committee oversaw distribution of money for vocational training and academic or professional education, including for "board, room, travel, and individual expenses as well as tuition, books, and supplies." The first two grants, made in the spring of 1988, went to a student at Gonzaga University and to one attending a technical school in Phoenix.[67]

During the 1980s and 1990s, the population at the Settlement remained near thirty. Children admitted in those decades included many who had lived with parental drug addiction and in abject poverty. Others came from such traumatic situations as those of the brother and sister whose mother had been living in destitution and "in hiding from her third husband for several years, in fear for her life." The Settlement provided "stability over and beyond that of the usual foster-care situation"; more than a few Hutton kids had moved through a series of foster homes before arriving on the campus. Although the state Department of Social and Health Services gave priority to foster home placement, it now made referrals to the Settlement as well. As in the past, children were also referred by those who held custody—grandparents, aunts, uncles, or a parent who could no longer cope.[68]

Parental custody laws still allowed parents to take children from the Settlement for whatever reason, even though they may be thriving there. Removal of children caused considerable anguish for board members. As one expressed it, "Lots of times they just want them home so they get their support checks . . . or the parents are more needy than the children, and the children end up at home taking care of the parents. It's a vicious circle—so discouraging." All felt it "hard to 'let them go' and know they are returning to a sad and deplorable life again," and by 1999 most agreed that educating parents to allow and encourage their children to stay at the Settlement through high school graduation was a major challenge.[69]

The board aggressively sought new admissions, and sibling groups remained a priority. The six Metreveli children came to the Settlement after having lived at St. Joseph's Children's Home in Spokane for some time. Their mother, in poor health and unable to care for them, wanted them to stay together; as she later said, "I knew they had a right to a decent life and I couldn't give it to them." St. Joseph's closed in 1980, and the children moved to the Settlement that fall; on their weekends away from the campus, they took turns staying in town with their mother.[70]

Mrs. Metreveli was one parent who wanted her children to stay at the Hutton Settlement through high school, where they were active in school activities. Marianne, for example, played soccer and played clarinet in the West Valley band, which in her junior year went to San Diego to perform and visited Disneyland. All the Metrevelis took part in the 4-H club and the lamb project. Board members relished the story of Jimmy Metreveli's deciding once, when a little boy, to run away and take his lamb with him; the animal was nearly as large as he and they did not go far. They followed the siblings with interest beyond their campus years and were delighted that Marianne later used an alumni scholarship when she returned to school to prepare for a career as a personal trainer and health and fitness consultant.[71]

Hutton kids in the 1960s had been limited to only one weekend a month away from the campus. During the next thirty years campus personnel and the board recognized the importance of relationships beyond the campus. By the end of the century, children frequently spent time with family members

> often times every other weekend. And in some cases, [for] kids who aren't able to visit parents—we have . . . what we call a friendship family—[people] in the community who serve as kind of surrogate parent[s] who bring the children into their home for the weekends—just as a way to make those connections outside of Hutton.[72]

An integral part of the Settlement program today, the friendship family concept had its origins in the 4-H activities of the sixties. Dorothy Revel recalled:

> We always had a wonderful camaraderie with everybody in the sheep business. They loved our children, and Bob and I always went everyplace with them. . . . We had a lot of friends, and that's how a lot of our children got their friendship families. . . . And then our kids always were winners, so they always stood out. . . . [People] would come up and ask . . . could they have them for a day, and take them to dinner, and—you know, something like that.

Board women embraced the idea of friendship families, provided there were proper screening and safeguards to prevent "the friendship family [from] interfering with the real family relationship." By 1983 they had called on Patsy Gottschalk to draft formal policy and procedures governing the program, which had grown to the point where "just about everyone had a friendship family. . . . [and] a place to stay over Thanksgiving."[73]

Friendship families came from groups other than the lamb fraternity. Many were members of the Millwood Presbyterian Church and others were valley neighbors. These ties often endured, as in the case of Debbie Finley; her friendship mother, Mary Floyd, remained part of her life after Debbie left the Settlement, hosting her wedding and later accepting Debbie's children as her own grandchildren.[74]

Weekly church attendance remained mandatory throughout the last two decades of the century, and Hutton kids with no congregation of their own went to Millwood Presbyterian. In the 1980s, Marilyn McIntosh, a congregation stalwart, connected with the Metrevelis in the friendship family program. Marianne Metreveli cited "getting to be with Herb and Marilyn McIntosh" as one of the good things in Settlement life.

> Their daughter would pick me up for Church, and . . . one Christmas they asked which kid didn't have a family to go to, and it just happened to be me. . . . And so I just got lucky, and I got to spend Christmas with them, and then it just developed from there. I got to [spend] breaks a lot of the times, and then it became holidays, and then when I graduated, they really worked at staying in touch with me.

She added that when she married Eric Taylor in 1998, at Millwood Presbyterian Church, Herb McIntosh "walked me down the aisle, and so they've been a part of my life."[75]

The McIntoshes did in fact play a part in the lives of all the Metrevelis and other Hutton kids as well, but they took pains never to supplant the children's own parents. They simply offered friendship, Marilyn said: "They come to Church, they're with us, it's their time to do their thing, and what we can share in activities and things is what we do, just as an extra-curricular activity." The McIntoshes lived adjacent to the campus on the north. She volunteered at the Settlement, and they not only served as a friendship family but also hired Settlement boys to do chores on their property—stack wood or "haul hay for us and put it in the barn. Whenever it needed to be done, I'd just call . . . [and ask], 'Do any of the boys want to work?' And Sam . . . [would] see who was available." She had high regard for Skogsbergh, who even recruited her for a few emergency stints in the cottages as backup housemother.[76]

Friendship families stand in a long line of people and organizations who have supported Levi Hutton's enterprise. Husbands of board members constitute another group who contributed in no small way to the good of the Settlement. The men made donations in kind and in cash, backed their wives' work on behalf of the Settlement, and supported it with their own time and talent as well. They faithfully attended events ranging from picnics and Christmas programs to annual livestock shows and often filled the role of master of ceremonies at Settlement functions. Following the precedent set by Eric Johnston at early thirties' Founder's Day dinners, Robert Brown was the first to preside at an

Achievement Dinner. Haydn Morgan's rich Welch baritone highlighted many Christmas programs; Clinton Corliss was a mainstay of Settlement tours in the Idaho mining country; and Tom Hyslop always supported the children at the Junior Livestock Show.

For decades, before the availability of health insurance, board members' husbands in the medical and dental communities had been involved with the care of Settlement children. In the late 1960s Dr. Fred Grant persuaded the local dental association to resume the lapsed practice of giving reduced-fee or pro bono dental services. Beginning with D. R. Glasgow in the late 1920s, attorney-husbands had constituted a legal resource pool for board and administrators; none contributed more to the Settlement than Herbert Hamblen. Although his firm received fees for extended work such as that in the continual bouts with the Internal Revenue Service, Hamblen himself donated untold hours of legal work, carried the Settlement's banner in the state legislature, and served on a number of ad hoc board committees and task forces. Ben Nielsen contributed the architectural work required for the window replacement project. In 1994, Bernard (Kop) Kopczynski supervised the Settlement swimming pool renovation without compensation; his construction company played a major role in the campus five-year capital improvement program in the mid-1980s.[77]

As the twentieth century drew to a close, community groups continued to donate events tickets for Settlement children and to provide Christmas parties and entertainments much as they always had. Life on the campus incorporated changes, yet its patterns remained much as they always had. The board had debated long and hard about giving allowances to Hutton kids and permitting them to hold jobs off campus, but both had become routine. Weekly allowances were hardly extravagant; in 1990 they ranged from $.60 per week for those in the primary grades to $2.50 for high school seniors. Settlement teenagers found summer jobs through a federally funded program known as SPEEDY (Summer Program for the Employment, Education and Development of Youth). Younger children could take part in activities that individual board members brought to the campus, such as the instructional sewing sessions arranged by Sharon Cortner in conjunction with the Women of Rotary.[78]

Throughout the year traditional campus recreations, such as sledding on the hill behind the cottages, were augmented by activities of the eighties and nineties—such as in-line skating and skateboarding. When Spokane became obsessed with a passion for running, the Hutton Settlement was captivated as well, and Hutton kids competed as far afield as Coulee Dam. But Spokane's own Bloomsday event remained the most important on their running calendar. This annual "12 kilometer road race/fun run" attracted upwards of 50,000 entrants, from world-class runners to recreational joggers.[79]

Unlikely as it may seem, Bloomsday presented a late-century cohort of Hutton kids an opportunity to know Margaret Cowles as generations before them had.

One remembered her this way:

> She used to run Bloomsday and bring her running shoes. We adored her. She was very approachable. You could tell that she really loved children. . . . When you saw her, you knew you could go up and hug her. She was our height. . . . We had a lot of respect for her. . . . I think just her always going after Bloomsday, and being the oldest runner reminded us that we could do anything that we put our minds to.[80]

Not all board members took as personal a role in the children's lives as some of their prewar predecessors had, but they still encouraged aspiration to higher goals and greater accomplishment.

For eighty years, bonds of sisterhood had sustained a unique volunteer enterprise; work in common cause had forged cherished and enduring friendships. At century's end the Board Ladies still found the greatest satisfaction of their stewardship in the happiness and success of the children. They took great pleasure in attending or playing a role in an alumni wedding, in awarding scholarships, and in learning of later employment and career successes. They took genuine pride in the children's accomplishments from winning ribbons and championships at stock shows, participating in sports and cheerleading, to earning membership in the National Honor Society and becoming an Eagle Scout.[81] Above all, they delighted in seeing children flourish in a stable environment, knowing that the Hutton Settlement remained the safe haven that Levi Hutton had created.

Notes

Preface

1. For the definitive history of the Hercules Mine, see the excellent account by John Fahey, *The Days of the Hercules* (Moscow: University of Idaho Press, 1978).

2. Spokane *Daily Chronicle,* January 20, 1909. The newspaper listed the names of the city's millionaires on its front page, followed by those of men worth a half or a quarter of a million.

3. Cletis Hydrick (resident, 1970–81), statement for Settlement 75th anniversary time capsule, July 1994, Hutton Settlement papers, Eastern Washington State Historical Society archives, Northwest Museum of Arts and Culture, Spokane.

Chapter 1

1. Levi Hutton to "Any and all interested," June 28, 1919, statement in Settlement cornerstone (quotation), copy in Hutton Settlement papers, Eastern Washington State Historical Society archives, Northwest Museum of Arts and Culture (NMAC); N. W. Durham, *History of the City of Spokane and Spokane County, Washington: From Its Earliest Settlement to the Present Time* (Spokane: S. J. Clarke Publishing, 1912), p. 374.

2. Murray Morgan, *Puget's Sound: A Narrative of Early Tacoma and the Southern Sound* (Seattle: University of Washington Press, 1979), p. 192; Carlos A. Schwantes, *Railroad Signatures across the Pacific Northwest* (Seattle: University of Washington Press, 1993), p. 58.

3. Transcript of Charles Gonser statement to Hutton Settlement board, n.d., Hutton Settlement papers, NMAC; LH cornerstone statement (quotation).

4. Gonser statement to Settlement board, John Fahey interview with Charles Gonser, February 21, 1972, copy in author's possession; Lucille Johnson interview with Charles Gonser, 1964, oral history archives, NMAC.

5. LH cornerstone statement (quotation); Fahey–Gonser interview, February 21, 1972; untitled fact sheet, Hutton Settlement papers.

6. Durham, *History of Spokane*, p. 376; John Fahey, *Inland Empire: D. C. Corbin and Spokane* (Seattle: University of Washington Press, 1965), pp. 174 and 175 (quotations).

7. Fahey–Gonser interview, February 21, 1972; Fahey, *The Days of the Hercules,* p. 27 (quotation).

8. Powers, Dorothy R., *Heritage from Heroes* (Spokane: Fairmount Memorial Association, 1993), p. 188.

9. Hutton did not like his first name. His wife and friends called him Al; for business purposes, he preferred L. W. Hutton. The board and staff of the Hutton Settlement always referred to and addressed him as Mr. Hutton. Historically, Spokane has known him as Levi Hutton.

10. Benjamin H. Kizer, "May Arkwright Hutton," *Pacific Northwest Quarterly,* Vol. 57 (April 1966), p. 49 (first quotation); Powers, *Heritage from Heroes,* p. 187 (second quotation); Debra E. Lish, "Aspiring to Eminence: The Lives of May and Al Hutton," Ph.D. dissertation (University of Idaho, 1999), p. 36; Patricia Voeller Horner, "May Arkwright Hutton: Suffragist and Politician," in *Women in Pacific Northwest History: An Anthology,* edited by Karen J. Blair (Seattle: University of Washington Press, 1988), p. 27.

11. Spokane *Daily Chronicle,* October 6, 1915; for Arkwright's various names, see the will of Mary Arkwright Hutton and the deed for Idaho property in the name of Mamie Arkwright in Hutton Settlement papers.

12. Lish, "Aspiring to Eminence," p. 14; MH quoted in Horner, "May Arkwright Hutton," p. 30; see also May Hutton papers, NMAC.

13. Lish, "Aspiring to Eminence," p. 12; Horner, "May Arkwright Hutton," p. 25.

14. Horner, "May Arkwright Hutton," p. 27.

15. NP pamphlet quoted in Lucille Fargo, "Mrs. Hercules" (typescript, n.d.), Spokane Public Library, p. 28; Horner, "May Arkwright Hutton," p. 27.

16. MH to William E. Borah, September 28, 1909; the letter was read aloud during Louis Livingston interview with Charles Gonser, March 6, 1973, Hutton Settlement papers.

17. James W. Montgomery, *Liberated Woman: A Life of May Arkwright Hutton* (Fairfield, Wash.: Ye Galleon Press, 1985), pp. 14 and 28; Horner, "May Arkwright Hutton," p. 27.

18. Montgomery, *Liberated Woman,* p. 29; Fahey, *The Days of the Hercules,* pp. 22–24.

19. Spokane *Spokesman-Review,* May 5, 1968 (first quotation); Bob Briley interview with Gonser, December 3, 1974, oral history archives (second quotation), NMAC.

20. Fahey, *The Days of the Hercules,* pp. 1, 27 (first quotation), 28, and 29; Johnson–Gonser interview, 1964 (last quotation).

21. Fahey, *The Days of the Hercules,* p. 35.

22. Ibid., p. 36 (quotation); Grace Roffey Pratt, "The Great-hearted Huttons of the Coeur d'Alenes," *Montana, the Magazine of Western History,* Vol. 17 (Spring 1967), p. 30.

23. Lish, "Aspiring to Eminence," p. 54; Fahey, *The Days of the Hercules,* p. 37.

24. Fahey, *The Days of the Hercules,* p. 37.

25. Ibid., pp. 29, 39.

26. Pratt, "The Great-hearted Huttons," p. 24; Kizer, "May Arkwright Hutton," p. 54; Fahey, *The Days of the Hercules,* pp. 41 and 50 (quotation).

27. Fahey, *The Days of the Hercules,* pp. 104 and 316.

28. Horner, "May Arkwright Hutton," p. 27; Pratt, "The Great-hearted Huttons," p. 31. May Hutton's novel is now a highly prized collector's item.

29. Horner, "May Arkwright Hutton," p. 27 (first quotation); Fahey, *The Days of the Hercules,* p. 215 (second quotation).

30. MH to Mrs. Thomas Follett, November 28, 1908, the letter was read aloud in Livingston–Gonser interview, March 6, 1973.

31. John Fahey, *Shaping Spokane: Jay P. Graves and His Times* (Seattle: University of Washington Press, 1994), pp. 37–39.

32. Fahey, *The Days of the Hercules*, pp. 217 and 218; Livingston–Gonser interview, March 6, 1973. Three stories were later added to the Hutton Building and the residential floor was converted to commercial use.

33. Kizer, "May Arkwright Hutton," p. 55.

34. LH quoted in Livingston–Gonser interview, March 6, 1973.

35. Pratt, "The Great-hearted Huttons," p. 25; Horner, "May Arkwright Hutton," p. 28; MH quoted in Horner, p. 28.

36. Horner, "May Arkwright Hutton," pp. 28 and 29.

37. Cora Eaton, treasurer, quoted in Horner, p. 31. May Hutton later converted the Political Equality League into the Non-Partisan League, which supported the Democratic party's candidates.

38. Ibid., p. 33.

39. Ibid., p. 35.

40. Fahey, *The Days of the Hercules*, p. 223 (first quotation); Pratt, "The Great-hearted Huttons," p. 27 (second quotation).

41. Horner, "May Arkwright Hutton," p. 39 (first quotation); Pratt, "The Great-hearted Huttons," pp. 29 (second quotation) and 30.

42. MH to George W. Fuller, May 29, 1912, May Hutton papers (first quotation); Kizer, "May Arkwright Hutton," p. 54 (second quotation); Otto Wilson, *Fifty Years' Work with Girls, 1882–1933* (Alexandria, Va.: National Florence Crittenton Mission, 1939), p. 450; Montgomery, *Liberated Woman*, p. 98 (third quotation).

43. Jonathan Edwards, *An Illustrated History of Spokane County, State of Washington* (Spokane: W. H. Lever, 1900), p. 244; Kizer, "May Arkwright Hutton," p. 54; MH quoted in Fahey, *The Days of the Hercules*, p. 219. Fahey estimates that May donated $457,551 to Spokane charities (p. 224). Secretary reports of the Ladies' Benevolent Society list donations from L. W. Hutton as early as 1909.

44. Fahey, *The Days of the Hercules*, p. 223; Livingston–Gonser interview, March 6, 1973 (cost of home); Pratt, "The Great-hearted Huttons," p. 31 (quotation). Visiting Lincoln Park on a warm, pleasant evening in early August 2001, the present writer found a large number of children enjoying the playground, dogs kept on leash, and families picnicking; no one knew about May or Levi Hutton.

45. Fahey, *The Days of the Hercules*, pp. 223 and 224.

46. Pratt, "The Great-hearted Huttons," p. 31 (second quotation); funeral booklet, Hutton biography file, Northwest Room, Spokane Public Library; *Daily Chronicle*, October 6, 1915 (first and third quotations).

47. *Spokesman-Review*, August 25, 1973.

48. Livingston–Gonser interview, March 6, 1973; *Spokesman-Review*, November 11, 1921 (quotation).

Chapter 2

1. "Last Will and Testament of Mary A. Hutton," May Hutton papers, Eastern Washington State Historical Society archives, Northwest Museum of Arts and Culture (NMAC).

2. Spokane *Spokesman-Review,* May 2 (first quotation), 1917; James W. Montgomery, *Liberated Woman: A Life of May Arkwright Hutton* (Fairfield, Wash.: Ye Galleon Press, 1985), p. 131 (second quotation).

3. Spokane *Daily Chronicle,* March 20, 1917; *Spokesman Review,* May 3, 1917.

4. LH to John Wiley, April 26, 1917 (quotation); to George Grombacher, May 3 and 25, 1917; to Lyman B. Arkwright, January 31, 1918; to Old National Bank, February 9, 1918; all in Hutton Settlement papers. That 1917 payment of $175,000 had an estimated value of $327,700 when he died in 1928.

5. Draft will of Levi Hutton (unsigned), ibid.

6. Mrs. H. J. Cole to LH, May 11, 1917, Ladies' Benevolent Society (LBS) Secretary Reports, LBS papers, NMAC (quotation); John Fahey, *The Days of the Hercules* (Moscow: University of Idaho Press, 1978), p. 224.

7. LBS Secretary Reports, June 7 and 14, 1917. In his ledgers, Hutton noted that he bought a new Pierce-Arrow on June 19, 1917, and paid $78.27 for "repairing and painting old auto for Home." LH ledgers, Hutton Settlement papers. Eventually he paid the Children's Home mortgage in full.

8. LH record book.

9. *Spokesman-Review,* August 29, 1917; P. T. Becher to Charles Gonser, October 30, 1929, Hutton Settlement papers; LH ledgers, June 10, 1913–January 16, 1918.

10. Hutton press release, September 1917, Hutton Settlement papers.

11. *Spokesman-Review,* November 11, 1921.

12. LBS Secretary Reports, September 6, 1917 (first quotation); Mrs. Agnes Cowley Paine to LH, September 11, 1917, LBS papers.

13. The present writer is indebted to the Spokane architect Ben Nielsen for information on the Keith association and an inventory of Whitehouse designs; Sally Byrne Woodbridge, *Building through Time: The Life of Harold C. Whitehouse, 1884-1974* (Portola Valley, Calif.: American Lives Endowment, 1981), pp. 2 through 8; Harold C. Whitehouse, "A Modernly Planned Orphanage," *Architectural Forum,* Vol. 33 (December 1920), and "The Cottage Planned Orphanage," pt. 1 and pt. 2, *Architectural Forum,* Vol. 30 (February 1919 and March 1919).

14. "Statement by the Architect," June 28, 1919, in Hutton Settlement cornerstone (quotation). Whitehouse's trip cost Hutton $1,212.62.

15. E. Wayne Carp, *Family Matters: Secrecy and Disclosure in the History of Adoption* (Cambridge, Mass.: Harvard University Press, 1998), p. 5.

16. Ibid., pp. 9 (first quotation) and 11; Brace quoted in *Children and Youth in America: A Documentary History,* Vol. 2: *1866–1932,* edited by Robert H. Bremner, John Barnard, Tamara K. Hareven, and Robert M. Mennel (Cambridge: Harvard University Press, 1971), p. 291; Howard Goldstein, *The Home on Gorham Street and the Voices of Its Children* (Tuscaloosa: University of Alabama Press, 1996), p. 29.

17. LeRoy Ashby, *Endangered Children: Dependency, Neglect, and Abuse in American History* (New York: Twayne Publishers, 1997), pp. 59 and 63 (quotation); Matthew A. Crenson, *Building the Invisible Orphanage: A Prehistory of the American Welfare System* (Cambridge: Harvard University Press, 1998), p. 18.

18. Ashby, *Endangered Children,* pp. 63 (quotation) and 75–77; Michael B. Katz, *In the Shadow of the Poorhouse: A Social History of Welfare in America,* rev. ed. (New York: Basic Books of Harper Collins Publishers, 1996), p. 117.

19. Katz, *In the Shadow of the Poorhouse,* pp. 125, 128, and 133; Crenson, *Building the Invisible Orphanage,* p. 3. For an account of the drive for mother's pensions, see Theda Skocpol, *Protecting Soldiers and Mothers: The Political Origins of Social Policy in the United States* (Cambridge, Mass.: Belknap Press, 1992).

20. Ashby, *Endangered Children,* p. 79 (first quotation); Katz, *In the Shadow of the Poorhouse,* pp. 124 (second quotation) and 128.

21. Architect's cornerstone statement; Carp, *Family Matters,* p. 17; Bremner et al., *Children and Youth in America,* p. 262; Goldstein, *The Home on Gorham Street,* p. 39.

22. "The William L. Gilbert Home," September 1928, booklet in Hutton Settlement papers.

23. Guy H. Fuller, "Mooseheart," pp. 31–33 (first two quotations), and 42 (last quotation), from Moose Charity publications courtesy of Robert Zaininger, Curator of the Museum of Moose History, Mooseheart, Illinois.

24. Whitehouse, "The Cottage Planned Orphanage," pt. 1, p. 33.

25. Ibid., p. 40.

26. LBS Secretary Reports, November 17 and 24, 1917.

27. LBS Statement in Hutton Settlement cornerstone (first quotation); LBS information sheet and LBS Secretary Reports, November 24, 1917 (second quotation); Crenson, *Building the Invisible Orphanage,* pp. 5 and 20; Ashby, *Endangered Children,* p. 80.

28. Mrs. F. B. Lewis to Rudolph Reeder, December 5, 1917, LBS papers.

29. Goldstein, *The Home on Gorham Street,* p. 39; sample of New York Orphan Asylum children's compositions reprinted in Bremner et al., eds., *Children and Youth in America,* p. 288.

30. Whitehouse to Edwin Reeder, December 13, 1917, and Reeder to Whitehouse, December 22, 1917, Hutton Settlement papers.

31. Architect's cornerstone statement.

32. LBS Secretary Reports, December 1917.

33. *Spokesman-Review,* February 14, 1920 (first and last quotations); Ashby, *Endangered Children,* pp. 63 and 71 (second quotation); LH record book, Hutton Settlement papers.

34. LH record book.

35. Ibid.

36. Gonser, text of 1969 address, Hutton Settlement papers (first quotation); LH record book.

37. LH record book.

38. Ibid.; W. H. Slingerland to Whitehouse, May 10, 1918, Hutton Settlement papers.

39. Hart quoted in Whitehouse, "The Cottage Planned Orphanage," pt. 1, p. 33.

40. Ibid., p. 34 (first quotation); Louis Livingston interview with Gonser, March 6, 1973, oral history archives, NMAC (second and third quotations). P. L. Peterson had built the house on 17th for May and Levi in 1914.

41. Author's interview with Helen Whitehouse Hamblen, June 8, 1999.

42. Whitehouse to C. Midjo, May 10, 1918, and April 29, 1919 (quotations), Hutton Settlement papers.

43. Whitehouse, "The Cottage Planned Orphanage," pt. 1, p. 39 (quotations), and "A Modernly Planned Orphanage," pp. 206–10.

44. Undated clipping, ca. August 1919, Whitehouse papers, NMAC (first quotation); Whitehouse, "The Cottage Planned Orphanage," pt. 1, p. 36 (other quotations), and "A Modernly Planned Orphanage," pp. 205 and 210.

45. Whitehouse, "A Modernly Planned Orphanage," pp. 206–10.

46. LH to Lyman B. Arkwright, July 10, 1918, Hutton Settlement papers.

47. LH cornerstone statement (quotation); Mutual Materials price list, October 18, 2001, Seattle (by telephone); Washington State Department of Labor and Industries, Prevailing Wages List, summer 2001, Olympia (by phone).

48. Information sheet, ca. 1994, Mason/Shrine file, Northwest Room, Spokane Public Library.

49. Pieroth–Hamblen interview, June 8, 1999; Whitehouse, "The Cottage Planned Orphanage," pt. 1, p. 34 (quotation); LBS Secretary Reports, June 5, 1919.

50. Roy Lubove, *The Professional Altruist: The Emergence of Social Work as a Career, 1880–1930* (Cambridge: Harvard University Press, 1965), p. 16 (first quotation); Ashby, *Endangered Children,* p. 80 (second quotation).

51. LBS Secretary Reports, March 19, 1917. Levi Hutton supplied the car three months later.

52. Ibid., April 3, 1919.

53. Ibid., April 3 and May 1, 1919.

54. Ibid., May 1, 1919.

55. Letter to Jesse Huxtable, June 29, 1919 (quotations), appended to LBS Secretary Reports, July 3, 1919.

56. LBS papers.

57. LBS Secretary Reports, August 7 and September 3, 1919.

58. Edwards, p. 184; LBS Board Minutes, December 11, 1922, LBS papers; *Spokesman-Review,* January 31, 1919.

59. LBS Secretary Reports, March 6, 1919.

60. Ibid., March 6, (first quotation) and November 6, 1919 (second quotation). Not all Children's Home residents were orphans; some parents who placed a child in the facility did so reluctantly, visited, and hoped to reunite the family when circumstances improved.

61. Fahey, *The Days of the Hercules,* p. 224; Statement of Whitehouse & Price, April 1, 1920, Hutton Settlement papers; Livingston–Gonser interview, March 6, 1973 (quotation). It took Hutton years to repay the entire $160,000 he had been forced to borrow.

62. LH ledgers, October 31, 1921 (first quotation), January 8, 1923 (second quotation), and September 27, 1920 (last quotations).

63. Frank Paine to LH, August 30, 1917; Miles Poindexter to LH, April 1, 1918; Margaret Ross to LH, September 3, 1917 (quotations), Hutton Settlement papers.

64. Author's interviews with 1920s residents of the Hutton Settlement. Jane Wiese Anderson to Robert Revel, ca. 1966–69, Hutton Settlement papers.

Chapter 3

1. LeRoy Ashby, *Endangered Children: Dependency, Neglect, and Abuse in American History* (New York: Twayne Publishers, 1997), pp. 67 and 68.

2. Gladys Guilbert interview with Charles Gonser, May 10, 1960, oral history archives, Eastern Washington State Historical Society, Northwest Museum of Arts and Culture (NMAC).

3. *Word,* December 1969, Mason/Shrine file, Spokane Public Library.

4. Ladies' Benevolent Society (LBS) Secretary Report, December 4, 1919, Ladies' Benevolent Society papers, NMAC.

5. Hutton Settlement Superintendent's Report, January 1920, Hutton Settlement office, Spokane; LBS Secretary Report, January 8, 1920.

6. Articles of Incorporation, Hutton Settlement papers.

7. Ibid.

8. Ibid.

9. LBS Secretary Reports, February 6, 1920; Last Will and Testament of L. W. Hutton, dated August 26, 1927, Hutton Settlement papers.

10. Deed of Trust, Hutton Settlement papers.

11. Ibid.

12. Ibid.

13. Ibid.

14. The Hutton Settlement Oath of Trustees. Signing the oath did not become an established practice; the original notarized document hangs in the Settlement office.

15. HS Board Minutes, March 20, 1920, Hutton Settlement office, Spokane.

16. "By-Laws of the Hutton Settlement," approved April 6, 1920, ibid.

17. LBS Secretary Reports, July 3, 1924, through March 1, 1928.

18. Ibid.

19. Karen J. Blair, *Clubwoman as Feminist: True Womanhood Redefined, 1869-1914* (New York: Homes and Meier Publishers, 1980), pp. 118 (quotation), xiii, and xiv.

20. Ibid., p. xiii (second quotation); Anne Firor Scott, *Natural Allies: Women's Associations in American History* (Urbana: University of Illinois Press, 1991), p. 13 (first quotation). Scott's excellent book traces the roots of benevolent societies to the late 18th- and early 19th-century United States.

21. The term "Board Ladies" first appeared in Hutton Settlement Board Minutes for June 1, 1920, in a report that four Board Ladies had visited Cottage One the previous month.

22. Cowley quoted in Clifford M. Drury, *A Tepee in His Front Yard: A Biography of H. T. Cowley, One of the Four Founders of the City of Spokane, Washington* (Portland, Ore.: Binfords & Morts, [1949]), p. 6; transcript of Margaret Cowles' speech, January 7, 1989, NMAC; transcript of Margaret Cowles' talk, May 7, 1970, Tape 27, Interview 50, Spokane Public Library.

23. Lori D. Ginzberg, "The 'Joint Education of the Sexes': Oberlin's Original Vision," in *Educating Men and Women Together: Coeducation in a Changing World,* edited by Carol Lasser (Urbana: University of Illinois Press, 1987), pp. 68–71 and 75. The later 19th-century period at Oberlin produced another person who had an impact on the creation of the Hutton Settlement: Hastings H. Hart, longtime director of the Russell Sage Foundation's Department of Child-Helping and a leading figure in social work in the United States, graduated from Oberlin in 1875.

24. Drury, *A Tepee in His Front Yard,* pp. 11, 42, and 192; transcript of Margaret Cowles speech, January 7, 1989.

25. Drury, *A Tepee in His Front Yard,* pp. 98, 107, 108, and 150 (quotation); Dorothy R. Powers, *Heritage from Heroes* (Spokane: Fairmount Memorial Association, 1993), p. 145.

26. Transcript of Margaret Cowles speech, January 7, 1989.

27. Joan Hollowell interview with Margaret Cowles, April 24, 1984, oral history archives.

28. Hutton will (first quotation); Levi Hutton record book, p. 43 (second quotation), Hutton Settlement papers.

29. Waller Shobe to Harold Whitehouse, February 2 and March 18, 1918, and undated clipping, ca. August 1919, Harold Whitehouse papers, NMAC; L.W. Hutton ledgers, January 16, 1918–June 30, 1924, Hutton Settlement papers; Hutton Settlement Superintendent's Report, Hutton Settlement office, Spokane.

30. Superintendent's Report, January–December 1920.

31. Kenneth Knoll, "When the Plague Hit Spokane," *Pacific Northwesterner,* Vol. 30 (1989), 6–7; Superintendent's Reports, 1920; Board Minutes, September 1, 1920.

32. Tape recording of alumni group discussion, October 6, 1999, Anita Abramson Woslager (quotation) and Bob Clark.

33. Author's interview with Mike Mateef, June 7, 1999; Board Minutes, June 5, 1928.

34. Board Minutes, November 2 and December 7, 1920 (quotation), October 4, 1921; Superintendent's Report, January 1921.

35. LH ledgers, Jan 16, 1918–June 30, 1924; author's interview with Mabel Maley Maxwell, May 1, 2001 (quotation).

36. Board Minutes, September 1 (first quotation), October 5, 1920 (second quotation), January 4 (third quotation), and March 1, 1921 (last quotation); LH ledgers, July 1, 1924 through June 30, 1927 and July 1, 1927 through September 30, 1931.

37. LH ledgers, Jan 16, 1918–September 30, 1931.

38. Board Minutes, May 1, 1928 (quotation), and February 1, 1927; Settlement Date Book, 1927, p. 160, Hutton Settlement papers.

39. Board Minutes, February 1, 1921; LH ledgers, Jan 16, 1918–September 30, 1931; "By-Laws of the Hutton Settlement" (quotation).

40. Financial Report, Board Minutes, February 1, 1921 (first quotation); Louis Livingston interview with Charles Gonser, March 6, 1973, oral history archives (second quotation), NMAC.

41. LH to Yakima County Commissioners, February 11, 1925, Hutton Settlement papers.

42. Board Minutes, January 1, 1927 (first quotation); October 2, 1928 (second quotation).

43. Bob Briley interview with Gonser, December 3, 1974, oral history archives.

44. Spokane *Spokesman-Review,* January 23, 1922, March 20, and June 9, 1925.

45. Board Minutes, passim, July 6, and December 6, 1927 (quotation, emphasis added). The author is forever indebted to Mrs. Edna Glasgow, who in her twenty-one years as recording secretary submitted typewritten minutes; she was the first to do so.

46. Addendum to Board Minutes, dated December 11, 1922.

47. Author's interview with Clara Scott Simons, June 7, 1999 (quotation), with Mike Mateef, June 7, 1999, and Mabel Maley Maxwell, May 1, 2001. Browne's Addition, a residential area west of downtown Spokane, was home to many of Spokane's affluent elite.

48. LBS Secretary Reports, November 24, 1917; Board Minutes, January 4, 1921 (quotation).

49. Secretary, Washington State Conference of Social Work, to Hutton, May 31, 1923, Hutton Settlement papers.

50. *Spokesman-Review,* September 4, 1926; Board Minutes, August 3, 1926.

51. Board Minutes, January 4, 1921, October 6, 1925; undated clippings, ca. October 31, 1925 and November 1926 (quotation), Hutton Settlement papers; Livingston–Gonser interview, March 6, 1973.

52. Stephen B. L. Penrose to LH, May 5, 1928, Hutton Settlement papers.

53. Board Minutes, June 5, 1928.

54. James W. Montgomery, *Liberated Woman: A Life of May Arkwright Hutton,* p. 131; John Fahey, *The Days of the Hercules,* p. 226; Livingston–Gonser interview, March 6, 1973; Gonser to Mrs. Nellie Hutton Newton, November 4, 1928, Hutton Settlement papers.

55. Livingston–Gonser interview, March 6, 1973; *Spokesman-Review,* November 7, 1928 (quotation).

56. Clipping, November 3, 1928, Hutton Settlement papers.

Chapter 4

1. Hutton Settlement Superintendent's Report, July 1928, Hutton Settlement office, Spokane.

2. Alumni statements in document prepared for Internal Revenue Service, 1971, Hutton Settlement papers, Eastern Washington State Historical Society archives, Northwest Museum of Arts and Culture (NMAC).

3. Ibid.

4. Ibid.

5. Author's interview with Clara Scott Simons, June 7, 1999; tape recording of alumni group discussion, October 6, 1999 (last quotation).

6. Spokane *Spokesman-Review,* July 20, 1969.

7. Author's interview with Mike Mateef, June 7, 1999.

8. Author's interview with Mabel Maley Maxwell, May 1, 2001.

9. Harold C. Whitehouse, "The Cottage Planned Orphanage," pt. 1, *Architectural Forum,* Vol. 30 (February 1919), p. 33; Gladys Guilbert interview with Charles Gonser, May 10, 1960, oral history archives, NMAC (quotation).

10. Hutton Settlement Board Minutes, February 1, 1921, Hutton Settlement office.

11. Pieroth–Mateef interview, June 7, 1999. Pasadena School stood on the site of the present Argonne Library, at the corner of Argonne and Upriver Drive.

12. Ibid. (first quotation); Pieroth–Scott Simons interview, June 7, 1999.

13. Pieroth–Mateef interview, June 7, 1999; Pieroth–Maley Maxwell interview, May 1, 2001; Pieroth–Scott Simons interview, June 7, 1999.

14. Board Minutes, November 2, 1920, and April 3, 1928.

15. May Hutton to John D. Rockefeller, March 4, 1910, and to George Fuller, May 29, 1912, May Arkwright Hutton papers, NMAC.

16. Superintendent's Report, May 1923.

17. S. B. L. Penrose to LH, April 17, 1924, Hutton Settlement papers.

18. *Spokesman-Review,* November 3, 1928.

19. Ibid., July 20, 1969 (first quotation); Pieroth–Maley Maxwell interview, May 1, 2001 (second quotation).

20. Pieroth–Mateef interview, June 7, 1999. Others recalled the same sort of routine.

21. Pieroth–Scott Simons interview, June 7, 1999; Pieroth–Maley Maxwell interview, May 1, 2001.

22. Pieroth–Maley Maxwell interview, May 1, 2001.

23. Pieroth–Scott Simons interview, June 7, 1999; Pieroth–Mateef interview, June 7, 1999.

24. Board Minutes, February 5, 1929.

25. Pieroth–Mateef interview, June 7, 1999; Pieroth–Maley Maxwell interview, May 1, 2001.

26. Matthew A. Crenson, *Building the Invisible Orphanage: A Prehistory of the American Welfare System* (Cambridge: Harvard University Press, 1998), p. 6.

27. Ladies' Benevolent Society (LBS) Secretary Reports, March 1920, Ladies' Benevolent Society papers, NMAC.

28. Hutton ledgers, Jan 16, 1918–June 30, 1924, Hutton Settlement papers; *Spokesman-Review,* March 31, 1918. The Olsons lived in a small house on Upriver Drive just at the entrance to the campus; his salary as the Settlement farmer remained $75 per month through the 1920s.

29. List of produce, 1926, Hutton Settlement papers; Board Minutes, June 7, 1927.

30. Author's interview with Gordon Windle, June 10, 1999.

31. Pieroth–Mateef interview, June 7, 1999.

32. Pieroth–Maley Maxwell interview, May 1, 2001; *Spokesman-Review,* July 20, 1969.

33. Pieroth–Mateef interview, June 7, 1999.

34. Ibid., June 7, 1999.

35. Board Minutes, October 2, 1929, and February 1, 1927; Settlement Date Book, 1927, p. 44, Hutton Settlement papers; Pieroth–Scott Simons interview, June 7, 1999.

36. Pieroth–Scott Simons interview, June 7, 1999.

37. Pieroth–Mateef interview, June 7, 1999.

38. Ibid.

39. Ibid.

40. Memo re: movie policy, ca. 1924, Hutton Settlement papers; Pieroth–Mateef interview, June 7, 1999.

41. Memo re: movie policy, ca. 1924.

42. Bob Briley interview with Charles Gonser, December 3, 1974, oral history archives NMAC; Pieroth–Scott Simons interview, June 7, 1999; Pieroth–Mateef interview, June 7, 1999.

43. Board Minutes, January 4, 1921, August 6, 1927, and passim; author's interviews with various former Settlement residents; Jay F. Kalez, *Saga of a Western Town: Spokane* (Spokane: Lawton Printing, 1972), pp. 74–77. For some Hutton kids, wearing ribbon tags and being introduced to the crowd as a group were embarrassments that stigmatized them and negated the pleasure of Settlement outings.

44. Interviews with former Settlement residents; "Children's Voices," sheet music, NMAC; *Spokesman-Review,* June 14, 1933. In the 1930s, community and service groups in Spokane began bringing all the Settlement children into the city for elaborate parties during the holidays.

45. Board Minutes, January 4, 1921.

46. LBS Board Minutes, March 4, 1920; Superintendent's Report, January 1933 (quotation).

47. Pieroth–Maley Maxwell interview, May 1, 2001.

48. Howe, author of "The Battle Hymn of the Republic," quoted in Wendy Kaminer, *Women Volunteering: The Pleasure, Pain, and Politics of Unpaid Work, from 1830 to the Present* (New York: Anchor Press/Doubleday, 1984), p. 25; *Spokesman-Review,* July 20, 1969.

49. Pieroth–Scott Simons interview, June 7, 1999.

50. Clara Scott Simons's statement for Settlement 75th anniversary time capsule, July 1994, Hutton Settlement papers.

51. *Spokesman-Review,* July 20, 1969.

52. Pieroth–Scott Simons interview, June 7, 1999.

53. Pieroth–Mateef interview, June 7, 1999.

54. *Spokesman-Review,* July 20, 1969.

55. Alumni statements in document prepared for IRS, 1971.

56. Tape recording of alumni group discussion, October 6, 1999, Clara Scott Simons (quotation); Board Minutes, August 6, 1929; Author's interviews with Maley Maxwell, May 1, 2001, Mateef, June 7, 1999, Bob Baker, July 15, 1999, and Cletis Hydrick, October 24, 2001.

57. Board Minutes, May 3, 1927.

58. Ibid., February 5, 1929. Records do not indicate how closely these later policies were followed.

59. LH ledgers, January 16, 1918–June 30, 1924, Hutton Settlement papers.

60. Pieroth–Mateef interview, June 7, 1999; Pieroth–Scott Simons interview, June 7, 1999; Pieroth–Maley Maxwell interview, May 1, 2001.

61. Tape recording of alumni group discussion, October 6, 1999 (Scott Simons quotation); Board scrapbook, alumni comments at Settlement 75th anniversary, 1994 (Susie Dubuque quotation), Hutton Settlement papers.

62. Pieroth–Maley Maxwell interview, May 1, 2001.

63. Pieroth–Mateef interview, June 7, 1999.

64. Briley–Gonser interview, December 3, 1974 (first quotation); Louis Livingston interview with Gonser, March 6, 1973, oral history archives, NMAC. Another reason that Hutton resisted a closed car was that he thought it looked too much like a hearse.

65. Briley–Gonser interview, December 3, 1974 (first quotation); Settlement Date Book, 1927, passim and p. 248 (quotation).

66. John Fahey, *The Days of the Hercules*, p. 225; *Spokesman-Review*, October 12, 1969 (quotations).

67. Settlement Date Book, 1927, pp. 219 (quotation) and 221.

68. Jane Wiese to Robert Revel, ca. 1960, Hutton Settlement papers; Pieroth–Mateef interview, June 7, 1999; Pieroth–Maley Maxwell interview, May 1, 2001.

69. Last Will and Testament of L. W. Hutton, dated August 26, 1927, Hutton Settlement papers; *Spokesman-Review*, November 7, 1928; Masonic *Word*, December 1969, Mason/Shrine file, Northwest Room, Spokane Public Library.

70. James W. Montgomery, *Liberated Woman: A Life of May Arkwright Hutton*, p. 132; *Spokesman-Review*, November 7, 1928 (quotation).

71. Jane Wiese to Robert Revel, ca. 1960, Hutton Settlement papers; *Spokesman-Review*, November 7, 1928.

Chapter 5

1. Hutton Settlement Board Minutes, November 7, 1928, Hutton Settlement office, Spokane.

2. Last Will and Testament of L. W. Hutton, dated May 17, 1926, and Last Will and Testament of L. W. Hutton, dated August 26, 1927, both in Hutton Settlement papers, Eastern Washington State Historical Society archives, Northwest Museum of Arts and Culture (NMAC).

3. Joel Ferris to Charles Gonser, November 9, 1928, R. W. Butler to Gonser, November 8, 1928, and Paul Robertson to Gonser, November 16, 1928, all in Hutton Settlement papers; "Voices of the Pioneers," Gladys Guilbert interview of Charles Gonser, ca. 1957, tape 12, interview 21, Spokane Public Library (last quotation).

4. Elizabeth Bender to Gonser, ca. November 15, 1928 and Gonser to board, November 17, 1928, both in Hutton Settlement papers; Board Minutes, December 4, 1928.

5. Hutton will, dated August 26, 1927.

6. Ibid. Many of the imposing furnishings from the home continued to grace the administration building on the Settlement campus at century's end.

7. Louis Livingston interview with Gonser, March 6, 1973, oral history archives, NMAC.

8. Spokane *Daily Chronicle*, June 16, 1970; Livingston–Gonser interview, March 6, 1973 (quotation).

9. *Daily Chronicle*, June 16, 1970.

10. Author's interview with Ed McWilliams, July 13, 1999. Gonser's cigar habit may well have stemmed from his association with Levi Hutton.

11. Author's interview with Philip Stanton, October 4, 1999; Board Minutes, passim, 1929–70; Author's interview with Clara Scott Simons, June 7, 1999; tape recording of alumni group discussion, October 6, 1999, Anita Abramson Woslager and Dorothy Grater.

12. R. H. Back to Gonser, April 23, 1929, Hutton Settlement papers; Spokane *Spokesman-Review,* May 7, 1929. There was correspondence between Gonser and May Hutton's half sister's daughter-in-law, Mrs. E. R. Grombacher of Lakewood, Ohio, throughout the litigation, Hutton Settlement papers. LH's German shepherd, Peter, also went to his brother, Stephen; the dog died in February 1929.

13. *Spokesman-Review,* May 7, 1929.

14. Ibid.

15. Board Minutes, June 4, 1929.

16. *Spokesman-Review,* October 28 (quotation) and 29, 1929.

17. LH to Asa Hutton, July 24, 1922, Hutton Settlement papers.

18. LH to Will Hutton, August 14, 1922, ibid.

19. Deed of Trust, Hutton Settlement papers.

20. Nellie Hutton Newton to Gonser, April 7, 1931, ibid. Gonser estimated that Hutton had spent $816,909 of the Hutton money on the Settlement by the time of his death; *Spokesman-Review,* March 28, 1931.

21. *Spokesman-Review,* October 30, 1929.

22. Board Minutes, December 3, 1929.

23. John H. Wourms to Gonser, May 3, 1930, Hutton Settlement papers; *Spokesman-Review,* March 25, 1931.

24. *Daily Chronicle,* August 3, 1931 (quotation); *Spokesman-Review,* June 25, 1932.

25. *Spokesman-Review,* December 22, 1914.

26. John Fahey, *The Days of the Hercules,* p. 218; clipping, ca. January 1915, Hutton Settlement papers (quotations); Livingston–Gonser interview, March 6, 1973.

27. Livingston–Gonser interview, March 6, 1973; Board Minutes, November 2, 1926.

28. Board Minutes, February 5, 1935; Margaret Bean, "Hutton Settlement Faces Cash Shortage," *Spokesman-Review,* undated clipping, ca. March 1936, Hutton Settlement papers.

29. Josephine C. Sherwood had left $2,000 to both the Hutton Settlement and the Ladies' Benevolent Society in 1923; Board Minutes, October 2 and November 5, 1929 (quotation), May 6 and June 3, 1930, and July 11, 1944; Financial Advisory Committee Minutes, July 30, 1935, Hutton Settlement office.

30. Undated *Spokesman-Review* clippings, ca. 1936, Hutton Settlement papers.

31. Roy Lubove, *The Professional Altruist: The Emergence of Social Work as a Career, 1880–1930* (Cambridge: Harvard University Press, 1965), pp. 162, 163, and 164. Lubove's book gives an excellent account of the birth and growth of social work as a profession.

32. E. Wayne Carp, *Family Matters: Secrecy and Disclosure in the History of Adoption* (Cambridge: Harvard University Press, 1998), p. 13 (first quotation); Lubove, *The Professional Altruist,* p. 5 (second quotation).

33. Carp, *Family Matters,* p. 24 (second quotation); Lubove, *The Professional Altruist,* pp. 19 (first quotation), 124, 127, and 157 (last quotation).

34. Lubove, *The Professional Altruist,* p. 52 (first two quotations) and 50 (last quotation); Board Minutes, passim 1930–45.

35. Author's interview with Nancy Anderson, August 7, 2001; Mrs. Anderson, Gonser's step-daughter, heard his sentiments regarding social workers expressed many times. Board Minutes, February 4 and March 3, 1936, May 2, 1939, June 5, 1940, March 10, 1942, and April 6, 1943.

36. Lubove, *The Professional Altruist,* pp. 178–202.

37. Ibid., pp. 190 and 196; Community Welfare promotional brochure, 1921, Spokane Public Library Collection; clipping, *Spokesman-Review,* May 29, 1929, Hutton Settlement papers; *Spokane Woman,* January 29, 1925, Spokane Public Library.

38. Community Welfare promotional brochure, 1921; Gonser's undated "Synopsis of finances relating to the Community Chest," Hutton Settlement papers.

39. Livingston–Gonser interview, March 6, 1973; Financial Advisory Committee Minutes, June 26, 1934, Hutton Settlement office; Board Minutes, Special Meeting, December 12, 1934.

40. Board Minutes, February 2, special meeting June 23, and September 7, 1937 (last quotation); Author's interview with Philip Stanton, October 4, 1999 (first quotation).

41. Gonser's "Synopsis of finances, Community Chest." For an account of the Hercules reorganization, see Fahey's *Days of the Hercules.*

42. Regina G. Kunzel, *Fallen Women, Problem Girls: Unmarried Mothers and the Professionalization of Social Work, 1890–1945* (New Haven, Conn.: Yale University Press, 1993), pp. 119 and 120 (quotation).

43. Board Minutes, August 4, 1936 (first quotation), May 3 (second quotation) and 6, 1938 (third quotation).

44. Ibid., April 22, 1942, July 6, 1943 (quotation from letter dated June 15), and June 1, 1948; and Gonser's "Synopsis of finances, Community Chest."

45. Board Minutes, November 5, 1929 (quotation), October 7, 1930, September 1, 1931, October 5, 1932.

46. Hutton Settlement Superintendent's Report, November 1933 (quotations), Hutton Settlement office; Board Minutes, November 11, 1933.

47. Board Minutes, April 2, 1929, March 4 (first quotation) and August 2, 1930 (second quotation); clipping, *Spokesman-Review,* May 1, 1929, Hutton Settlement papers.

48. Board Minutes, September 2, October 7 (quotation), and December 3, 1930; Livingston–Gonser interview, March 6, 1973.

49. O. S. Burkholder letter of resignation, appended to Board Minutes, December 15, 1934 (quotations); Livingston–Gonser interview, March 6, 1973; Board Minutes, July 2, 1935.

50. Board Minutes, August 11, 1936 (quotations) and April 30, 1941.

51. Pieroth, World War II segment, "Home, Frontier, Crossroads," Washington State Historical Society museum permanent exhibit story line, 1989, Tacoma.

52. Board Minutes, March 17, special board meeting, March 25 (first quotation), and special joint meeting with Financial Advisory Committee, April 22, 1942 (other quotations).

53. Board Minutes and Superintendent's Reports, 1930–44.

54. Superintendent's Report, August (first quotation) and October 1943 (last quotations).

55. Board Minutes, January 6, 1942, November 2, 1943; Superintendent's Report, December 1943.

56. Board Minutes, December 7, 1943, January 1, April 4, and June 6, 1944.

57. Protective School proposal, Hutton Settlement papers; Board Minutes, June 6 and 22 (first quotation), 1944, and May 1, 1945 (second quotation).

58. Board Minutes, June 1, 1943; Financial Advisory Committee Minutes, January 26, 1944 (quotation).

Chapter 6

1. Clipping, Spokane *Spokesman-Review*, ca. June 15, 1929, Hutton Settlement papers, Eastern Washington State Historical Society archives, Northwest Museum of Arts and Culture (NMAC) (quotation); Dorothy R. Powers, *Heritage from Heroes*, pp. 177 and 179. Spokane's Mrs. John Bruce Dodd had recently put forth the concept of Father's Day as a national day of recognition.

2. Hutton Settlement Board Minutes, April 5, 1932, Hutton Settlement office, Spokane; "Some statistics for the year 1933," Hutton Settlement papers.

3. Hutton Settlement Superintendent's Report, November 1931 and January 1933, Hutton Settlement office; Author's interview with Gordon Windle, June 10, 1999 (first two quotations); alumni statements in document prepared for Internal Revenue Service, 1971, Hutton Settlement papers (last quotation).

4. Superintendent's Report, May and December 1931.

5. Author's interview with Clara Scott Simons, June 7, 1999.

6. Superintendent's Report, October 1930.

7. *Spokesman-Review*, July 16, 1989.

8. Alumni statements in document prepared for IRS, 1971; Pieroth–Scott Simons interview, June 7, 1999.

9. Board Minutes show frequent discussions of reminding young people of their debts, e.g., December 5, 1939.

10. Superintendent's Report, October 1931; Board Minutes, January 6, 1931 (quotation) and passim, 1931–33, Special Meeting, September 19, 1932, June 6 and September 5, 1933; *Pow Wow,* Summer 1963, Hutton Settlement papers.

11. Board Minutes, April 5 and October 5, 1932.

12. Ibid., January 2, 1934, April 6 and May 5, 1937.

13. Alumni statements in document prepared for IRS, 1971.

14. Board Minutes, February 2 (quotation) and March 1, 1932.

15. Ibid., February 3, 1931, July 2, 1932, and September 5, 1933; Superintendent's Report, March 1935 (quotation); alumni statements in document prepared for IRS, 1971.

16. Board Minutes, May 5 (first two quotations), June 2 (third quotation), and September 4, 1936.

17. Excerpt from Smith will attached to Financial Advisory Committee Minutes, July 27, 1938, Hutton Settlement office.

18. Board Minutes, March 5, 1929 (first quotation), February 17, 1930 (second quotation), and July 7, 1931 (last quotation).

19. Ibid., March 1, 1932; Author's interview with Mabel Maley Maxwell, May 1, 2001; Ira Sisson in document prepared for IRS, 1971.

20. Superintendent's Report, December 1930; Board Minutes, January 5, 1932.

21. Author's interview with Dorothy Fuller Grater, May 1, 2001; author's telephone interview with Pearle Grater LaLumia, May 18, 2001; Author's telephone interview with Glen Grater, May 23, 2001.

22. Author's interview with Bob Baker, July 15, 1999. The Board Lady who facilitated the Bakers' move to the Settlement could well have been Mrs. Northrop, who had always served as something of a Settlement liaison with the Spokane medical community.

23. Author's interview with Jim Taylor, July 16, 1999.

24. Board Minutes, October 10, 1946.

25. Author's interview with Clara Aldridge Demmer, July 14, 1999; Board Minutes, June 2, 1948.

26. Author's interview with Sylvia Olsen Slatky, May 1, 2001.

27. Ibid., May 1, 2001.

28. 1920s Superintendent's Reports; Board Minutes, e.g., March 7, 1933; Financial Advisory Committee Minutes, August 28, 1934.

29. Author's interview with Anita Abramson Woslager, July 12, 1999.

30. Author's interview with Kenneth Dunlap, July 13, 1999.

31. Ibid..

32. Ibid.; Board Minutes, January 7, 1941.

33. Board Minutes, March 1932 (quotation) and passim, 1930–34.

34. Superintendent's Report, October 1930 (first quotation) and April 1931 (second quotation).

35. Ibid., October (first quotation) and December 1930 (second quotation), and January 1931 (third quotation).

36. "Spizzerinkeum" (Hutton Settlement newspaper) 1931, Hutton Settlement papers.

37. Author's interview with Mike Mateef, June 7, 1999.

38. Board Minutes, April 5, 1932 (first two quotations); interviews with Settlement alumni; and alumni statements in document prepared for IRS, 1971 (last quotation). Mike Mateef had reached the age to leave the campus but could have stayed until he graduated from West Valley.

39. Barbara Brecheen, comp., *Washington State Developmental Disability Services: An Historical Outline, 1861-1980* (Olympia, Wash.: Department of Social and Health Services, 1988), pp. 29 through 31.

40. Superintendent's Report, January and February 1935.

41. Pieroth–Olsen Slatky interview, May 1, 2001 (quotation); tape recording of alumni group discussion, October 6, 1999, Anita Abramson Woslager; Superintendent's Report, January 1935.

42. Pieroth–Taylor interview, July 16, 1999, Pieroth–Dunlap interview, July 13, 1999, and Pieroth–Baker interview, July 15, 1999.

43. Superintendent's Report, March 1940; Pieroth–Dunlap interview, July 13, 1999.

44. Pieroth–Taylor interview, July 16, 1999; Pieroth–G. Grater interview, May 23, 2001.

45. Pieroth–Abramson Woslager interview, July 12, 1999.

46. Baker account, Hutton Settlement picnic, August 17, 1999.

47. Pieroth–Abramson Woslager interview, July 12, 1999; Pieroth–Aldridge Demmer interview, July 14, 1999; Pieroth–Baker interview, July 15, 1999.

48. Written recollections of Kathryn Metrovich Riddell, supplement to tape recording of alumni group discussion, October 6, 1999; Pieroth–Olsen Slatky interview, May 1, 2001; Olsen Slatky comments at Hutton picnic, August 17, 1999, and at the alumni group discussion, October 6, 1999.

49. Pieroth–Abramson Woslager interview, July 12, 1999; Pieroth–Dunlap interview, July 13, 1999; handwritten notes on payments for lessons, ca. 1940, Hutton Settlement papers; Board Minutes, February 1, 1944 (Schrader connection).

50. Pieroth–Dunlap interview, July 13, 1999; unidentified alumna recorded at Hutton picnic, August 17, 1999 (quotation).

51. Pieroth–Dunlap interview, July 13, 1999.

52. Pieroth–Baker interview, July 15, 1999; Pieroth–Scott Simons interview, June 7, 1999; Superintendent's Report, May and August 1931.

53. Sylvia Olsen Slatky and Anita Abramson Woslanger (quotations), tape recording of alumni group discussion, October 6, 1999.

54. Ibid., October 6, 1999, and at Hutton picnic, August 17, 1999.

55. Superintendent's Report, July 1935, July 1940, August 1941; and Board Minutes, July 10, 1942.

56. Board Minutes, February 4 and May 6, 1930, and passim through 1945; Superintendent's Report, July 1947.

57. Board Minutes, December 1, 1936 (first quotation), March 4, 1941 (second and third quotations), October 14, 1938, and October 7, 1941 (last quotation); Metrovich Riddell recollections, alumni group discussion, October 6, 1999 (fourth quotation); Pieroth–Grater LaLumia interview, May 18, 2001; Pieroth–D. Grater interview, May 1, 2001.

58. Pieroth–Baker interview, July 15, 1999, and Pieroth–D. Grater interview, May 1, 2001.

59. Pieroth–Grater LaLumia interview, May 18, 2001; Metrovich Riddell recollections, alumni group discussion, October 6, 1999.

60. Board Minutes, September 1, 1942; Pieroth–Abramson Woslager interview, July 12, 1999.

61. Superintendent's Report, October 1940.

62. Ibid., April 1941 (first two quotations), February 1940 (third quotation); Board Minutes, November 4, 1941 (last quotation). Billings was on guard duty at Pearl Harbor when the attack occurred on December 7, 1941.

63. Board Minutes, January 6 (first quotation), February 3, 1942 (second quotation).

64. Ibid., July 4, 1942 (quotation).

65. Dorothy Grater, tape recording of alumni group discussion, October 6, 1999; Pieroth–Grater LaLumia interview, May 19, 2001; Pieroth–G. Grater interview, May 23, 2001.

66. Board Minutes, March 5 and April 2, 1946.

67. Pieroth–D. Grater interview, May 1, 2001; Bob Grater to D. Grater, Sept. 30, 1945, copy in author's possession; Board Minutes, January 2, 1934; Dorothy Grater, tape recording of alumni group discussion, October 6, 1999.

Chapter 7

1. Jeffrey K. Ochsner, "Willis A. Ritchie: Public Architecture in Washington, 1889–1905," *Pacific Northwest Quarterly*, Vol. 87 (1996), pp. 209 (quotation) and 211. Ritchie is perhaps best known for his design of the "chateauesque" Spokane County Courthouse. Various spellings of her first name exist, but Mrs. Ritchie herself signed as Miriam.

2. Hutton Settlement Board Minutes, July 3, 1934, Hutton Settlement office, Spokane; Ladies' Benevolent Society (LBS) Secretary Report, October 2, 1924, Ladies' Benevolent Society papers, Eastern Washington State Historical Society archives, Northwest Museum of Arts and Culture (NMAC). Honorary status is customarily bestowed on board members who resign after long tenures; it does not preclude returning as an active member. Mrs. Ritchie may have been the first so honored.

3. Hutton Settlement Superintendent's Report, November 1944, Hutton Settlement office.

4. Author's interview with Clara Aldrich Demmer, July 14, 1999; Superintendent's Reports, August 1944 through 1950.

5. Superintendent's Report, July 1949 and September 1950.

6. Board Minutes, December 4, 1956, and January 8, 1957.

7. Ibid., April 5 and December 5, 1932, March 7 and April 4, 1933, January 2 and February 9, 1934.

8. Ibid., March 1933 through April 1952 passim, and April 1, 1952 (quotation).

9. Board Minutes, March 4, 1936, (first quotation), November 7, 1933 (second quotation), and December 1, 1936 (third quotation).

10. Board Minutes, May 7, 1935, and December 1, 1936; Author's interview with James and Wanda Cowles, March 4, 2002.

11. Settlement Date Book, 1927, Hutton Settlement papers, NMAC (first quotation); Ralph E. Dyar, *News for an Empire: The Story of the "Spokesman-Review" of Spokane, Washington, and of the Field It Serves* (Caldwell, Idaho: Caxton Printers, 1952), p. 99 (second quotation).

12. Board Minutes, October 6, 1936, and March 7, 1939.

13. http://www.jlspokane.org (quotation). The Association of Junior Leagues is a "conglomeration of 250 separate organizations. . . . Local autonomy is deeply treasured and stoutly defended," in Janet Gordon and Diana Reische's complete history of the organization, *The Volunteer Powerhouse: The Junior League* (New York: Rutledge Press, 1982), p. 13.

14. Author's interview with Evelyn Morgan, July 13, 1999 (quotation); Board Minutes, 1920–45.

15. Board Minutes, special joint meeting with Financial Advisory Committee, April 22, 1942 (first quotation), July 11, 1944 (second quotation), and January 5, 1943 (final quotation).

16. Board Minutes, November 7, 1944.

17. Spokane *Spokesman-Review,* October 4, 1952 (quotation), and October 22, 1970.

18. Author's interview with Helen Whitehouse Hamblen, June 8, 1999; Board Minutes, April 5, September 6, and November 1, 1955.

19. Board Minutes, February 3, 1948 (first quotation), March 3 (second quotation), and April 7, 1959 (last quotation).

20. Author's interview with Dorothy Rochon Powers, June 25, 2001 (quotations); John Fahey, *Shaping Spokane: Jay P. Graves and His Times* (Seattle: University of Washington Press, 1994), p. 100.

21. Margaret Bean's article, in *Spokesman-Review,* February 25, 1951, and manuscript, Hutton Settlement papers.

22. Ibid. (quotations); Board Minutes, 1950–67, passim.

23. Board Minutes, October 20, 1950.

24. Ibid., March 6, 1951.

25. Ibid., March 6, September 4 (first quotation), and October 2, 1951 (second quotation); Author's interview with Philip Stanton, October 4, 1999 (last quotation). Gonser told the Financial Advisory Committee that the Settlement preferred the term "'fees' rather than payment for board and keep, as the cost per child is far in excess of the price paid"; Financial Advisory Committee Minutes, April 27, 1956, Hutton Settlement office.

26. Michael Reese, "'To Help Her Live the Right Kind of Life': Mothers Pensions in King County, 1913–1937," in *More Voices, New Stories: King County Washington's First 150 Years,* edited by Mary C. Wright (Seattle: Pacific Northwest Historians Guild, 2002).

27. Michael K. Green, "The Development of Human Services in Washington, 1933–1960," in *A Shared Experience* (Olympia, Wash.: Department of Social and Health Services, 1989), p. 32; Reese, "'To Help Her Live the Right Kind of Life,'" pp. 207–209.

28. Green, "The Development of Human Services in Washington," pp. 32 and 35 (quotation).

29. Board Minutes, June 7, 1938.

30. Ibid., February 6, 1945, and February 5, 1946 (quotation).

31. Superintendent's Report, April 1947; Board Minutes, March 4 (first quotation) and May 6, 1947 (second quotation).

32. Superintendent's Report, May 1947.

33. Board Minutes, April 6, 1954.

34. Ibid., July 8 (first quotation) and October 7, 1947 (second quotation), December 6, 1949 (third quotation).

35. Ibid., January 6, October 25, 1948, January 4, February 1, and October 4, 1949 (quotations), September 5, 1950 (last quotation); Financial Advisory Committee Minutes, January 28, 1948.

36. Board Minutes, September 6, 1949.

37. Ibid., May 4 and October 4, 1948 (quotations).

38. Elaine Tyler May, *Homeward Bound: American Families in the Cold War Era* (New York: Basic Books, 1988), p. 121 (first quotation); E. Wayne Carp, *Family Matters: Secrecy and Disclosure in the History of Adoption*, pp. 28 and 29 (other quotations); Children's Home Society of Washington, *A Century of Turning Hope into Reality* (Seattle: Children's Home Society of Washington, 1996), pp. 50–55.

39. Board Minutes, January 4, 1955–January 5, 1960.

40. Ibid., September 9, 1958; Financial Advisory Committee Minutes, February 27, 1959.

41. Board Minutes, August 2, 1960 (quotation), and August 29, 1961.

42. Ibid., February 1, 1955.

43. Financial Advisory Committee Minutes, March 27, 1959 (first quotation); Board Minutes, June 2, 1959, and April 4, 1961 (last quotation); *Spokesman-Review,* January 22, 1961, and May 2, 1975.

44. Board Minutes, March 6, 1951 (quotation), and June 1, 1954.

45. Financial Advisory Committee Minutes, March 27, 1946 (quotation), and September 30, 1949.

46. Ibid., January 28, 1948, and January 26, 1949; Board Minutes, February 5, 1952 (quotation).

47. Board Minutes, June 6, 1944, and November 7, 1944; Financial Advisory Committee Minutes, July 27, 1944 (quotation).

48. Financial Advisory Committee minutes, September 26, 1945 (quotation); Board Minutes, August 7 and October 2, 1945.

49. Board Minutes, February 3, 1959.

50. Ibid., June 7, 1955 (first quotation), and joint special meeting of board and Financial Advisory Committee, June 17, 1955 (second quotation), July 5, 1955, February 7, 1956; "Financial History of the Hutton Settlement, Inc., November 3, 1928 to May, 1969," Hutton Settlement papers.

51. Financial Advisory Committee Minutes, November 30, 1956 (quotation); Board Minutes, February 5, 1957, and January 7, 1958.

52. Board Minutes, October 25, 1957, and April 25, 1958 (quotation), January 30, February 27, and March 27, 1959, and joint meeting with Financial Advisory Committee, January 29, 1960.

53. Financial Advisory Committee Minutes, November 27, 1959 (quotation), June 30, 1961; Board Minutes, July 11, 1961.

54. Hutton Settlement audit records, Hutton Settlement office.

Chapter 8

1. William H. Chafe, *The Unfinished Journey: America since World War II*, 4th ed. (New York: Oxford University Press, 1999), pp. 111–45 (quotations, 111, 113, 117).

2. Spokane *Spokesman-Review*, September 18, 1999 (quotations); Florence Boutwell, *The Spokane Valley*, Vol. 2: *A History of the Growing Years, 1921–1945* (Spokane: Arthur H. Clark, 1995), p. 140.

3. Hutton Settlement Financial Advisory Committee Minutes, January 28, 1955, Hutton Settlement office, Spokane (quotations); Hutton Settlement Board Minutes, February 1, 1955, ibid.

4. Financial Advisory Committee Minutes, February 25, 1955 (first quotation); Board Minutes, March 1, 1955 (second quotation).

5. Board Minutes, February 5, 1957, August 4, 1959, and October 4, 1960; Financial Advisory Committee Minutes, July 30, 1959, and September 30, 1960 (quotation).

6. Hutton Settlement Superintendent's Report, October 1946, Hutton Settlement office.

7. Board Minutes, June 16, 1942, August 1 (first quotation), August 14, 1950, February 6, 1951 (second quotation), and September 1950–April 1951.

8. Board Minutes, April 18, 1951.

9. Ibid., May 1, 1951; Author's interview with Pamela Yoho Crouse, March 7, 2002; Author's interview with John Thurber, February 26, 2002 (quotations).

10. Superintendent's Report, May 1951 (first quotation); Board Minutes, December 7, 1954 (second quotation); Financial Advisory Committee Minutes, March 25, 1955.

11. Board Minutes, March 25, August 2 (first quotation), September 6, and October 4, 1955 (second quotation).

12. Ibid., November 4 and December 2, 1958, June 2, 1959; Pieroth–Thurber interview, February 26, 2002.

13. Board Minutes, May 7, 1957.

14. Ibid., August 6, 1957 (quotation); *Spokesman-Review*, September 26, 1957.

15. Pieroth–Thurber interview, February 26, 2002; Board Minutes, July 1, 1958.

16. Board Minutes, November 4, 1959 (first quotation), January 5, 1960, and January 3 and April 4, 1961 (second quotation).

17. Ibid., December 12, 1950, January 2 and September 4, 1951.

18. Ibid., January 3, 1956, October 1, 1957, and April 5, 1960.

19. Deed of Trust, Hutton Settlement papers, Eastern Washington State Historical Society archives, Northwest Museum of Arts and Culture (NMAC); Board Minutes, February 2, 1954.

20. Board Minutes, February 7, 1950 (first quotation), and June 5, 1947 (second quotation).

21. Ibid., passim, 1946–61.

22. Ibid., July 8, 1949 (first quotation); Gonser referrals report to board, ca. July 1949, Hutton Settlement office (other quotations).

23. Board Minutes, May 2, 1950.

24. Ibid., October 9, 1948 (quotation), and December 6, 1949.

25. Gonser's admissions report to the board, September 1961, Hutton Settlement office.

26. Board Minutes, February 5, 1946 (first quotation), and June 7, 1949 (second quotation).

27. Ibid., March 7, 1961.

28. Ibid., March 18 and April 5, 1960.

29. Board Minutes, October 7, 1958, January 6 and February 3, 1959.

30. Hutton press release dated September 1917, Hutton Settlement papers; clipping from *Spokesman-Review,* ca. September 1917, Harold Whitehouse papers, NMAC.

31. Board Minutes, December 1, 1953, and January 5, 1954.

32. Ibid., August 5, September 2, November 4, 1958, and February 3, 1959.

33. Ibid., October 7, 1958.

34. Board Minutes, February 1, 1955 (first quotation), February 5, 1957 (second quotation), and April 5, 1955 (last quotation).

35. Pieroth–Yoho Crouse interview, March 7, 2002; Pieroth–Thurber interview, February 26, 2002.

36. Pieroth–Thurber interview, February 26, 2002.

37. Pieroth–Yoho Crouse interview, March 7, 2002.

38. Pieroth–Thurber interview, February 26, 2002.

39. Ibid., February 26, 2002; Board Minutes, July 6, 1954.

40. Board Minutes, March 8 (first quotation) and May 2, 1950 (second quotation), March 30, 1954 (last quotation), and April 1, 1958—the lease agreement phased out by 1958; Superintendent's Report, April 1942.

41. Board Minutes, May 5, August 4, September 1, and December 1, 1953; Pieroth–Thurber interview, February 26, 2002; Jim Thurber to Pieroth, July 28, 2002; Pieroth–Yoho Crouse interview, March 7, 2002 (quotation).

42. Board Minutes, April 6, 1954 (first quotation); Author's interviews with Bob Baker, July 15, 1999, and Clara Aldrich Demmer, July 14, 1999; Jim Thurber to Pieroth, July 28, 2002 (second quotation); tape recording of alumni group discussion, October 6, 1999 (third quotation); Pieroth–Yoho Crouse interview, March 7, 2002 (last quotation).

43. Pieroth–Yoho Crouse interview, March 7, 2002 (quotation).

44. Board Minutes, 1952–59, passim, and November 6, 1956.

45. Pieroth–Thurber interview, February 26, 2002; Pieroth–Yoho Crouse interview, March 7, 2002.

46. Pieroth–Thurber interview, February 26, 2002; Pieroth–Yoho Crouse interview, March 7, 2002.

47. Board Minutes, July 10, 1951; Pieroth–Yoho Crouse interview, March 7, 2002.

48. Pieroth–Thurber interview, February 26, 2002 (quotations); Pieroth–Yoho Crouse interview, March 7, 2002.

49. Pieroth–Thurber interview, February 26, 2002.

50. *Spokesman Review,* September 18, 1999; Pieroth–Thurber interview, February 26, 2002.

51. Board Minutes, August 7, 1956.

52. Ibid., December 4, 1956, and September 3, 1957, March 4 (first quotation), April 1 (second quotation), May 6, and June 6, 1958 (third quotation), and March 3, 1959.

53. Financial Advisory Committee Minutes, October 31, 1958.

54. Board Minutes, November 6, 1956, April 1, 1952, and December 2, 1958 (quotation).

55. Ibid., October 4, 1949 (quotation) and passim, 1949–60.

56. Conversation with Linda Hansford, Spokane Public Library, June 26, 2001.

57. Pieroth–Yoho Crouse interview, March 7, 2002 (quotation); alumni statements in document prepared for Internal Revenue Service, 1971, Hutton Settlement papers.

Chapter 9

1. Levi Hutton record book, p. 43, Hutton Settlement papers, Eastern Washington State Historical Society archives, Northwest Museum of Arts and Culture (NMAC).

2. Hutton Settlement Financial Advisory Committee Minutes, February 24, 1961, Hutton Settlement office, Spokane; Hutton Settlement Board Minutes, March 7, 1961, ibid.; Author's interview with Marilyn Stocker, May 2, 2001; Author's interview with Robert Revel, July 19, 1999.

3. Pieroth–Revel interview, July 19, 1999; Author's interview with Evelyn Morgan, July 13, 1999.

4. Author's interview with Dorothy Revel, October 4, 1999.

5. Author's interview with Dana Finley Kirklin, June 25, 2001; Pieroth–Revel interview, July 19, 1999.

6. Pieroth–Revel interview, July 19, 1999 (quotations); Pieroth–D. Revel interview, October 4, 1999.

7. Pieroth–Revel interview, July 19, 1999. After three years as superintendent, with the board's blessing, Revel returned to school two days a week to complete his bachelor's degree; Board Minutes, October 6, 1964.

8. Pieroth–Revel interview, July 19, 1999. The board hired the first campus secretary in February 1971; Lorna Diehl started as a part-time employee.

9. Board Minutes, October 4, 1960 (quotation), July 11, August 1, September 5, and October 2, 1961.

10. Ibid., September 5 (quotation), October 2, and June 5, 1961.

11. Ibid., July 11 (quotation), October 2, 1961.

12. Board Minutes, September 5, 1961.

13. Ibid., November 6, 1962 (quotation).

14. Pieroth–Revel interview, July 19, 1999.

15. Author's interview with Lois and Russell Riddell, October 5, 1999.

16. Pieroth–Revel interview, July 19, 1999; Pieroth–D. Revel interview, October 4, 1999.

17. Pieroth–D. Revel interview, October 4, 1999; Pieroth–Morgan interview, July 13, 1999; Author's interview with Marion Phillips, July 16, 1999.

18. Author's interview with Diane Hunt Hamilton, July 25, 2001, and Nancy Hoyle Skillman, September 24, 2002; and Joy Brady Zerba to Pieroth, July 1, 2002.

19. Personnel Committee minutes, February 9, 1971 (quotation), Hutton Settlement office; Board Minutes, July 5, 1962, April 5, 1966, and September 5, 1972.

20. Pieroth–Phillips interview, July 16, 1999 (first quotation); Board Minutes, February 4, 1964 (last quotation).

21. Board Executive Committee minutes, May 3 (first quotation), September 20, 1965 (second quotation), Hutton Settlement office; Board Minutes, May 4, 1965, November 15 and December 6, 1966.

22. Board Minutes, May 16, November 22, 1968, and March 3, 1970 (quotation); Board President's Report, 1969, Hutton Settlement office; Executive Committee minutes, June 13, 1969.

23. Board Minutes, July 7, 1970, and July 11, 1972; Personnel Committee minutes, July 7, November 1 (quotation) and 12, 1971.

24. Personnel Committee minutes, November 12, 1971, December 8, 1972, and July 7, 1975; Board Minutes, July 1 and August 5, 1975 (quotation).

25. Board Minutes, June 1, October 5, 1976 (second quotation); Personnel Committee minutes, September 15, 1976 (first quotation); Resident Director's Report, June and July 1976, Hutton Settlement office.

26. Board Minutes, March 1, 1977.

27. Author's interview with Sam Skogsbergh, July 15, 1999. Once Skogsbergh became resident director, camping treks soon topped the list of Hutton Settlement activities.

28. Board Minutes, January 6, 1959–February 6, 1979; Cottage captains reports, January–March 1962, Hutton Settlement office; President's Report, 1972; Resident Director's Report, December 1979.

29. Board Minutes, June 5 (first quotation), August 7, 1962 (second quotation), and September 7, 1965 (third quotation).

30. Ibid., January 3, 1967.

31. Ibid., April 3, 1962 (first quotation) and October 8, 1969; Admissions Committee minutes, September 18, 1969 (second quotation), Hutton Settlement office.

32. Board Minutes, June 1, 1976.

33. Ibid., January 3, 1967; Admissions Committee minutes, August 31, 1972.

34. Personnel Committee minutes, March 2, 1972 (first quotation); Admissions Committee minutes, February 14, 1975 (second quotation); Board Minutes, July 11, 1967, and May 6, 1975; Financial Advisory Committee Minutes, February 28, 1975 (third quotation).

35. Resident Director's Report, May 1979 (quotation); Board Minutes, May 1, 1979.

36. Gonser's report to the board, July 30, 1960; Board Minutes, July 11, 1961, and May 4, 1965.

37. Pieroth–Finley Kirklin interview, June 25, 2001.

38. Author's interview with Dick Hamilton, July 25, 2001.

39. Brady Zerba to Pieroth, July 1, 2002; Author's interview with Tere Hoyle Hall, September 18, 2002; Pieroth–Finley Kirklin interview, June 25, 2001.

40. Pieroth–Finley Kirklin interview, June 25, 2001 (first and fourth quotations); Pieroth–Hoyle Hall interview, September 18, 2002 (second and third quotations); Brady Zerba to Pieroth, July 1, 2002 (last quotation).

41. Pieroth–D. Revel interview, October 4, 1999.

42. Board Minutes, December 7, 1971.

43. Pieroth–Finley Kirklin interview, June 25, 2001 (quotations); Pieroth–Hamilton interview, July 25, 2001.

44. Pieroth–Hamilton interview, July 25, 2001; Pieroth–Finley Kirklin interview, June 25, 2001 (quotation).

45. Pieroth–Hoyle Hall interview, September 18, 2002 (first quotation); Pieroth–Finley Kirklin interview, June 25, 2001 (second quotation); Pieroth–Revel interview, July 19, 1999 (third quotation).

46. Pieroth–Revel interview, and D. Revel comment, July 19, 1999.

47. Pieroth–Finley Kirklin interview, June 25, 2001 (quotations); Pieroth–Hamilton interview, July 25, 2001; and Pieroth–Hunt Hamilton interview, July 25, 2001.

48. Joy Brady Zerba, "My Years at the Hutton Settlement" May 2002 (first quotation) copy in Pieroth's possession; Board Minutes, December 7, 1971, and January 2, 1973; President's Report, 1971 (last quotation).

49. Pieroth–Revel interview, July 19, 1999; Pieroth–Hunt Hamilton interview, July 25, 2001; Pieroth–Finley Kirklin interview, June 25, 2001; and Pieroth–Hoyle Hall interview, September 18, 2002.

50. Pieroth–Hoyle Hall interview, September 18, 2002; Pieroth–Hoyle Skillman interview, October 24, 2001 (last quotation).

51. Author's interview with Cletis Hydrick, October 24, 2001.

52. Pieroth–Hoyle Hall interview, September 18, 2002 (first quotation); Pieroth–Hoyle Skillman interview, October 24, 2001 (second quotation); and Brady Zerba to Pieroth, July 1, 2002.

53. Pieroth–Riddell interview, October 5, 1999; Author's interview with Jesse Satre, October 24, 2001.

54. Personnel Committee minutes, June 19, 1972, October 24, 1973, and March 5, 1974; Board Minutes, October 5, 1976.

55. Pieroth–Riddell interviews, October 5, 1999.

56. Ibid., October 5, 1999.

57. Pieroth–Hoyle Skillman interview, September 24, 2002 (first two quotations); Resident Director's Report, April and October 1977 (third quotation), and March 1978; Hutton Settlement real estate and financial records, Hutton Settlement office. The Honolulu property is the Settlement's only holding outside the city of Spokane, and at century's end it yielded annual returns in excess of $50,000.

58. Resident Director's Report, August 1979.

59. Board Minutes, February 2, 1965 (quotations), March 4 and June 3, 1969, and March 7 and November 7, 1978.

60. Cottage captains report, September 27, 1971; Board Minutes, August 4, 1964, and June 3, 1975; Brady Zerba, "My Years at the Hutton Settlement."

61. Itinerary for May 4, 1968, mining district tour, Hutton Settlement papers; Board Minutes, November 1, 1966, January 2, 1979; President's Report, 1974; Resident Director's Report, October 1977 and October 1979; Brady Zerba to Pieroth, July 1, 2002 (quotation).

Chapter 10

1. Hutton Settlement Board Minutes, October 2 and December 4, 1962, Hutton Settlement office, Spokane.

2. Board Minutes, January 4 and August 2, 1966, January 2 and September 3, 1968, February 3 and December 1, 1970, and March 2, 1971; Author's interview with Carol Wendle, May 2, 2001 (quotation).

3. Board Minutes, February 6, 1962, April 2, and December 3, 1963 (quotation).

4. Ibid., December 3, 1963, and June 6, 1967 (quotation)

5. Ibid., January 2, 1968 (first quotation), January 6, December 1, 1970 (second quotation), April 6, 1971 (third quotation), March 20, June 6 (last two quotations), December 5, 1972.

6. Board Minutes, May 2, 1972, July 2, 1974.

7. Board President's Report, 1972, Hutton Settlement office; Board Minutes, May 6, 1975, and May 4, 1976.

8. Education Committee minutes, September 9, 1975, Hutton Settlement office; Board Minutes, October 7, 1975. In 1985 Carol Wendle won election to the Spokane School District 81 Board of Directors.

9. Board Minutes, February 1, 1977.

10. Ibid., April 5, 1977 (first quotation); Hutton Settlement Financial Advisory Committee Minutes, April 1, 1977, Hutton Settlement office (second quotation).

11. Author's interviews with Catherine Hyslop (quotation), June 9, 1999, Catherine Bernhard, June 9, 1999, and Regina Manser, October 5, 1999.

12. Pieroth–Hyslop interview, June 9, 1999 (quotations); Pieroth–Bernhard interview, June 9, 1999; and Author's interview with Evelyn Morgan, July 13, 1999.

13. Board Minutes, October 12, 1970 (first quotation); Author's interview with Robert Revel, July 19, 1999 (last quotations).

14. Author's interview with Corine Brown, June 11, 1999 (first quotation); Pieroth–Hyslop interview, June 9, 1999 (second quotation); Board Minutes, August 1, 1972.

15. Pieroth–Revel interview, July 19, 1999.

16. Board Minutes, February 2, 1965, April 5 and November 15, 1966; Spokane *Spokesman-Review,* May 13, 1966.

17. Ray Haman to Republican Legislators from Spokane County, March 20, 1967, and his accompanying Memo on Constitutionality of House Bill 76, both in Hutton Settlement papers; RCW 74.15.170. The provision remains in effect.

18. Author's interviews with Zelma Ellis, October 24, 2000 (first quotation), Dorothy Rochon Powers, June 25, 2001 (second quotation), and Ed McWilliams, July 13, 1999 (third quotation).

19. Author's interview with Nancy Henry, October 23, 2001; Pieroth–Morgan interview, July 13, 1999 (quotations).

20. Author's interviews with Betty Corliss, June 9, 1999 (second quotation), and Helen Hamblen, June 8, 1999; Pieroth–Manser interview, October 5, 1999 (first quotation); Pieroth–Morgan interview, July 13, 1999; and Pieroth–Bernhard interview, June 9, 1999.

21. Board Minutes, December 4, 1962 (quotations), February 5, 1963, and August 3, 1971. An umbrella pension plan finally emerged in August 1971, only to be phased out early in 1979 because of changed legal interpretations.

22. Pieroth–Morgan interview, July 13, 1999; Board Minutes, April 3 and December 10, 1962, and passim, 1950–62.

23. Board Executive Committee minutes, September 25, 1963, Hutton Settlement office; Board Minutes, November 5, 1963 (second quotation).

24. Executive Committee minutes, November 11, 1963; Board Minutes, Executive Session, December 3, 1963 (quotations).

25. Charles Gonser to Margaret Cowles, January 3, 1964, Hutton Settlement papers, Eastern Washington State Historical Society archives, Northwest Museum of Arts and Culture (NMAC).

26. Gonser to Virginia Osborn, July 27, 1968, ibid.

27. Handwritten text of Cowles's remarks, September 16, 1967, ibid.

28. Board Minutes, June 2, 1970, February 1, 1972, and January 2, 1973; Pieroth–Revel interview, July 19, 1999.

29. Author's interview with Philip Stanton, October 4, 1999.

30. Ibid.; Financial Advisory Committee Minutes, March 27, 1959 (first quotation). The committee always met at the old Crescent Tea Room, in which over the years innumerable Spokane business transactions occurred during lunch.

31. Financial Advisory Committee Minutes, January 26, 1962, and March 27, 1964; Board Minutes, October 1 and November 29, 1963, and April 17, 1964; J. William T. Youngs, Jr., *The Fair and the Falls: Spokane's Expo '74: Transforming an American Environment* (Cheney, Wash.: Eastern Washington University Press, 1996), p. 113. Youngs's excellent book is the definitive story of Expo '74.

32. Undated clipping, ca. 1970, Hutton Settlement Board Scrapbook, Hutton Settlement office.

33. Board Minutes, January 2, 1951, July 5, 1962 (first quotation); Financial Advisory Committee Minutes, April 28, 1967 (second quotation), February 23, November 6, 1973 (third quotation).

34. Board Minutes, April 4, 1961, and July 5, 1962; Financial Advisory Committee Minutes, March 31 (first quotation) and July 28, 1961, March 30, 1962, and February 22, 1963 (second quotation).

35. Board Minutes, March 1, 1966, March 7, 1967 (second quotation), May 26, 1969, and February 6, 1973; Financial Advisory Committee Minutes, January 27 (first quotation), June 30, and October 27, 1967 (last quotation).

36. Financial Advisory Committee Minutes, August 30, September 27, 1974; Board Minutes, October 1, 1974, and February 4, 1975 (quotation); *Spokesman-Review,* January 31, 1975. Inter Mountain Investment Corporation could have been the same as the Intermountain Mortgage Company that had sought to buy Settlement land in the valley twenty years earlier.

37. *Spokesman-Review,* February 26, 1964; Author's interview with Jessie Satre, October 24, 2001 (last quotation); Pieroth–Revel interview, July 19, 1999; Financial Advisory Committee Minutes, August 26, 1966 (second quotation). Mrs. Satre was board president when the sale was finalized.

38. Financial Advisory Committee Minutes, October 30, 1970, October 29, 1971 (first quotation), November 25, 1977 (second quotation), April 27 (third quotation), May 31, 1979; Board Minutes, August 1, 1972, May 1, 1979.

39. Financial Advisory Committee Minutes, June 29 and July 27 1979; Board Minutes, August 7, 1979.

40. Board Minutes, June 5, 1962.

41. Financial Advisory Committee Minutes, June 29 and July 27, 1962; Board Minutes, July 5, 1962 (quotation).

42. Financial Advisory Committee Minutes, November 30, 1962; Board Minutes, March 5, 1963.

43. Memo from Gonser, December 5, 1962, Hutton Settlement office; Board Minutes, January 8, April 2, and October 1, 1963 (quotation); Financial Advisory Committee Minutes, July 26, 1963.

44. Financial Advisory Committee Minutes, August 28, 1964 (quotation); Board Minutes, January 27–October 15, 1964, passim.

45. Financial Advisory Committee Minutes, November 27, 1964 (quotation), and November 11, 1965; conversation with Ben Nielsen, architect, October 29, 2002; Board Minutes, December 7, 1965; Seattle *Post-Intelligencer,* December 3, 1965. At century's end the Settlement still owned the IBM building, but its occupant was then the Itronix Corporation.

46. Board Minutes, February 1 and March 1, 1977, June 6, 1978, and June 5, 1979; Financial Advisory Committee Minutes, August 26 and November 25, 1977; Pieroth–Revel interview, July 19, 1999; President's Report, 1978 (first quotation) and 1979 (last quotation).

47. Board Minutes, January 8, 1963 (quotation), and January 2, 1979; Financial Advisory Committee Minutes, May 26, 1967; Hutton Settlement Balance Sheet, December 31, 1979, Hutton Settlement office.

48. Pieroth–Hyslop interview, June 9, 1999.

49. Ibid., June 9, 1999 (quotations); Board Minutes, August 18 and November 4, 1969.

50. Pieroth–Henry interview, October 23, 2001 (first quotation); Cottage captains meeting minutes, January 12, 1970, and Personnel Committee minutes, November 12, 1971 (second quotation), both in Hutton Settlement office; Board Minutes, January 5, 1971, and special meeting, January 24, 1972; Financial Advisory Committee Minutes, February 2, 1971.

51. Pieroth–Hyslop interview, June 9, 1999 (quotations); Cottage captains minutes, March 29, 1971; and *Spokesman-Review,* May 17, 1971.

52. Pieroth–Stanton interview, October 4, 1999.

53. Charles T. Russell, IRS deputy commissioner, to Hutton Settlement, July 9, 1937, Hutton Settlement papers; Financial Advisory Committee Minutes, June 29, 1951.

54. Herbert Hamblen to Revel, November 25, 1970, Fred Emry to Revel, April 1, 1972, Hutton Settlement papers; Board Minutes, September 1, 1970 (quotation).

55. Hamblen to Hutton Settlement, Inc., November 11, 1971, Hutton Settlement papers.

56. Hutton Settlement documents submitted to IRS, ca. October 1971, copies in ibid.; Board Minutes, June 1 and July 6, 1971. Seventy-two percent is an extraordinary return for any questionnaire.

57. Warren Magnuson to John Walters, IRS commissioner, November 30, 1971 (quotation), and Revel correspondence with Magnuson and Thomas Foley, November and December 1971, Hutton Settlement papers; Board Minutes, March 7, 1972.

58. Pieroth–Manser interview, October 5, 1999 (first quotation); Financial Advisory Committee Minutes, December 29, 1972; President's Report, 1972 (second quotation).

59. Board Minutes, June 6, 1972 (first quotation) and January 22, 1973 (other quotations).

60. Ibid., March 13, April 10, May 1, and September 4, 1979.

61. Hutton Settlement Accounting Statement, October 15, 2002, Hutton Settlement office.

62. Financial Advisory Committee Minutes, March 30, 1973, September 27, 1975; Board Minutes, October 3, 1972, March 30, 1973, October 7, 1975, September 6, 1977.

63. Pieroth–Stocker interview, May 2, 2001.

64. Board Minutes, June 7, 1960, June 7, 1966, and February 23, 1968 (quotation).

65. Ibid., May 5, 1970 (first quotation); Hyslop to Bruce McPhaden, August 18, 1972, Hutton Settlement papers; Pieroth–Hyslop interview, July 12, 1999.

66. Financial Advisory Committee Minutes, November 1976; Board Minutes, December 7, 1976 (quotation); Board Minutes, December 4, 1979.

67. Executive Committee minutes, April 13, 1978 (quotation); Financial Advisory Committee Minutes, September 29, 1978.

68. Author's interview with Ruth Jensen, October 23, 2001 (quotation); Board Minutes, July 5 and December 5, 1978.

69. President's Report, 1976 (first quotation); Pieroth–Manser interview, October 5, 1999 (second quotation); Pieroth–Henry interview, October 23, 2001; Pieroth–Wendle interview, May 2, 2001 (third quotation); Pieroth–Morgan interview, July 13, 1999 (fourth quotation).

Chapter 11

1. Author's interviews with Corine Brown, June 11, 1999 (quotation), and Ruth Jensen, October 23, 2001.

2. Hutton Settlement Board Minutes, February 7, 1972, Hutton Settlement office, Spokane.

3. Author's interviews with Nancy Henry, October 23, 2001, and Carol Wendle, May 2, 2001.

4. Author's interviews with Marion Phillips, July 16, 1999, Ruth Jensen, October 23, 2001, and Jo Ann Nielsen, April 30, 2001; Hutton Settlement Yearbook, 2002, Hutton Settlement papers, Eastern Washington State Historical Society archives, Northwest Museum of Arts and Culture (NMAC)

5. Board Minutes, January 1935 to present, passim; Author's interviews with Patty Skogsbergh, July 15, 1999, and Kay Stipe, October 23, 2001; Pieroth–Phillips interview, July 16, 1999.

6. Board Minutes, September 3, 1985 (first quotation), and January 7, 1992 (second quotation).

7. "By-Laws of the Hutton Settlement," Revised December 1989, Hutton Settlement office, Spokane; Board Minutes, June 4, August 6, and September 3, 1985.

8. Amendment to Articles of Incorporation of The Hutton Settlement, May 9, 1997, Hutton Settlement papers.

9. Pieroth–Jensen interview, October 23, 2001 (first quotation); Author's interview with Maxine Kopcynski, October 23, 2001; and Pieroth–Henry interview, October 23, 2001 (second quotation).

10. Financial Advisory Committee Minutes, September 28, 1979, Hutton Settlement office; Board Minutes, May 5, 1987; Board President's Report, 1986 (quotation), ibid.

11. Board Minutes, January 9, 1996; Pieroth–Nielsen interview, April 30, 2001 (quotation).

12. Board Minutes, April 1, 1980 (quotation), October 6, 1981, July 6, 1982–February 7, 1984, September 6–December 6, 1994, January 10, 1995, and August 5, 1997. Congressman Foley himself donated a speaking honorarium to the Settlement in 1982 and returned a fee for speaking on the campus in 1984.

13. Board Executive Committee minutes, September 22, 1982, Hutton Settlement office; Financial Advisory Committee Minutes, September 24, 1982; Board Minutes, October 6, 1992 (quotation).

14. Board Minutes, February 2, June 4, and September 30, 1985, October 5, 1987; Robert Brown to Evelyn Morgan, n.d. (Cox information), Hutton Settlement papers; Hutton Settlement Balance Sheet, December 31, 1987 (assets), Hutton Settlement office.

15. Board Minutes, October 3, 1983, April 6, 1993; Financial Advisory Committee Minutes, May 3, 1985, and November 28, 1990 (quotation).

16. Nielsen and Phillips responses to Board questionnaire, 2002, Hutton Settlement papers; Board Minutes, December 7, 1993, October 4, 1994, and March 7, 1995 (quotation).

17. Author's interview with Mike Butler, March 4, 2002.

18. Board Minutes, January 10, 1995, and February 7, 1992; RCW 30.24.020 (quotation); Pieroth–Nielsen interview, April 30, 2001.

19. Board Minutes, October 3, 1983, and September 8, 1987.

20. Ibid., November 2, 1993; Author's interview with Catherine Hyslop, June 9, 1999; "By-Laws of the Hutton Settlement," Revised March 7, 1995 (quotation); Pieroth–Butler interview, March 4, 2002. Even as the board contemplated bylaw changes, John Wagner of SeaFirst-Bank of America proved an exception to the "absentee banker" description; he has continued to serve on the consulting committee and to provide sound advice.

21. Hutton Settlement IRS Form 990 for the year 1999, Hutton Settlement office. At century's end the board numbered twenty-one, plus five ex officio financial advisers. Not long after Mr. Hutton's death, the women trustees decreed that his seat, the twenty-seventh, remain empty.

22. President's Report, 1988; Board Minutes, passim, February 4, 1997–November 2, 1999, and August 5, 1999.

23. Board Minutes, July 1, August 5 and 18, and September 2, 1969.

24. Ibid., April 1, 1986 (first quotation), September 6, December 2, 1988, May 2, 1989 (second quotation); Spokane *Spokesman-Review,* July 8, 1993 (third quotation).

25. Board Minutes, May 4 and November 2, 1993; *Spokesman-Review,* July 8, 1993.

26. Board Minutes, June 7, 1994; *Spokesman-Review,* May 26, 1994; Pieroth–Nielsen interview, April 30, 2001.

27. Board Minutes, June 5, 1984; Pieroth–Nielsen interview, April 30, 2001; Author's interview with Sharon Cortner, March 6, 2002 (quotation).

28. Financial Advisory Committee Minutes, June 25, 1982; Board Minutes, August 1 and October 3, 1995 (first quotation); Teresa L. Brum to Michael Butler, September 19, 1995 (second quotation), Hutton Settlement papers.

29. Board Minutes, May 5, 1994, August 1, November 7, and December 5, 1995; Comstock Foundation to Butler, February 16, 2000, Comstock Foundation papers, NMAC; *Tower Topics,* Vol. 24, no. 1, Spring 1995 (quotation), Hutton Settlement papers; Author's interviews with Jim Taylor, July 16, 1999, and Ken Dunlap, July 13, 1999. The Comstock Foundation had awarded a $15,000 grant for needed repairs of the Settlement swimming pool in 1994.

30. Board Minutes, May 7 and June 3, 1996; President's Report, 1996. Regina Manser headed grantwriting for the project.

31. Board Minutes, October 8 and November 4, 1969, July 3, 1979, and July 5 (first quotation) and August 1, 1989; President's Report, 1989 (second quotation).

32. Board Minutes, August 2, 1994; President's welcoming remarks, July 16, 1994 (quotation), copy in Hutton Settlement papers; President's Report, 1994. In 1999, eighty years after Levi Hutton carried Jane Wiese into Cottage One, the Hutton Settlement administrator served as her guardian and encouraged board members to visit her in the Spokane nursing home where she lived.

33. Board Minutes, December 2, 1986, May 5 (quotation), August 4, November 3, and December 1, 1987; Notes from Hutton Settlement Future Planning Task Group, January 8, 1987, Hutton Settlement office.

34. Pieroth–Butler interview, March 4, 2002. Butler also has a Master of Education degree from the University of Portland.

35. Ibid.

36. Ibid.

37. Board Minutes, January 3, 1984, August 6, 1991 (second quotation); President's Report, 1984 (first quotation).

38. Board Minutes, February 1, 1994 (first quotation), July 11, 1995, February 6, 1996 (second quotation), and March 1, 1997.

39. "Remarks from the Board of Trustees," Staff Luncheon, April 18, 1991, Hutton Settlement papers (quotations); *Spokesman-Review,* June 29, 1995 (last quotation).

40. Board Minutes, July 5, 1994, and June 6, 1991; Pieroth–Butler interview, March 4, 2002.

41. Pieroth–Butler interview, March 4, 2002; Author's interviews with numerous board members, and with Robert Revel, July 19, 1999; Samuel Skogsbergh, July 15, 1999, Mary Jo Lyonnais, March 6, 2002, and Bernie Nelson, September 16, 2002. Nelson was regional director of DSHS in Spokane in the 1970s and 1980s.

42. Author's interview with Margie Hemming, September 18, 2002 (quotation); Board Minutes, May 1, 1979.

43. Pieroth–Lyonnais interview, March 6, 2002.

44. President's Report, 1983 (first quotation); Board Minutes, March 1, 1983 (second quotation); and Resident Director's Report, September 1983 (third quotation), Hutton Settlement office.

45. Board Minutes, July 7, 1987, March 5 and June 7, 1988, January 3 and February 5, 1989, February 5, 1991, and April 7, 1992.

46. Ibid., February 7, 1984, June 2, 1992, and December 3, 1996 (quotation); Pieroth–Stipe interview, October 23, 2001.

47. Executive Committee minutes, August 4, 1987; Board Minutes, July 7 and September 1, 1992 (quotation), February 1, 1993, January 10 and October 4, 1994, and February 7, 1995.

48. Board Minutes, November 3, 1983, December 4, 1984, March 6, 1990, and November 2, 1993, February 2, 1999; Pieroth–Lyonnais interview, March 6, 2002 (first quotation); Pieroth–Butler interview, March 4, 2002; Hutton Settlement Manual for the Board of Trustees, 2002, Hutton Settlement office; Author's interview with David Milliken, March 6, 2002 (last quotation).

49. Hutton Settlement Deed of Trust, Hutton Settlement papers (quotation); Five–Ten Year Planning Committee minutes, April 26, 1993, Hutton Settlement office; report of pediatric study on use of psychiatric drugs, New York *Times,* January 14, 2003.

50. Author's interview with Pam Hydrick, October 25, 2001 (quotation); Pieroth–Butler interview, March 4, 2002; and Pieroth–Milliken interview, March 6, 2002.

51. Pieroth–Milliken interview, March 6, 2002.

52. Ibid.

53. Board Minutes, August 7, 1973; Resident Director's Report, December 1978 and February 1979. Sam's entertaining reports were small gems, surpassing the board minutes kept by Lee Nielsen in the 1960s in entertainment value.

54. Board Minutes, June 7 and November 1, 1988, April 7 and July 7, 1992, and March 2 and April 6, 1993.

55. President's Report, 1988 (quotation); Board Minutes, February 5, and September 30, 1985, January 7, 1992, and September 5, 1995; Pieroth–P. Hydrick interview, October 25, 2001. The Settlement hired a girls counselor in 2001, but Lyonnais still carried the load as girls caseworker.

56. Author's interview with Cletis Hydrick, October 24, 2001.

57. Author's interview with Kayla Skillman, September 15, 2002; Board Minutes, July 11, 1995.

58. Author's interview with Nancy Skillman, October 24, 2001; Pieroth–P. Hydrick interview, October 25, 2001.

59. Pieroth–N. Skillman interview, October 24, 2001.

60. Pieroth–Hemming interview, September 18, 2002.

61. Ibid.; Pieroth–Milliken interview, March 6, 2002.

62. Pieroth–Hemming interview, September 18, 2002.

63. Board Minutes, September 6, 1983 (first quotation), July 3, 1984, and May 6, 1997; President's Report 1988 (second quotation) and 1997.

64. Numerous board member interviews; President's Report, 1984 (quotation); Board Minutes, July 6, 1993, October 4, 1994, July 2, 1996, and January 1, 1997; Hutton Settlement Manual for the Board of Trustees, 2002.

65. Board Minutes, 1970–80, passim, and July 1, 1980; Author's interview with Regina Manser, October 5, 1999; Author's interview with Anita Abramson Woslager, July 12, 1999, and Dorothy Grater, tape recording of alumni group discussion, October 6, 1999.

66. Author's interview with David Smith, August 17, 1999; Board Minutes, April 6, 1982, March 30, 1984, February 5 and March 2, 1991.

67. Board Minutes, March 3 and April 7, 1987 (quotation), February 7, 1989, and January 4, 2000; President's Report, 1988.

68. Ibid., August 6, 1985 (first quotation), and June 4, 1991 (second quotation).

69. Pieroth–Henry interview, October 23, 2001 (first quotation); Pieroth–Wendle interview, May 2, 2001; Board Minutes, March 3 and August 4, 1992, and June 7, 1994; responses to Board questionnaire, 2002 (last quotations).

70. Board Minutes, November 4, 1980; *Spokesman-Review,* May 15, 1991 (quotation); Author's interview with Marianne Metreveli Taylor, February 7, 2002.

71. Pieroth–Metreveli Taylor interview, February 7, 2002; Pieroth–Stocker interview, May 2, 2001; and Pieroth–Nielsen interview, April 30, 2001.

72. Pieroth–Milliken interview, March 6, 2002.

73. Author's interview with Dorothy Revel, October 4, 1999 (first quotation); Pieroth–Revel interview, July 19, 1999 (second quotation); and Board Minutes, December 6, 1983 (last quotation).

74. Pieroth–Revel interview, July 19, 1999.

75. Pieroth–Metreveli Taylor interview, February 7, 2002.

76. Author's interview with Marilyn McIntosh, March 6, 2002.

77. Author's interview with Zelma Grant Ellis, October 24, 2000; Pieroth–Revel interview, July 19, 1999; Pieroth–Butler interview, March 4, 2002; Board Minutes, 1920–2000, passim; Revel to Comstock Foundation, October 5, 1994, Comstock Foundation papers; President's Report, 1988.

78. Board Minutes, July 3, 1990, July 6 and August 3, 1999; Pieroth–Cortner interview, March 6, 2002.

79. Charles N. LeWarne, track coach, to Pieroth, January 10, 2003; Board Minutes and Resident Director's Reports, passim.

80. Pieroth–Metreveli Taylor interview, February 7, 2002.

81. Board Minutes, 1980–2000, passim, August 5, 1980, November 1, 1994. Cletis Hydrick spent a semester in Germany as a Rotary Exchange student in 1980.

Appendix

Presidents of the Hutton Settlement Board of Trustees

Agnes Cowley Paine, 1920-23
Kate H. Bean, 1924-25
Miriam Ritchie, 1926-29
Pauline Blackwell, 1930-32
Myrtle Osgood, 1933-34
Pearl Hutton Schrader, 1935-38
Cazenovia Cowley Weaver, 1939-40
Pearl Hutton Schrader, 1941-42
Lena M. Smith, 1943-45
March Pike, 1946-48
May Kizer, 1949-52
Mae Costello Bright, 1953-54
Marjorie Greene, 1955-57
Marian Marshall, 1958-59
Alice Leonard, 1960-61
Margaret Paine Cowles, 1962-64
Evelyn Morgan, 1965-66
Virginia Osborn, 1967-68
Lee Nielsen, 1969-70
Catherine Hyslop, 1971-73
Corine Brown, 1974-75
Elizabeth Corliss, 1976
Ruth Jensen, 1977-78
Jessie Satre, 1979-80
Maxine Kopczynski, 1981-82
Marilyn Stocker, 1983-84
Donna Greenough, 1985-86
Marion Phillips, 1987-88
Nancy Henry, 1989-90
Kay Stipe, 1991-92
Jo Ann Nielsen, 1993-95
Carol Wendle, 1996
Carole Walker, 1997
Marion Phillips, 1998
Sharon Cortner, 1999-2001
Renee Rigsby, 2002
Janice Boots, 2003

List of Interviews

Trustees
Catherine Bernhard, June 9, 1999
Corine Brown, June 11, 1999
Elizabeth Corliss, June 9, 1999
Sharon Cortner, March 3, 2002
Wanda Cowles, March 3, 2002
Zelma Ellis, October 24, 2000
Helen Hamblen, June 8, 1999
Nancy Henry, October 23, 2001
Catherine Hyslop, June 9, 1999 and July 12, 1999
Ruth Jensen, October 23, 2001
Maxine Kopczynski, October 23, 2001
Regina Manser, October 5, 1999
Evelyn Morgan, July 13, 1999
Jo Ann Nielsen, April 30, 2001
Marion Phillips, July 16, 1999
Jessie Satre, October 24, 2001
Connie Stacey, March 5, 2002
Kay Stipe, October 23, 2001
Marilyn Stocker, May 2, 2001
Carol Wendle, March 2, 2002

Former Residents
Bob Baker, July 15, 1999
Pamela Yoho Crouse, March 7, 2002
Clara Aldrich Demmer, July 14, 1999
Ken Dunlap, July 13, 1999
Glen Grater, May 23, 2001 (by phone from Fond du Lac, Wisconsin)
Tere Hoyle Hall, September 18, 2002
Cletis Hydrick, October 24, 2001
Pam Croff Hydrick, October 25, 2001
Diane Hunt Hamilton, July 25, 2001
Richard Hamilton, July 25, 2001
Dana Finley Kirklin, June 25, 2001
Pearle Grater LaLumia, May 18, 2001 (by phone from Lansing, Michigan)
Mike Mateef, June 7, 1999
Mabel Maley Maxwell, May 1, 2002
Clara Scott Simons, June 7, 1999
Nancy Hoyle Skillman, October 24, 2001

Former Residents *(continued)*

Sylvia Olsen Slatky, May 1, 2002
David Smith, August 17, 1999
Jim Taylor, July 16, 1999
Marianne Metrovelli Taylor, February 7, 2002
John Thurber, February 26, 2002
Gordon Windle, June 10, 1999
Anita Abramson Woslager, July 12, 1999

Settlement Administrators

Michael Butler, March 5 and September 17, 2002
Robert Revel, July 19, 1999

Settlement Staff

Patsy Gottschalk, January 25, 2002
Margie Hemming, September 18, 2002
Mary Jo Lyonnais, July 14, 1999 and March 6, 2002
David Milliken, March 6, 2002
Lois Riddell, October 5, 1999
Russell Riddell, October 5, 1999
Dorothy Revel, October 4, 1999
Sam Skogsbergh, July 15, 1999
Patty Skogsbergh, July 15, 1999

Others

Nancy Anderson, August 6, 2001
Ben Eide, June 21, 2001
Dorothy Fuller Grater, May 1, 2002
Marilyn McIntosh, March 6, 2002
Ed McWilliams, July 13, 1999
Bernard Nelson, September 16, 2002
Dorothy Rochon Powers, June 25, 2001
Kayla Skillman, September 14, 2002
Philip Stanton, October 4, 1999

Tapes of Group Discussions

Trustees and Dorothy Revel, June 8, 1999
Former residents, October 6, 1999
Former residents, August 17, 1999
Alumni at Settlement picnic, August 17, 1999

Trustees of the Hutton Settlement, 1920 through 2003

The following is the most complete list of trustees that can be determined.
Names appear in the order of election; records do not contain given names for everyone.

Kate H. Bean, 1920; died 1925
Addie Cole, 1920; resigned 1926
Ruth C. Corbet, 1920; resigned 1923
Jennie E. Dodd, 1920; resigned 1938
Maggie Dodd, 1920; died 1922
Harriet Ross Gandy, 1920; died 1923
Rebecca Graves, 1920; no resignation date
Pearle Jones, 1920; resigned 1939
Laura Northrup, 1920; died 1951
Ada O'Dell, 1920; resigned 1922
Agnes C. Paine, 1920; died 1952
Ella V. Paterson, 1920; resigned 1926
Matilda Prescott, 1920; resigned 1938
Miriam Ritchie, 1920; died 1959
Mary Robison, 1920; no resignation date
Louise M. Sargent, 1920; resigned 1921
Pearl Hutton Schrader, 1920; died 1964
Helen W. Smith, 1920; resigned 1923
Mollie Stephens, 1920; no resignation date
Ursula Ruch Sutherland, 1920; died 1953
Katherine Tate, 1920; resigned 1939
Elizabeth Bender, 1921; died 1934
Rose V. Sivyer, 1921; resigned 1922
Cazenovia Cowley Smythe Weaver, 1921; died 1944
Fannie Wentworth, 1921; resigned 1922

Nevada Taylor, 1921; resigned 1926
Cleora M. Merryweather, 1922; resigned 1936
Elsie Hansen, 1922; resigned 1925
Pauline Blackwell, 1922; resigned 1942
Alice McVay, 1922; died 1927
Belle Michael, 1922; no resignation date
Margaret Argall, 1923; no resignation date
Belle Hanauer, 1923; resigned 1930
Carre Ward, 1924; no resignation date
Maude Lindsley, 1926; resigned 1926
—— Murray, 1926; resigned 1932
Myrtle Osgood, 1926; died 1962
Arley Katz, 1926; resigned 1929
Edna Glasgow, 1927; resigned 1956
Helen Reinhardt, 1929; resigned 1933
Bess Williams, 1930; resigned 1938
Kate W. Farnham, 1929; resigned 1942
Dorothy Bean Humbird, 1932; resigned 1934
May Armstrong Kizer, 1933; died 1964
Ina Hughes Johnston, 1933; resigned 1947
Lena M. Smith, 1934; died 1972
Helen S. Paine, 1935; resigned 1947
Margaret Paine Cowles, 1935; died 1991
Lillian Rusch, 1936; resigned 1940
Harriet McElroy, 1937; resigned 1967

Dorothy Perham, 1938; resigned 1951
Florence Rucker, 1938; resigned 1961
Ethel Thomson, 1939; resigned 1949
Lena Brown, 1939; resigned 1940
March Pike, 1939; resigned 1969
Leora S. Telyea, 1939; resigned 1943
Mae Costello Bright, 1940; died 1970
Edna Smith Gilbert, 1939; died 1945
Ruth Anderson, 1940; died 1941
Julia C. Lindsay, 1941; resigned 1966
Helen H. Gamble, 1943; resigned 1944
Zula Weiss, 1945; resigned 1960
Charlotte Decker, 1945; died 1959
Lillian Steinheiser, 1946; resigned 1970
Marjorie Greene, 1946; died 1985
Virginia Coffin, 1948; resigned 1980
Marian Marshall, 1948; died 1976
Betty Harvey, 1948; resigned 1955
Alice Leonard, 1952; resigned 1968
Helen Whitehouse Hamblen, 1952; resigned 2001
Lee Nielsen, 1954; resigned 1984
Virginia Osborn, 1956; resigned 1970
Margaret Bean, 1959; resigned 1970
Evelyn Morgan, 1959; died 2002
Muriel S. Veasey, 1961; resigned 1966
Edith Whitney, 1961; resigned 1977
Wanda Cowles, 1962; resigned 1974
Elizabeth Corliss, 1965; resigned 1993
Mildred Smith, 1965; resigned 1972
Catherine Hyslop, 1966
Jeannette Brooke, 1966; resigned 1973
Janet Salladay, 1966; resigned 1970
Catherine Bernhard, 1968; resigned 1997

Corine Brown, 1968
Regina Manser, 1970; resigned 1995
Joan Fergin, 1970; resigned 1974
Martha Reid, 1970; resigned 1982
Zelma Grant Ellis, 1970; resigned 2000
Jessie Satre, 1971; resigned 1982
Ruth Jensen, 1972
Nancy Henry, 1973
Marion Phillips, 1974
Donna Greenough, 1974; resigned 1995
Carol Wendle, 1975
Maxine Kopczynski, 1975; resigned 2001
Lorna Diehl, 1976; resigned 1978
Marilyn Stocker, 1978
Kay Stipe, 1980
Connie Moore Stacey, 1981
Carole Walker, 1982; resigned 1999
Jo Ann Nielsen, 1984
Carol Wilson, 1986; resigned 1996
Karen Damon, 1992; resigned 1999
Gail Stevenson, 1993; resigned 1997
Sharon Cortner, 1995
Lani Ellingsen, 1996; resigned 2001
Janet Moffitt, 1997
Renée Rigsby, 1997
Janice Boots, 1997
Janet Goebel, 1999
Loreen McFaul, 2000
Melissa Coffin Willis, 2000
Stella DeBarros, 2001
Linda Hendricksen, 2002
Virginia Hinch, 2002
Suzanne Lynch, 2003

Index